The *Kasrils* AFFAIR

JEWS AND MINORITY POLITICS
IN POST-APARTHEID SOUTH AFRICA

THE *Kasrils* AFFAIR

JEWS AND MINORITY POLITICS
IN POST-APARTHEID SOUTH AFRICA

JOEL B POLLAK

In association with the
Isaac and Jessie Kaplan Centre
for Jewish Studies and Research,
University of Cape Town

The Kasrils Affair – Jews and Minority Politics in post-apartheid South Africa

First published 2009

Juta & Company Ltd
PO Box 14373, Lansdowne, 7779, Cape Town, South Africa

© **2009** Juta & Company Ltd

ISBN 978-1-91989-507-9

All rights reserved. No part of this publication may be reproduced or transmitted in any form or by any means, electronic or mechanical, including photocopying, recording, or any information storage or retrieval system, without prior permission in writing from the publisher. Subject to any applicable licensing terms and conditions in the case of electronically supplied publications, a person may engage in fair dealing with a copy of this publication for his or her personal or private use, or his or her research or private study. See Section 12(1)(a) of the Copyright Act 98 of 1978.

Project Manager: Seshni Moodley-Kazadi
Editor: Wendy Priilaid
Proofreader: David Merrington
Typesetter: PETALDESIGN
Cover designer: PETALDESIGN
Indexer: Lindsay Jane Norman
Printed in South Africa by Print Communications

Typeset in 10/15pt Adobe Garamond

The authors and the publisher have made every effort to obtain permission for and to acknowledge the use of copyright material. Should any infringement of copyright have occurred, please contact the publisher, and every effort will be made to rectify omissions or errors in the event of a reprint or new edition.

CONTENTS

- vii — Preface
- 1 — Chapter One – **Introduction**
- 12 — Chapter Two – **Politics and South African Jewry before 1994**
- 38 — Chapter Three – **The Post-Apartheid Jewish Community**
- 61 — Chapter Four – **The Kasrils Affair**
- 86 — Chapter Five – **The Aftermath**
- 114 — Chapter Six – **Challenging the Board's Strategy**
- 135 — Chapter Seven – **Conclusions and Comparisons**
- 165 — Epilogue – **The Zuma Era**
- 169 — Appendix – **The Kasrils Declarations**
- 177 — Bibliography
- 191 — Index

To my parents, Raymond and Naomi.

✡

In memory of Abe Barron,
a man who believed in the future
of South African Jewish leadership
and led by bold example.

PREFACE

This book describes the 'Kasrils affair', a debate about the Israeli–Palestinian conflict that took place in the South African Jewish community in late 2001 and early 2002. The affair began when Minister of Water Affairs and Forestry (now Minister of Intelligence) Ronnie Kasrils issued a declaration on behalf of 'South Africans of Jewish Descent' in which he criticised Israeli policies in the West Bank and Gaza. He later circulated the declaration as a petition among South African Jews. Though relatively few signed the declaration, Jewish leaders considered the Kasrils affair to be the first major political crisis for South African Jewry in the democratic era.

The book explores what the Kasrils affair reveals about, and how it has affected, politics in the South African Jewish community and its institutions after apartheid. The book also examines the broader implications of the Kasrils affair for minority and interest-group politics in South Africa's single-party-dominant democracy and constitutional state.

This is a contemporary analysis, based largely on published commentary and on interviews conducted with the members and staff of the South African Jewish Board of Deputies. Few public minutes of the Board's meetings, and very little of the Board's correspondence on the issue, are available. The book also draws heavily on my own insights and experiences, as I was personally involved in the debates and discussions surrounding the Kasrils affair. At one point I made suggestions to Kasrils as to how the original text of the declaration should be amended, and some of these changes were incorporated into the final draft. I was among the original signatories, but later dissented from the declaration, due to various disagreements of principle and tactics with Kasrils and his supporters. I was also employed as a speechwriter and researcher in the office of the Leader of the Opposition in the Parliament of South Africa from December 2002 to July 2006. In that capacity, I assisted the Democratic Alliance leader at the time, Tony Leon, in preparing remarks to and correspondence with the Board of Deputies in exchanges about the Board's political stance. As such, this is a deeply 'embedded' account of events and ideas, albeit one that strives to reach an objective standard. The book does not focus on the merits of the arguments used by Kasrils and his opponents. Rather, it describes those arguments, how they were used, and by whom.

Kasrils later recalled the affair in an update to his autobiography, *Armed and Dangerous*:

> *A group of 300 South Africans of Jewish origin signed a declaration of conscience formulated by ANC activist Max Ozinsky and myself. We reiterated the growing call around the world for Israel to withdraw its troops from the occupied territories and resume negotiations for a peaceful settlement. Virtually all the signatories had participated in the struggle against apartheid. Some adopted the title 'Not in my Name'.*
>
> *We were repudiated by South Africa's orthodox rabbis and were castigated by most publicists of the Jewish community. We expected opposition but not the degree of venom and distortion that spewed forth. This was almost exclusively of a personal nature and failed to deal with the issues we raised ... were Jews not meant to act 'as the leaven unto bread'—the biblical phrase for a chosen few whose duty it was to show humanity the righteous path?*

For Kasrils and some of his supporters, the campaign was a homecoming of sorts, a way to connect to a sense of Jewish identity, long dormant in some cases, that was compatible with the ideological and political commitments of the 'struggle' experience. There were other sides to the story, however, and much that held broader political significance for South African Jews and other minority communities as well.

In order to consider the impact of the Kasrils affair, the book investigates broader patterns of Jewish political behaviour prior to the normalisation and democratisation of South African society. It describes subsequent debates within the Jewish community about the approach of communal leadership towards the government. It also examines aspects of political behaviour among other minorities and interest groups in South Africa, and compares the experience of the South African Jewish community in the Kasrils affair with the recent experiences of Jewish communities in Britain, France and the US.

The book observes that the South African Jewish community remains in a state of political transition, well over a decade into the democratic era. The central political question facing Jewish institutions at the end of apartheid was whether the community should be more politically outspoken than it had been in the past, or whether it should behave as an intercessor, using quiet tactics to achieve influence. The leadership of the Jewish community attempted to do both at once.

The book concludes that the Kasrils affair encouraged the communal leadership to cultivate a far closer relationship with the ruling party. It observes that new and independent voices began to emerge in the community, but that the community struggled to incorporate and tolerate diverse perspectives. It also suggests that institutional and political diversity are essential for minority groups and interest groups to affect policy debates in contemporary South Africa and to avoid co-option or isolation by the ruling party. This conclusion may apply to minorities in other democracies as well.

A brief editorial note: I have used the term "antisemitism" (and "antisemitic", "antisemite", etc.) in this book in contrast to the more common spelling, "anti-Semitism". The term "anti-Semitism" was developed in Germany in the late nineteenth century to give a pseudo-scientific, racial veneer to the hatred of Jews. It was intended to refer solely to Jews and not to "Semitic" peoples as such. In my view, and in the view of many scholars in the field of Jewish Studies, the word "antisemitism" is preferable because the hyphenated form of the term may preserve the old scientific and racist pretenses. Where the term "anti-Semitic" appears in block quotes, I have left it as is, even in quotes from texts that use the hyphen but (incorrectly) use lower case for both words (e.g. "anti-semitism").

I would like to thank Professor Milton Shain of the Isaac and Jessie Kaplan Centre for Jewish Studies for encouraging me to undertake this project as an MA thesis, and for providing constant support, assistance and encouragement throughout its preparation. The Kaplan Centre was particularly generous in granting me bursaries to fund my studies in 2004, 2005 and 2006. The South African Jewish Board of Deputies and its archives in Johannesburg were invaluable resources. Thanks are also due to the staff of the Jacob Gitlin Library in Cape Town, as well as the Jewish Studies Library at the Kaplan Centre, for their continued interest and assistance in my research, and their patience with me as I hoarded long-overdue books. I am also indebted to award-winning bloggers Michael Kransdorff and Steve Magid for their archive of opinion articles and their support.

In addition, I would like to thank Sandy Shepherd, Seshni Moodley-Kazadi, David Merrington, Lindsay Jane Norman and Wendy Priilaid for their assistance in bringing this book to publication.

My friend and intellectual co-conspirator, Theo Schkolne, provided and provoked many insights, both as I wrote my thesis and as I participated in some of the debates that are its focus. Rhoda Kadalie was generous with her home-cooked meals, and offered me a healthy motivational wager in the form of the bottle of wine of my choice should I finish my thesis on time. The Perkel family was a constant source of support, with Adrian attending my public talk, Jonah and Maisie accommodating me in their Johannesburg home, Jenny providing Shabbat hospitality, and Michaela producing ample amusement. Tony Leon of the Democratic Alliance gave me the opportunity to study and write about politics from the halls of Parliament. Bronagh Casey covered for me while I was out of the office on long lunch breaks. My father Raymond and my mother Naomi read preliminary drafts and offered suggestions. Above all, I want to thank my girlfriend Julia Bertelsmann for her unbounded love, lively enthusiasm and critical advice.

Finally, I must thank Ronnie Kasrils. Though he may not have intended any encouragement, in my arguments with him I began to discover and hone my political voice. Without his contributions to public debates about Israel and Zionism, however controversial, this book would never have been written.

CHAPTER ONE

INTRODUCTION

On Thursday 23 October 2001, the National Assembly of the Parliament of South Africa convened in Cape Town to consider and debate the report of a fact-finding mission that had been sent to Israel and the Palestinian territories three months before.[1] The task of the multiparty delegation had been to study the ongoing *intifada*, the latest tragic chapter in the decades-old conflict between Jews and Arabs over a land claimed by both. The hope was that South Africa's parliamentarians, with their fresh experience of conflict resolution in their own country, could offer insights to Israelis and Palestinians, recommend ways of reviving the peace process, and suggest how the South African government could become involved.[2] The work of the delegates was now set before Parliament and the nation.

Exactly six weeks before, on Tuesday 11 September 2001, 19 Arab hijackers had crashed commercial passenger jets into the World Trade Center in New York and the Pentagon in Washington, DC. The former was destroyed and the latter was severely damaged. Nearly 3 000 people died, and the US declared a 'war on terror' that continues to this day.

A debate about the Israeli–Palestinian conflict would have been combative under any circumstances, but in the weeks after the '9/11' attack, discussions about the Palestinian *intifada* and the Israeli response to it had become more

---

1 Parliament of South Africa. 'Report of the fact-finding mission to Israel and Palestine from 9 to 19 July 2001.
2 Parliament of South Africa (Hansard). 'Consideration of report of fact-finding mission to Israel and Palestine from 9 to 19 July 2001'. *Debates of the National Assembly* no 19 (23 to 26 October 2001): 6813–6864.

heated and passionate than ever before. By the time the fact-finding mission's report came before Parliament, American-led forces had already begun bombing targets in Afghanistan, Muslims around the world were preparing to observe the fast of the holy month of Ramadan, and terror and its causes were being debated feverishly around the world. The arguments in the National Assembly that afternoon were therefore more dramatic and intense than usual.

The divisions, however, were along typical party political lines. Members of the ruling African National Congress (ANC) defended the report, which had largely reflected their party's position by calling for a tough line against Israel. 'The report,' said Thandi R Modise, an ANC Member of Parliament (MP) and chairperson of the National Assembly's Portfolio Committee on Defence, '... draws a parallel between apartheid South Africa and the situation that is obtaining now in Palestine ... there is no way that South Africans, those of us who profess to understand, to love and to fight for democracy, can keep quiet ...'.[3]

Members of the opposition, led by the Democratic Party (DP), and joined by smaller parties, criticised the report, arguing that it 'tends to take sides'.[4] Dr B L 'Boy' Geldenhuys, who had represented the New National Party on the fact-finding mission—and who would be named South Africa's ambassador to Jordan in 2004—added: 'To equate what the report calls the oppression experienced by Palestinians with apartheid is also invalid and an open attempt to isolate Israel internationally ...'.[5]

The rebuttals were sharp and often bitter. 'The defining difference between the ANC and the DP-led opposition is our recognition of the fundamental right of people to resist occupation of their land, and we make no apologies for that,' said Ebrahim Ismail Ebrahim, an ANC MP who had participated in the fact-finding mission.[6] Another, referring to members of the opposition, added: '... [T]hey could not learn to be neighbours with black children. They could not because they lived under the threat and insecurity that there was always this myth about the 'swart gevaar' [black peril]. In Palestine and Israel, the 'gevaar' are the Arabs.'[7]

---

3   Modise, T R. 2001. Speech in the National Assembly, Parliament of South Africa, Cape Town. 23 October. *Debates of the National Assembly* no 19 (23 to 26 October 2001): 6815.
4   Van der Merwe, J H. 2001. Speech in the National Assembly, Parliament of South Africa, Cape Town. 23 October. *Debates of the National Assembly* no 19 (23 to 26 October 2001): 6824.
5   Geldenhuys, B L. 2001. Speech in the National Assembly, Parliament of South Africa, Cape Town. 23 October. *Debates of the National Assembly* no 19 (23 to 26 October 2001): 6829.
6   Ebrahim, E I. 2001. Speech in the National Assembly, Parliament of South Africa, Cape Town. 23 October. *Debates of the National Assembly* no 19 (23 to 26 October 2001): 6836.
7   Modise, T R. 2001. Speech in the National Assembly, Parliament of South Africa, Cape Town. 23 October. *Debates of the National Assembly* no 19 (23 to 26 October 2001): 6857.

The opposition hit back. 'The governing party in Parliament has a long-standing relationship with the Palestine Liberation Organisation ... [I]n order to retain the trust of both parties, and to facilitate peace effectively in the area, South Africa will have to demonstrate its impartiality. We have, thus far, dismally failed to do so,' said Dr Geldenhuys.[8] Dene Smuts, the DP delegate to the mission, spoke about her discussions with Palestinian parliamentarians in Gaza 'with whom it is possible to discuss these matters on a more rational basis than with my colleagues [in Parliament]', provoking interjections from the ANC benches.[9]

The first speeches in the debate were made by those who themselves had participated in the fact-finding mission. Later, other MPs with strong views on the subject were given the chance to express themselves. It was then that Ronnie Kasrils, Minister of Water Affairs and Forestry, approached the podium to read a statement he said he had prepared jointly with Max Ozinsky, an ANC member of the provincial legislature in the Western Cape.

It was a statement, Kasrils informed the Assembly, that he wished to circulate as a petition among South African Jews: 'We are issuing this publicly to call on all South Africans of Jewish descent to join us in signing this statement.'[10] He was, he declared, speaking out against Israel as a Jew, and encouraging other Jews to do the same.

The statement did not dispute 'that sectors of the Palestinian population have resorted to terror', but described the 'fundamental cause of the conflict' as 'Israel's occupation of Palestine and the suppression of the Palestinians' struggle for national self-determination'. Kasrils argued that blaming Israel for the conflict did not constitute antisemitism, 'nor does it amount to a denial of Israel's right to exist. Rather, it constitutes an urgent call on the Israeli government to redress injustice and satisfy legitimate claims.' Kasrils added that he felt compelled by the lessons of the Holocaust to speak out against Israeli policies, and 'to support justice and freedom from persecution for all people, regardless of their nationality, ethnicity or religion'. He warned that '[r]epression and reprisals in response to rebellion provide no relief'. He called for Israel to take a number of actions, including a withdrawal

---

[8] Geldenhuys, Ibid. In 2004 Geldenhuys would be appointed South African ambassador to the Kingdom of Jordan.
[9] Smuts, D. 2001. Speech in the National Assembly, Parliament of South Africa, Cape Town. 23 October. *Debates of the National Assembly* no 19 (23 to 26 October 2001): 6819.
[10] Kasrils, R. 2001. Speech in the National Assembly, Parliament of South Africa, Cape Town. 23 October. *Debates of the National Assembly* no 19 (23 to 26 October 2001): 6850.

from the occupied territories and the resumption of negotiations towards a two-state solution to the conflict, and asked South African Jews 'to raise their voices and join all governments and people in support of justice for Palestine'.[11]

The 'Kasrils declaration', as it became known, caused immediate sensation and controversy, not only in South Africa but also abroad, where it attracted attention in the pages of the *Washington Post*, among other media.[12] It marked the first time in recent world history (certainly since the late Austrian chancellor Bruno Kreisky in the 1970s and 1980s) that a prominent Jewish public official outside Israel had attacked the Israeli government and its policies so vehemently —and had done so, publicly and self-consciously, as a Jew.

The South African media gave great prominence to Kasrils's story. The morning after the parliamentary debate, the front-page headline in *The Citizen*, a conservative national daily tabloid, announced: 'SA slams Israel'.[13] Other newspapers, notably the *Sunday Independent*, greeted the Kasrils affair with enthusiasm. His stance was also welcomed by Muslim leaders, pro-Palestinian activists and members of the ruling party. Opposition figures, however, kept their distance.

Nowhere was the reaction to the Kasrils declaration more intense than among South African Jews. The official leadership of the community, in the form of the South African Jewish Board of Deputies, the South African Zionist Federation and the Beth Din (ecclesiastical court), rejected the Kasrils declaration out of hand. Many Jews repudiated it in critical and often angry letters to community and national newspapers, and protested loudly on talk radio and other media. A small minority of Jews, however, rallied around Kasrils. They defended him against his detractors and formed a Cape Town-based organisation, 'Not in My Name', to support the Kasrils declaration and to represent Jewish dissent against Israeli policies. A similar group, 'SA Jewish Voices', was later formed in Johannesburg.

Debate over the declaration in the Jewish community raged throughout November and December 2001 and well into 2002. The main community organ, the *South African Jewish Report*, tried to encourage 'open debate in troubled times', as the title of one editorial put it.[14] But few South African Jews on either

---

11 Ibid, 6844–6852.
12 Jeter, J 2001. 'South African Jews polarized over Israel'. *Washington Post*, A35, 19 December.
13 'SA slams Israel' 2001. *The Citizen*, 1, 24 October.
14 'Open debate in troubled times' 2001. *South African Jewish Report*, 6, 9 November.

side of the issue were in the mood for patient debate, and the stakes only grew higher as the arguments within the community drew wider interest from the general public. Though Kasrils and Ozinsky would ultimately fail to gather more than 300 signatures for the declaration—less than one half of one per cent of the adult South African Jewish population in the country—members and staff of the Board of Deputies interviewed for this book would later describe the Kasrils affair as 'the community's first major crisis in the post-apartheid era'.[15]

Why did the Kasrils declaration cause such an upheaval? Part of the reason lay in the strong feelings of solidarity among South African Jews towards Israel, and the community's deep historical attachment to Zionism—broadly defined as the belief that Jews have a right to self-determination in their religious and cultural homeland in the Middle East. Kasrils had not only openly challenged Israeli policies but had also challenged Zionism itself and its prominence in the intellectual, political and cultural life of South African Jews. More than two months before making his declaration, for example, he wrote a letter to the *Sunday Independent* in which he claimed that few South African Jews who had supported the anti-apartheid struggle had been Zionists.[16] In Parliament, he concluded his remarks by declaring that most Jewish anti-apartheid activists 'were in fact anti-Zionists and rejected Zionism because they believed in a common humanity and that there should not be an exclusive state …'.[17] As the debate unfolded, Kasrils would continue to suggest that South African Jews abandon Zionism, and to imply that a belief in Zionism was incompatible with the norms of South Africa's new democratic political order.

Another reason the Kasrils declaration evoked such strong responses was the political context in which it had been introduced. The emergence of new and often angry debates about the Israeli–Palestinian conflict coincided with a surge in reported acts of antisemitism across the globe. These acts ranged from verbal abuse and vandalism to the destruction of synagogues, the attempted murder of Jewish leaders, and terrorist bombings aimed at Jews.[18] The wave of violence and hatred was described by some observers as the 'new antisemitism'.[19]

---

15 Personal interview for thesis. October 2005. Interviewees were given assurances of anonymity.
16 Kasrils, R. 2001. 'Few of struggle's Jewish heroes were Zionists'. *Sunday Independent*, 12 August.
17 Kasrils, R. 2001. *Debates of the National Assembly*: 6852.
18 Stephen Roth Institute, Tel Aviv University 2001. 'United Kingdom' n.d. *Antisemitism Worldwide: Annual Report 2000/1* [online report]. URL: http://www.tau.ac.il/Antisemitism/annual-report-00-01.html
19 See Iganski, P & Kosmin, B. (Eds) 2003. *A New Antisemitism? Debating Judeophobia in 21st-Century Britain*. London: Profile Books.

There were relatively few recorded incidents of antisemitic violence in South Africa, but intense anti-Israel propaganda often spilled over into blatant antisemitic rhetoric.[20] The world watched in fascination and dismay in August 2001—only two months before the Kasrils affair began—as the United Nations World Conference against Racism, held in the South African port city of Durban, became a platform for antisemitic hate speech that sprouted alongside militant criticism of Israel. Jews around the world were shocked by images and reports from the conference. None, however, were more traumatised than South African Jews, who had experienced the onslaught most directly and closest to home. The *South African Jewish Report* commented at the time that there was 'genuine cause for concern' for the safety and future of Jews in South Africa.[21] The attacks of 9/11, which occurred on the heels of the racism conference and just before Rosh Hashanah, the Jewish New Year—a time of spiritual trepidation even in peaceful circumstances—left nerves in the community more frayed than before. Kasrils chose this moment of vulnerability to challenge publicly the political beliefs of South African Jews and to canvass support for views that matched those held by the community's most strident adversaries. The angry reaction was almost inevitable.

Perhaps the most provocative feature of the Kasrils initiative was the way in which Kasrils used the weight of his ministerial office and his stature in Parliament and the ruling party to campaign against the prevailing ideas and opinions of a small minority community. Kasrils happened to be a member of that community—though, by his own admission, his religious and cultural connections to South African Jewry were minimal.[22] Nonetheless, his dissent from the Jewish mainstream and his efforts to promote a Jewish political alternative were a form of intervention by the state in the affairs of the community. Kasrils maintained that he was speaking and acting in his personal capacity, but his declaration and other documents relating to his initiative were posted in a special section on the website of the Department of Water Affairs and Forestry, blurring the boundary between his personal and official roles.[23]

At the time, the Kasrils declaration was not the only effort by the ANC government to shape opinions in a minority community. A similar initiative was the 'Home For

---

20 Saks, D. 'South Africa'. *Antisemitism Worldwide: Annual Report 2003/4* [online report of the Stephen Roth Institute]. URL: http://www.tau.ac.il/Antisemitism/asw2003-4/south_africa.htm.
21 'Hijacking of a grand idea'. 2001. *South African Jewish Report*, 6, 31 August.
22 Kasrils, R & Ozinsky, M. 2001. 'In a propaganda war, truth is the victim'. *South African Jewish Report*, 7, 9 November.
23 See URL: http://www.dwaf.gov.za/Communications/Articles/Israel.asp. Kasrils continued to post his views and activities relating to the Israeli-Palestinian conflict on the Department of Intelligence website after being named Minister of Intelligence after the 2004 elections.

All' campaign, launched on 16 December 2000 (the Day of Reconciliation, a public holiday) by white left-wing activists, most of whom had links to the ANC. The campaign centred on a petition entitled 'The Declaration of Commitment by White South Africans', which acknowledged 'the white community's responsibility for apartheid' and declared that its signatories would 'commit ourselves to redressing these wrongs … through individual and collective action …'.[24] The Home For All campaign never achieved wide support, but was enthusiastically praised and promoted by the ANC government.[25] In 2004, the ANC provincial government in the Western Cape even adopted the phrase 'Home For All' as the province's official motto.[26]

Other such efforts included the government's overtures to the Afrikaans-speaking community, which often took the form of well-publicised meetings between President Thabo Mbeki and leading Afrikaner dignitaries. These typically concluded with strong endorsements of the President and the government by the invited guests. A group of 'leading Afrikaners' told the President in November 2005: 'We would like to say to you personally, thank you for the leadership that you have given to establish constitutional democracy and to build on it. The economic and other policy directions that you and your government have put in place have made SA a home for all and is [sic] an example to many other countries'.[27]

Notwithstanding these sentiments, the vast majority of Afrikaans-speaking voters continued to support the opposition in overwhelming proportions.[28] That pattern partly reflected a deep sense of alienation from the new government, as did the popularity of *De la Rey*, a song about a Boer war hero, which was released in 2007 by musician Bok van Blerk. The song not only achieved great commercial success but also provoked a heated political debate about the continued challenge of reconciliation in South Africa. In response to these developments, the ANC conducted targeted political campaigns among minority groups in which it had fared poorly in elections, even as it expanded its overall share of the national vote. In each case it sought symbolic declarations of loyalty to the government, its ideals and its policies from representatives of those communities.

---

24 Nathan, L. 2001. *The Declaration of Commitment by White South Africans*. Presentation to Harold Wolpe Forum, Cape Town, 20 February [online notes]. URL: http://www.wolpetrust.org.za/show.asp?inc=forums/2001/debate20.htm&menu=forummnu.htm
25 See Jordan, P. 2001. Speech during President's debate, National Assembly, Parliament, Cape Town, 14 February [online text]. URL: http://www.anc.org.za/ancdocs/speeches/2001/sp0214.html
26 Rasool, E. 2004. Speech at the launch of the Home For All logo, Cape Town, 16 December [online text]. URL: http://www.polity.org.za/pol/speech/2004/?show=61019
27 Hartley, W. 2005. 'Mbeki lauded by group of leading Afrikaners'. *Business Day*, 3, 9 November.
28 Leon, A J. 2005. Speech to Democratic Alliance members in Citrusdal, Western Cape, 18 May.

The Kasrils declaration can therefore be examined not only in the context of debates about Israel and the rise of the 'new antisemitism' worldwide but as part of a pattern of behaviour by an increasingly dominant majority party towards ethnic, religious and political minorities in South Africa. For Jews, the Kasrils declaration was not just a challenge to cherished Zionist beliefs but an instrument of political pressure applied to the community and its institutions to push them into agreement with the ANC's worldview and its policies on international affairs.

It was not the first time in South African history that the government had used disapproval of Israel in an attempt to prod South African Jews towards closer alignment with the ruling party. An earlier example, somewhat ironically, was the 'Verwoerd affair' of the early 1960s, when Prime Minister Hendrik Verwoerd—one of the chief architects of apartheid—attacked Israel's voting behaviour at the United Nations. Israel had joined African and Asian nations in votes in the UN General Assembly against apartheid. In one such episode in October 1961, it voted to censure South African foreign minister Eric Louw and to support diplomatic sanctions against South Africa.[29] Louw declared that he was certain that 'South African citizens who have racial and religious ties with Israel' would disagree with Israel's 'hostile and ungrateful' stance.[30] Verwoerd himself not only criticised Israel's actions publicly but, in a private letter that was leaked to the media, he also took the South African Jewish community to task. He noted in the letter that many South African Jews had voted for the anti-apartheid Progressive Party, and suggested ominously that antisemitism might rise in South Africa if the community did not distance itself from Israel's foreign policy.[31]

Verwoerd's statements ignited a vigorous public debate. The Prime Minister was roundly criticised in the English-language press, which accused him of trying to drive South African Jews into the ruling party's white ethnic *laager*.[32] He found support, however, in the Afrikaans press, where some commentators attempted to draw parallels between Zionism and apartheid as forms of ethnic nationalism, and to argue that it was hypocrisy to support the former and not the latter.[33]

---

29 Shimoni, G. 1980. *Jews and Zionism: The South African Experience 1910–1967*. Cape Town: OUP, 305–8.
30 Shimoni 1980, 308.
31 Shimoni 1980, 310–1.
32 Shimoni 1980, 311. The *laager* was a defensive circle of ox wagons, frequently used by the Voortrekkers in their clashes with African warriors in the 19th century.
33 Shimoni 1980, 312–3.

In the Jewish press, the complaint was that Verwoerd had implied that the Jewish future in South Africa was to be conditional on the community's support for government policies, even it that meant dissociation from Israel. An editorial in the *South African Jewish Times* protested: 'If words mean anything—and we must assume that the head of the State chooses his words meticulously—the Jews of South Africa are being regarded as hostages in forcing Israel's hand at the UN'.[34]

Kasrils did not directly threaten the Jewish community with antisemitism, or openly object to the tendency of Jews to vote for opposition parties. Yet, like Verwoerd, he implied that the community's support for Israel was seen by the ruling party as a potential obstacle to full political acceptance.

During the apartheid era, Jewish leadership had often buckled under such pressure. The Board of Deputies, the umbrella body of the community's various organisations, adhered—at least officially—to a longstanding policy of political neutrality and non-involvement, except in cases in which the civil rights and interests of Jews were directly affected. However, as historian Gideon Shimoni has observed, '… it cannot be said that the Board always passed the test of consistency'.[35] At times, in fact, the Board appeared eager to appease the apartheid government. For example, after Louw's rebuke it issued a press statement criticising Israel's votes against South Africa at the UN, much to the consternation of the Israeli government and to Jewish critics of apartheid.[36]

Though the Board often opposed racial discrimination in general terms, and never supported apartheid policies or racial ideologies, it often deferred to the government in circumstances in which stronger opposition may have been a reasonable or practicable course of action. Its official policy of non-involvement in broader political affairs allowed room for individual Jews to express their personal views and vote with their conscience. Yet the Board frequently failed to defend the civil liberties of many Jews, including rabbinical leaders who had incurred the displeasure of the government by protesting against apartheid. Indeed, the Board often tried to distance itself and the broader Jewish community from the beliefs and activities of dissident Jews.[37]

---

[34] Quoted in Shimoni. 1980, 314.
[35] Shimoni, G. 2003. *Community and Conscience: The Jews in Apartheid South Africa*. Hanover, NH: University Press at New England, 112.
[36] Shimoni 1980, 308–10.
[37] Shimoni 2003, 113–4.

The end of apartheid and the beginning of non-racial, constitutional democracy in the 1990s allowed the Jewish community to examine and debate its past behaviour and that of its leadership, as well as to set a new course for the future. The central political question facing Jewish institutions soon became whether, in a more democratic era but one dominated by a hegemonic ruling party, the Jewish community should be more politically outspoken than it had been in the past, or whether it should revert to a deferential posture in relation to a new government that had—as its predecessor did not—a true popular mandate.

Initially, the community's leaders opted for an active approach, rather than a deferential one. The Board redefined itself in the 1990s in a new 'mission statement': it would now move beyond the narrow task of defending Jewish liberties and interests and towards 'work for the betterment of human relations between Jews and all other peoples of South Africa', alongside a commitment to '… a new South Africa where everyone will enjoy freedom from the evils of prejudice, intolerance and discrimination'.[38] Shimoni has described this as a shift to an 'advocacy' role.[39]

The new 'advocacy' approach, which implied a more assertive public political role for the Board, was evinced in the community's reactions to the Kasrils declaration. In November 2001, at the height of the Kasrils affair, the Board's national vice-chairman, Michael Bagraim, declared: 'No longer can we say as we did in the '60s, '70s and '80s that "we must not rock the boat", and no longer can we say as we did in the '90s that we are doing things "behind the scenes". It is now necessary for us to be in your face.'[40]

Three years later, however, in September 2004, as national chairman of the Board, writing in his weekly column in the *South African Jewish Report*, Bagraim took a different stance: 'In order to fulfil our mandate of protecting South African Jewry, we need to influence those who are in a position to assist us. It is unreasonable for us to publicly attack someone one week and then ask him for favours the next.'[41] This indicated a dramatic change in the Board's political tactics. It no longer defined itself as an advocacy organisation but as a 'lobbying' organisation, one focused on building relationships with the ruling party. As Bagraim wrote in his message for

---

38　Quoted in Shimoni 2003, 258.
39　Shimoni 2003, 258.
40　Bagraim, M. 2001/2. Quoted in 'SAJBD Cape Conference faces the future'. *Cape Jewish Chronicle*, 4, December/January.
41　Bagraim, M. 2004. 'Above Board: Reiterating Board's view'. *South African Jewish Report*, 5, 10 September.

the Board's 43rd national conference in Johannesburg in August 2005, 'The Board is primarily a lobbying organisation, one that seeks to promote the interests of the Jewish community through the politics of influence'.[42] Whatever outrage Kasrils provoked within the Jewish community and among most of its leaders, Jewish institutions were closer to the orbit of the ruling party at the affair's end than at its beginning.

It is difficult to determine precisely what caused the Board to change its approach. Its shift was not the result of any public decision, nor did the Board's political posture come up for discussion or debate at any of its annual conferences, where most of its major policies are determined.[43] The personal idiosyncrasies of Board members may have played a role. A new national executive took office in August 2003, and regional executives elected in that year included some new faces with connections to the ANC, such as Justice Dennis Davis in the Cape, a prominent jurist and former anti-apartheid activist.

Yet the timing of the Board's shift strongly suggests that the Kasrils affair had a significant impact on the community's political posture. Even as Bagraim was promising 'in your face' tactics in 2001, the Board's Cape Council chairman, Philip Krawitz, complained: 'We no longer have the ear of government.'[44] This exclusion presented a great challenge to the Board in its advocacy role at the very moment that its mandate to speak on behalf of all South African Jews was being contested by Kasrils and his supporters. The Board's reaction to these circumstances had a profound effect on its broader political posture.

Finally, it is important not to overstate the degree to which the South African Jewish community regards the South African government as an external entity. The Jewish community is not in opposition to the government, nor should it be; South African Jews have a great stake in the success of the government and of South Africa's new democracy more generally. At the same time, the Jewish community is a defined group with distinct interests. Even within the ruling ANC, there are factions and interest groups vying for attention, influence and power. The Jewish community, whether for or against the government of the day on specific issues, is no different. The task of this book is to describe, understand and explain the community's political behaviour and that of its leadership.

---

42 Bagraim, M. 2005. *National Chairman's Message*. South African Jewish Board of Deputies' 43rd National Conference programme, 7, August.
43 An attempt at raising some of these issues at the Board's national conference in August 2007 was largely unsuccessful.
44 Krawitz, P. 2001/2. Quoted in 'SAJBD Cape Conference faces the future'. *Cape Jewish Chronicle*, 4, December/January.

CHAPTER TWO

POLITICS AND SOUTH AFRICAN JEWRY BEFORE 1994

The political behaviour of the contemporary South African Jewish community emerges from, and responds to, a long history. Jewish political behaviour is also shaped by the social, economic, cultural and religious attributes of the community. To fully understand the choices made by South African Jews and Jewish leadership during the Kasrils affair, it is necessary to describe the community and to examine the history of its political behaviour, both prior to and after apartheid.

The South African Jewish community is unique within Diaspora Jewry. Small in number, nearly homogeneous in ethnic origin, rich in cultural and religious life, South African Jews have contributed to the country in many diverse fields of endeavour, and continue to play an important role in the life of the nation.

South African Jews today number roughly 80 000 people, about 0.2 per cent of the national population of 45 million.[45] Almost all are white,[46] forming less than 2 per cent of the white population,[47] and the overwhelming majority is Ashkenazic; i.e., of Eastern European origin. Most South African Jews trace their recent ancestors to the Baltic region, especially Lithuania, Poland and the north-western area of the Pale of Settlement to which Jews were confined in the Russian Empire.[48] Persecution, poverty and pogroms at home and new economic

---

45 Saks, D. 2003. *South African Jewry: A Contemporary Portrait*. Institute of the World Jewish Congress, Policy Study no 25, 3, 5–7.
46 Here I am referring to the general term of everyday use referring to skin colour or race—an ascribed, not an intrinsic, characteristic.
47 Saks 2003, 7.
48 Shimoni 2003, 2–3.

opportunities abroad prompted hundreds of thousands of these 'Litvak' Jews to emigrate in the late 19th and early 20th centuries.[49] Many went to North America, and some to South America or Palestine; roughly 40 000 also settled in South Africa prior to World War I.[50]

The 'Litvaks' were not the first Jews in South Africa, however. The earliest Jewish communities were of western European (primarily British and German) origin and were established in the mid-19th century.[51] These early immigrant outposts played a formative role in building the community's institutional framework. There is also today a sizeable number of Sephardic Jews, as well as a small population of Israeli immigrants, and Jews who have emigrated from other African countries.[52]

Today, Jews live almost exclusively in or near South Africa's two largest cities. Johannesburg, with over 52 000 Jews, and Cape Town, with just under 20 000, together account for almost 90 per cent of the Jewish population.[53] Several thousand Jews live in the 'country communities', the remnant of a rural Jewish population that was far larger in the late 19th and early 20th centuries.[54] Despite the humble origins of most South African Jews, the community is today an affluent one. Most Jews enjoy a comfortable quality of life, comparable to that of most affluent South Africans.[55]

One of the most distinguishing features of South African Jewry is the dominance of Orthodox Judaism. Only a small (but growing) proportion of the community is strictly observant. However, most South African Jews follow the traditional liturgy of Orthodox Judaism and acknowledge the authority of Orthodox rabbis. Some 88 per cent of all synagogues in South Africa are affiliated to the Orthodox movement.[56] The peculiar religious character of the South African Jewish community has been described as 'non-observant Orthodoxy'.[57]

---

49 See also Bradlow, E. 1978. *Immigration to the Union, 1910–1948: Policies and attitudes*. Unpublished PhD dissertation. University of Cape Town.
50 Saron, G. 2001. *The Jews of South Africa: An Illustrated History to 1953*, ed N Musiker. Johannesburg: Scarecrow Books, 54.
51 Shain, M. 1994. *The Roots of Antisemitism in South Africa*. Charlottesville, VA: Virginia University Press, 12.
52 DellaPergola, & Dubb. A A 1988. 'South African Jewry: A sociodemographic profile' in *American Jewish Year Book 1988*, 88, 66–7, eds D Singer & R R Seldin. New York: American Jewish Committee; Saks 2003, 7.
53 Saks 2003, 6.
54 Saks 2003, 6, 10.
55 Kosmin, B A et al. 1998. Jews of the 'new South Africa': Highlights of the 1998 national survey of South African Jews. *Institute for Jewish Policy Research*, 3, September.
56 Saks 2003, 11–2.
57 Hellig, J. 1984. 'Religious expression'. *South African Jewry: A Contemporary Survey*, ed M Arkin. Cape Town: OUP,. 95–116, cf. 102.

Another unique trait of South African Jewry is the community's fervent support of Zionism and the State of Israel, exceeding that of most other Diaspora communities. Although this passion is often said to have diminished somewhat in recent years, an observation reflected in declining emigration to Israel,[58] it remains strong. Zionism has been described as the 'civil religion' of South African Jewry,[59] and South African Jews follow events and trends in Israel with keen interest.

South African Jewry has a highly centralised institutional structure. The first countrywide Jewish institution was the South African Zionist Federation (SAZF), founded in 1898.[60] Though essentially based on a political ideology, the SAZF played a far broader communal role, and performed various cultural and social functions. It soon became, in Shimoni's words, 'the pre-eminent institution in the life of the community'.[61] Today the dominance of the SAZF has declined considerably. It maintains active branches throughout the country, however, and remains the Jewish community's primary representative voice on issues relating to Israel and the Middle East. Thousands of people attend Zionist lectures and events each year, and Jewish children continue to participate in Zionist youth movements and summer camps in large numbers.

Religiously, the affairs of Orthodox Jews—including more recently arrived sects such as Lubavitch Chabad—are managed by the national rabbinate through the Union of Orthodox Synagogues (UOS) and the Beth Din. The Reform Jewish minority is represented by the rabbis of the South African Union of Progressive Judaism. Relations between Orthodox and Reform rabbis are, unfortunately, uncomfortable and occasionally even hostile. In November 2005, Chief Rabbi Dr Warren Goldstein boycotted a memorial service in Johannesburg marking the 10th anniversary of the assassination of Israeli Prime Minister Yitzchak Rabin, because of the participation of a Reform rabbi in the ceremony, provoking a bitter public debate.[62]

---

58 Shain, M. 2002. 'South African Jewry: Emigrating? At risk? Or restructuring the Jewish future?' in *Continuity, Commitment, and Survival: Jewish Communities in the Diaspora*, eds S Encel & L Stein. Praeger Series on Jewish and Israeli Studies. Westport, CT: Praeger, 117.
59 Shain 2002, 106.
60 Shimoni 1980, 20.
61 Shimoni 2003, 4.
62 Halle, C. 2005. 'SA chief rabbi refused to attend Rabin memorial'. *Haaretz*, 11 November [Web article]. URL: http://www.haaretz.com/hasen/objects/pages/PrintArticleEn.jhtml?itemNo=647027; Schneider, M 2005. Goldstein sticks to his guns. *South African Jewish Report*, 1, 16 December.

The community also maintains an extensive network of charitable institutions. Organisations such as the Chevra Kadisha (burial society) have long provided for indigent members of the community. Newer institutions such as MaAfrika Tikkun conduct relief work and provide social services in South Africa's disadvantaged communities. Jewish educational institutions are also prominent, with 80 per cent of Jewish school-age children attending Jewish day schools—an unusually high rate compared to other Diaspora communities.[63] Other important institutions include the Israel United Appeal-United Communal Fund (IUA-UCF), which raises funds for various community purposes, and the Community Security Organisation (CSO), founded in 1993, which is a volunteer network that protects synagogues and Jewish institutions from crime and terror in coordination with the South African police and security services.

By far the most important institution in South African Jewish life historically and today is the South African Jewish Board of Deputies (SAJBOD or simply 'the Board'). The Board's leadership is 'deputised' by other Jewish institutions that appoint representatives, and by registered members of the community who vote for at-large positions on the Board's regional councils in elections held at regular intervals. The Board was formed in the Transvaal in 1903 and in the Cape in 1904 in response to immigration laws that were passed in those regions that would have kept Jews from entering the country.[64] A national organisation was formally amalgamated as the South African Jewish Board of Deputies in 1912 (coincidentally, the same year as the formation of the ANC), following the formation of the Union of South Africa in 1910.[65] Today, the Board serves as the central administrative institution of South African Jewry. It coordinates its activities with the UOS and other community institutions, though each is responsible for its own functions. In 2000, the Board, the SAZF and the UCF signed an administrative cooperation agreement and moved into a joint headquarters in the suburb of Raedene in Johannesburg.[66]

---

63 Saks 2003, 13.
64 Saron 1953, 80; Saron, G & Hotz, L. (Eds) 1955. *The Jews in South Africa: A History*. Cape Town: Oxford University Press (OUP), 226–269; Shain, M. 1983. *Jewry and Cape Society: The Origins and Activities of the Jewish Board of Deputies for the Cape Colony*. Cape Town: Historical Publication Society, 71–2.
65 Saron 1953, 84.
66 Shain, M. 2001. 'South Africa' in *American Jewish Year Book 2001*, eds D Singer & L Grossman, vol 101, 466. New York: American Jewish Committee.

Many South African Jews tend to choose vocations in professional fields such as medicine, law and accountancy; some are also among the country's business leaders. Roughly a third of South African Jews who are employed work as professionals.[67] Few choose political careers, and yet South African Jews have long played, and continue to play, a prominent role in South African political life. Historically, Jewish politicians have tended to represent opposition parties of various kinds, though some have aligned themselves with the government, both during the apartheid era and today. Jews who played emblematic roles during the political struggles of the apartheid era included the liberal anti-apartheid parliamentarian Helen Suzman, the communist leader Joe Slovo and the conservative state prosecutor Percy Yutar. In the post-apartheid era, Tony Leon led the Democratic Alliance from 1994 to 2007 and served as Leader of the Opposition from 1999 to 2007; Ronnie Kasrils serves in the Cabinet and has held high rank in the ANC and in the South African Communist Party (SACP).[68]

Jewish voters have tended to support moderate opposition parties since the National Party (NP) victory in 1948. In the years immediately prior to the apartheid era, and in its first three decades, Jewish voters backed the United Party (UP) in preference to the NP by overwhelming margins. The antisemitic ideologies and policies of the NP—Jews were disqualified for many years from membership in the NP in the province of Transvaal[69]—kept most Jewish voters away, even after the NP had dropped these offensive features. The NP began to attract more Jewish votes in the era of 'reformed' apartheid in the late 1970s and onward, but the majority of Jews still supported the opposition.[70] In addition to the UP, many Jews were also active members and supporters of anti-apartheid parties such as the Liberal Party, which was active in the 1950s and 1960s, and the Progressive Party (later the Progressive Federal Party, or PFP) which broke away from the United Party in 1959. By 1977 the PFP had replaced the UP as the favourite among Jewish voters.[71] Jews continued to vote for the PFP and its descendant, the Democratic Party, through the 1990s. A small minority of Jews joined radical

---

67 Kosmin 1999, 9.
68 Kasrils was voted off the Central Committee of the SACP in 2007 but was then 'co-opted' into its ranks. SACP Central Committee Press Statement, 19 August 2007 [online document]. URL: http://www.sacp.org.za/main.php?include=docs/pr/2007/pr0819a.html. See Epilogue.
69 Shimoni 1980, 123.
70 Shimoni 2003, 126–7.
71 Ibid, 126.

anti-apartheid organisations such as the Congress of Democrats, the ANC and the SACP, and Jewish names were prominent among those whites who had been banned, imprisoned or forced into exile by the South African government.[72]

Today, a small percentage of Jews continues to support the ANC. Most, however, vote for the opposition. In the 1994 elections, 56.4 per cent of Jews reported voting for the DP, 30.8 per cent for the NP and 11 per cent for the ANC.[73] In the years since then, support among Jews for the DP and its successor, the DA, increased while support for the NP and NNP collapsed, and support for the ANC declined considerably. The DP was estimated to have won 80 per cent of the Jewish vote in the 1999 elections (the most recent election for which such data are available)[74] and Jewish support for the DA probably remains at similar levels. In a municipal by-election in the Johannesburg suburb of Houghton in July 2005 in which all three candidates were Jewish, the DA won nearly 84 per cent of the vote, the ANC less than 9 per cent and the Independent Democrats (ID) less than 8 per cent.[75]

Despite the clear political preferences of most Jews, the community's leaders have long maintained that there is no 'Jewish vote'. The Board has insisted that individual Jews should vote as they feel best, but that the community as a whole can take no collective political stand. This is in keeping with the Board's official policy of non-involvement in political affairs, save where they directly concern Jews and Jewish interests. The Board has, with a few exceptions, maintained this policy almost since its inception.[76] In 1910, before the formation of the national Board, the Transvaal Board opposed an attempt by a Jewish candidate to call for a Jewish vote against Afrikaner nationalist parties, arguing that '… in politics the Jews are in no way distinct from other sections of the community …'.[77] The Board has clung to this neutral posture for a century, and has resisted

---

72 Ibid, 60–3.
73 Kosmin 1999, 23.
74 Saks 2003, 19.
75 Independent Electoral Commission of South Africa. 'By-election detailed results report for 27 July 2005' [online report]. URL: http://www.elections.org.za/InternetReportsIEC/DetailedReport/ByElectionDetailReport.asp?IWardID=79400074&IElectionID=91
76 By contrast, leaders in other minority groups often explicitly support political parties. In the 2004 election, Muslim leaders made clear that Muslims were expected to vote for the ANC and against the DA. See Vahed, G & Jeppie, S. 2004/5. 'Multiple communities: Muslims in post-apartheid South Africa'. State of the Nation: South Africa 2004–2005. Human Sciences Research Council [online document]. URL: http://www.hsrcpress.ac.za/download.asp?filename=2055_10_State_of_the_Nation_2004–2005–16112004105739AM.pdf. 278-9.
77 Raphaely, S. 1980. Quoted in Shimoni, 76.

appeals from both inside and outside the community for Jews to act as a group in support of any particular political cause outside of the narrow scope of Jewish affairs. During the apartheid era in particular, the Board avoided expressing opinions on general political matters, except in the vaguest terms and when such expressions were least likely to cause controversy.

The policy of non-involvement was severely tested and constantly contested by both supporters and opponents of the government, inside and outside the community. Debates about the stance that Jews should take were often passionate and sometimes acrimonious. In an exchange in 1957 in the pages of *Commentary*, a journal founded by the American Jewish Committee, critic Ronald M Segal charged that South African Jews, 'whether by commission or quiet omission', had been guilty of 'an abdication of their moral place in history'.[78] South African author Dan Jacobson replied that, while one could try to persuade South African Jews to oppose apartheid, to demand that they do so collectively amounted to an unreasonable demand for communal 'martyrdom'.[79] Only in apartheid's later years did the Board express a political opinion on the major issues facing the country. In 1985 it formally rejected apartheid for the first time. By then, many other religious groups and communities had already done so.[80]

In the post-apartheid era, the Board began to explore a more active public role, speaking out on such issues as the HIV/AIDS pandemic, racial tolerance and free speech. However, it still maintained a formal policy of political neutrality. This neutrality became somewhat compromised in the aftermath of the Kasrils affair (as I shall discuss in chapter five).

Among the dynamic and diverse political views held by South African Jews, one creed has remained constant: the community's commitment to Zionism. Typical Zionist activities include fundraising for Israel-related causes; public education on the Middle East; volunteering or travelling in Israel; participating in youth movements; and attending Israeli-themed cultural activities. In 1950, nearly half of all South African Jews held formal membership in the World Zionist Organisation, a percentage not matched by any other Diaspora commu-

---

78 Segal, R M & Jacobson, D. 1957. 'Apartheid and South African Jewry'. *Commentary*, November, 424–31.
79 Ibid.
80 Shimoni 2003, 138.

nity.[81] Fifty years later, enthusiasm for the cause remained strong: 5 000 Jews in Johannesburg and 4 000 in Cape Town attended celebrations to mark Yom Ha'atzmaut, the Israeli independence day, in 2001.[82] Subsequent years have also seen strong attendance at Israel-related events.

Support for Zionism among South African Jews, while staunch, has never been monolithic. The many different factions and opinions within the worldwide Zionist movement found their reflection in South African Jewry as well. Socialist and leftist Zionist youth movements such as Habonim and Hashomer Hatza'ir have existed in South Africa alongside religious Zionist movements such as Bnei Akiva and right-wing secular Zionist movements such as Betar. Among adults, there are organisations that support Israel's left-wing parties, such as Friends of Labour Israel, as well as those that support Israel's right-wing parties and religious movements.

There are various reasons for the Jewish community's strong attachment to Zionism in South Africa. Shimoni points out that 'the paramount political movement within Lithuanian Jewry was Zionism, and in no country was Zionism more firmly entrenched than in interwar independent Lithuania'.[83] Litvaks then brought their enthusiasm for Zionism with them to South Africa. In addition, Zionism was a form of positive ethnic and national identification for Jews in South Africa's highly group-conscious society.[84] For many Jews, Zionism provided an escape from or an answer to antisemitism. It offered a positive answer to the negative historical identity of Jews as victims. It also offered an alternative form of nationalism and national identification for Jews who yearned to belong to a national group but were troubled and excluded by the racially and ethnically narrow Afrikaner nationalism of the 20th century.

While Zionism was embraced by the overwhelming majority of South African Jews, a few dissented. Through the late 1940s, there was a small but visible anti-Zionist presence within South African Jewry,[85] which has been revived somewhat in recent times. Some Jewish immigrants, such as those who had been involved

---

81 Shimoni 2003, 5.
82 Shain, M. 2002. 'South Africa' in *American Jewish Year Book 2002*, eds D Singer & L Grossman, vol 101, 505. New York: American Jewish Committee.
83 Shimoni 2003, 4.
84 Ibid.
85 Adler, T. 1978. 'Lithuania's Diaspora: The Johannesburg Jewish Workers' Club, 1942–1948'. *Journal of Southern African Studies*, 6, no 1, 70–92.

in the socialist Bund movement or in community and trade union movements in Eastern Europe, advocated alternative solutions to the so-called 'Jewish Question', including migration to the semi-autonomous region of Birobidzhan in eastern Siberia.[86] However, these views and their proponents remained marginal in the community.

Zionist organisations in South Africa did not generally venture into or comment on local politics, but different views on the South African situation existed within the movement. Among youth movements, the leftist Habonim organisation preached racial and gender equality even at the height of apartheid.[87] The hawkish Revisionist Zionist movement did not support apartheid either, and backed Israel's opposition to it in the 1960s, but was critical of Israel's enthusiasm to align with African nations against South Africa.[88] Whatever their views on specific issues, Zionist organisations were careful to emphasise their South African patriotism. Displays such as an honour guard of Zionist youth at the 'Flame of Unity' at Parliament during the Union Jubilee Festival in 1960 were not uncommon.[89]

Today, the Zionist movement in South Africa has retreated somewhat from its dominance in the 1950s and 1960s, owing to a variety of factors. These include emigration, fundraising difficulties and the increasing religiosity of the Jewish community, especially in Johannesburg, which has seen worship and study replace Zionist activism as the cornerstone of communal social life. Emigration or *aliyah* to Israel has been relatively weak in recent decades, with anglophonic countries the destinations of choice for most Jewish families.[90] However, Zionist passions still run deep. In 1998, 54 per cent of South African Jews said they felt a 'strong attachment' to Israel, and 33 per cent said they felt a 'moderate attachment'. Only 12 per cent felt 'no special attachment', and 1 per cent felt 'negative feelings towards Israel'.[91] An unusually large 59 per cent of South African Jews reported having visited Israel at least once in the preceding decade.[92]

---

86 Ibid, 80.
87 Shimoni 2003, 117–9.
88 Shimoni 1980, 348–9.
89 Bernstein, E. 1968. 'A bird's-eye view of South African Jewry today'. *South African Jewry (1967/68 edition)*, ed L Feldberg. Johannesburg: Fieldhill. Reprinted by South African Jewish Board of Deputies c. 1975, 9. Following Zuma;s ascent within the ANC, Israeli officials expected a rise in South African immigrants, but a similar and perhaps greater rise occured elsewhere.
90 Saks 2003, 9.
91 Kosmin 1999, 15.
92 Ibid.

The importance of Zionist political ideology in communal life belies the fact that South African Jews have not always enjoyed the right to express their political beliefs. In fact, Jews suffered various forms of legal and religious discrimination for much of South Africa's history. This discrimination persisted through the mid 19th century and continued for many decades in certain parts of the country. Well into the 20th century, Jews had to struggle to defend their rights and their equal legal status in (white) South African society. These struggles shaped the subsequent political behaviour of the Jewish community and its institutions. The roots of the minority politics practised today by the Board and Jewish leadership in general can be traced to these early battles.

Prior to the 19th century, Jews, as non-Protestants, did not enjoy religious freedom in South Africa, which was then under Dutch rule. Individual Jews who arrived in the Dutch colony at the Cape hid their religion or had to undergo baptism before their arrival, since the Dutch East India Company required that all residents be Protestants.[93] The Batavian Republic introduced religious freedom at the Cape in 1803,[94] and the arrival of the British and their establishment of a colony in the Cape in 1806 led to increased religious freedom for Jews. Legal discrimination against Jews was only fully abolished in the Cape, however, in 1860.[95] Full equality led to the direct participation of individual Jews in political life. In the late 19th and early 20th century, several Jews ascended to high political office in the Cape, including Hyman Lieberman, who served as mayor of Cape Town for three years at the turn of the century. In Natal, Sir Matthew Nathan became the first Jew to represent the Crown in a British colony when he served as Governor from 1907 to 1910.[96]

For Jews living in the Boer republics of the Orange Free State and the Transvaal, where the Jewish population began growing rapidly in the late 19th century, life was more restricted. Jews often enjoyed good relations with Afrikaners and Afrikaner leaders, and were also granted religious freedom. However, Jews (along with Catholics) suffered certain forms of civil and political discrimination. Many Jews were considered foreigners or *uitlanders*, and therefore could

---

93 Shain 1983, xv.
94 Saron 1953, 7.
95 Ibid; Shain, M. 1994. *The Roots of Antisemitism in South Africa*. Johannesburg: Witwatersrand UP, 11.
96 Saron 1953, 49.

not vote.⁹⁷ Furthermore, those Jews who could vote were often barred from holding public office. Jewish intercessions with Transvaal President Paul Kruger failed to effect the full removal of these restrictions.⁹⁸

In addition to political discrimination, Jews also suffered a certain amount of social discrimination in both the Boer republics and the British colonies. However, in many places Jews also enjoyed a status that was rarely equalled elsewhere in the Diaspora. They were involved in the founding of several South African towns and cities, particularly in the Transvaal, and played a major role in South Africa's early agricultural, industrial and commercial development. Some Jews also fought in the South African War (Anglo-Boer War), mostly but not exclusively on the British side. The conclusion of that war in 1902 was followed by the formation of the Union of South Africa in 1910, after which Jews enjoyed full legal and political rights throughout the country. Five Jews were elected to the first Union Parliament in 1910, all representing the pro-British Unionist Party.⁹⁹

While individual Jews were beginning to play important political roles, a communal political identity began to emerge in battles against hostile and discriminatory immigration laws. Restrictive laws in the Transvaal and the Cape in 1903 and 1904 respectively were followed by the Immigration Act of 1913, passed by the Union Parliament, which allowed immigrants to be excluded on racial grounds.¹⁰⁰ The primary targets of this new legislation were Indian immigrants, but the government also wished to exclude those whites—primarily Jews—who were considered 'undesirable'. The proposed means of exclusion in early drafts of the legislation was a language test administered by an immigration officer, who would himself choose the language in which prospective immigrants would have to write out 50 words he dictated.¹⁰¹

Jews did their best to defend their liberty to immigrate. The Board of Deputies, newly amalgamated into a national organisation, worked actively to oppose the Immigration Bill and to encourage the government to amend it. The Board made use of the fact that Jews were now represented in the Union Parliament and could voice the community's concerns in the halls of power. One of these,

---

97 Shimoni 1980, 61.
98 Saron 1953, 20–8.
99 Shimoni 1980, 70.
100 Saron 1955, 104.
101 Shimoni 1980, 76–7.

Morris Alexander, spoke against the bill in Parliament on the grounds that it could allow an immigration officer to exclude Jews arbitrarily. He proposed that immigrants be asked to write the test in a European language, with Yiddish (spoken by most Jewish immigrants) included as such, and that an appeals board be created at which immigrants might have a second hearing.[102]

Ultimately, after much political wrangling—due largely to opposition in Parliament that was unrelated to the concerns of the Jewish community—a compromise was reached. A language test would be administered, but the immigrant him- or herself would choose the language. Critically (from a Jewish perspective), Yiddish would be included among acceptable European languages. An appeals board was established, to which the Board of Deputies insisted that a Jew be appointed. The government assured Jewish leaders that clauses in the legislation permitting the exclusion of poor immigrants would not be used to ban destitute Jews from entering the country. It was an early and important victory for the Board.[103]

The South African Indian community, however, was less pleased. Mahatma Gandhi—later to become the leader of the movement against British rule in India—had led his community's opposition to early versions of the Immigration Bill, yet his cause was not joined by the Board. As Shimoni notes: '… it was characteristic of the caste-like divisions in South African society that it did not occur to the Jewish leaders to link their objections to those of the Indians'.[104] The Jewish leadership had not opposed the principle of discriminatory legislation. It had merely sought to remove Jews from among those groups that were to be discriminated against. This occurred again in 1924, when the Board protested against the Class Areas Bill, a forerunner of the Group Areas Act. The Board's concern was that the bill should not attempt to impose segregation on Jews. No mention was made about the fate of Indians, who were again the primary target.[105]

These episodes highlighted an important but unspoken feature of the Board's policy of political non-involvement. Active and outspoken in defence of Jewish rights, the Board consciously chose to pursue Jewish rights separately from those of other vulnerable groups, and the rights of 'non-white' South Africans in

---

102 Ibid, 77.
103 Ibid, 78–9.
104 Ibid, 79.
105 Ibid, 79–80.

general. This meant not only that the Board would abstain from everyday politics but that the Jewish community would have no official voice in the debates and struggles that were to define South African politics in the 20th century. Shimoni notes that Jewish political activism on the community level was characterised by

> [a] detachment from the fate of the non-Whites which marked the Jewish community's development in South African society. Qua organised community, the Jews were preoccupied with looking after their own frequently vulnerable interests, and with seeking their own advancement in the host society'.

In mitigation, Shimoni adds that the era also 'reveals the equally characteristic fact that Jews nevertheless predominated amongst the few Whites who were dissenters and took up the cause of the underprivileged classes'.[106]

Meanwhile, the immigration issue refused to go away. The 'Red Scare' of the early 1920s and Afrikaner nationalist agitation of the 1930s also led to attempts to restrict Jewish immigration and civil rights. The Immigration Quota Act of 1930 was passed by the Nationalist government and excluded immigrants from certain—predominantly Eastern European—countries, with the deliberate intent of shutting Jews out of South Africa. The proposal had support in both the Afrikaans and English press, which supported a quota system similar to the one that the US had introduced in 1924. Opposition parties also supported the legislation, with the only real resistance coming from Jewish MPs and a few liberal politicians such as Jan H Hofmeyr.[107]

The Jewish community had been caught off guard when the bill was introduced. The Board and the SAZF organised protests of Jews all across the nation. Kentridge took up the cause in Parliament, while the Board attempted to intercede by meeting with government leaders. These efforts failed, and, after the bill was enacted into law, the Board contemplated a more far-reaching political response that included organising a 'Jewish vote', something the community's leaders had long resisted.[108] Such thoughts may have been prompted by the rising threat of Nazism. C P Robinson, a Jewish MP who had opposed the legislation, wrote: 'Do not tell me this is merely a bill for the exclusion of Lithuanian Jews. It sounds the death knell of any more Jews

---

106 Shimoni 1980, 80.
107 Ibid, 97–101.
108 Ibid, 106.

coming to South Africa. At present it is the poor Lithuanian, to-morrow it may be the Jew from Germany or France that will not be allowed to come in.'[109]

As he predicted, when the threat to German Jews in Europe became acute, and thousands of German Jewish refugees began arriving in South Africa in the 1930s, further legislative efforts were made to keep them out. Reaction to the new immigrant wave was particularly hostile among Afrikaner nationalists, who were becoming increasingly pro-Hitler in outlook and who staged a sensational protest in 1936 against the arrival of the *Stuttgart*, a ship that had been specially chartered to carry German Jewish refugees to safety.[110] The Fusion government (a coalition formed by Jan Smuts's South African Party and Barry Hertzog's National Party, which together formed the United South African National Party) responded by passing the Aliens Act of 1937, which cut off Jewish immigration altogether. In the parliamentary debate, Daniel François Malan—who had assumed the helm of a new right-wing opposition party, the *Gesuiwerde* (Purified) National Party—made explicit attacks against Jews and suggested that restrictions on Jews were necessary to allow white Afrikaners to prosper.[111]

Neither the Board of Deputies nor the Jewish MPs offered much opposition to the bill. Jewish leaders had become so overwhelmed by anxiety about antisemitism that they often chose to contain or appease it rather than confront it directly. As Shimoni notes:

> *Despite the crying moral need to assist its refugee brethren, the Board's Executive in fact capitulated to the public clamour against German-Jewish immigration which the anti-Semites had fanned into a hysteria: it appealed to the organizers of the immigration 'to bring about a dramatic diminution of the immigration' ... A strain of apologetics was evident in the Board's response to antisemitism. It attached importance to sensitizing and disciplining the behaviour of the individual Jew in his public and economic dealings; strained itself to avoid publicity about Jews, and favoured the production of enlightenment literature proving the value of the Jew.*[112]

---

109 Robinson, C P. Quoted in Shain 1994, 140.
110 Saron 2001, 155.
111 Saunders, C (ed) 1995. *Illustrated History of South Africa: The Real Story*. Cape Town: Reader's Digest. 347. See also Saron 2001, 155.
112 Shimoni 1980, 149–50.

The Board had little choice, however. Its attempts to take a more active political role had failed. In 1938, the Board experimented with direct intervention in politics, breaking its neutrality by explicitly encouraging Jews to oppose the *Gesuiwerde* National Party and to contribute towards the campaigns of the United Party. This tactic backfired when the United Party split over South Africa's involvement on the Allied side in the Second World War, and some of the MPs who had been helped by the Board actually defected to Malan's party.[113]

By the late 1930s, and throughout the 1940s, the struggle against antisemitism was the chief preoccupation of the community and its leaders. The rise of Afrikaner nationalism—and extremist right-wing politics on its fringes—had moved the 'Jewish Question' to the centre of national debates, with dire implications. Right-wing movements such as the Ossewa Brandwag and the Greyshirts openly identified with Nazi racial ideologies, symbols and leaders. Attacks on Jews increased in this period, and the basic elements of radical European antisemitism were imported, including Jewish conspiracy theories and propaganda such as the *Protocols of the Elders of Zion*.[114]

Mainstream nationalists often disapproved of aspects of the extremists' methods and political aspirations, but not of the racial, antisemitic core of their ideologies. Nationalist leaders such as Malan, Hendrik Verwoerd and Eric Louw not only supported immigration restrictions but also proposed more sweeping measures against Jews. Verwoerd suggested restricting Jewish participation in business and the professions according to the Jewish percentage of the white population.[115] Malan's National Party ran elections on explicitly antisemitic platforms, introduced legislation in Parliament that specifically targeted Jews as a 'problem'[116] and sided openly with Hitler. Several National Party leaders, including future prime ministers of South Africa, were jailed for their involvement in pro-Nazi and anti-war activities that included sabotage.

Despite the risks, Jewish leaders felt compelled to act. At its congress in May 1945, the Board developed a 'Nine-Point Programme' to fight antisemitism,

---

113 Shimoni 1980, 150–1.
114 Shain, M. 2005. *Humpty Dumpty was Pushed: Anti-Jewish Conspiracies and the South African Experience*. Seventeenth Jacob Gitlin Memorial Lecture, Cape Town, 28 June.
115 Shimoni 1980, 124–5.
116 Ibid, 126.

placing the struggle for Jewish rights alongside 'the defence of democracy and freedom'.'[117] The Board continued its political alignment with the United Party and other political groupings opposed to the Nationalists. The courts, too, offered recourse. In a celebrated libel case tried in Grahamstown in 1934, the rabbi of a Port Elizabeth synagogue won damages from members of the pro-Nazi Greyshirt movement who had accused him of plotting a conspiracy.[118] Their allegations were based on the *Protocols*, which were declared by the judge to be a forgery, setting an important international legal precedent.[119]

Jewish fears remained intense through the late 1940s. In the fateful election of May 1948, when the National Party ran on an apartheid platform, the Board again took action. Through a series of articles in the communal journal, *Jewish Affairs*, it attacked the National Party's apartheid policy. In an editorial before the election, it implicitly encouraged Jews to vote for the United Party of Prime Minister Jan Smuts rather than the National Party.[120] Jewish support for the United Party had also been encouraged by Smuts's support for the Zionist cause. Israel declared independence on 14 May 1948, just 12 days before South Africa's elections of 26 May 1948. Smuts was among the first to recognise the new State of Israel, against objections from some Afrikaner nationalists who, in their hostility towards Jews, regarded Zionism as incompatible with patriotism towards South Africa.[121] Despite its stand against the National Party, the Board stuck to its official policy of non-involvement, insisting that the community's leadership was concerned only with the antisemitic element of Afrikaner nationalism, not the Afrikaner nationalist cause itself.[122]

The attempt to prevent the National Party from taking power failed. However, Jewish fears of the negative consequences of nationalist rule were never realised. As brutal as the apartheid system was for black, coloured and Indian South Africans, Jews were never targeted. In fact, after taking power, newly elected Prime Minister Malan carefully distanced himself from his party's antisemitic pa attempted to mend relations with the Jewish community through such a

---

117 Shimoni 2003, 16.
118 Shain 2005.
119 Saron 2001, 139–41.
120 Shimoni 1980, 154.
121 Ibid, 202–3.
122 Shimoni 2003, 16–7.

visiting Israel in 1953, becoming the first sitting head of state to do so. Some Afrikaner nationalists discovered an affinity for Zionism—both in the early struggles of Jews in Mandatory Palestine against continued British rule, and in the rather contrived notion that Israel, like South Africa, was an ethnically defined polity surrounded by hostile and ethnically distinct neighbours.

In effect, Jews were offered a place in South Africa's elite, privileged white racial caste. Though most Jews still did not support the National Party, and many became increasingly perturbed at the decline of democratic freedoms under its government, the community came to an uneasy accommodation with the new political order. As Shimoni notes, the alliance of the Board with broader liberal democratic political forces in the 1990s 'turned out to be a temporary linkup based on convergence of interests, rather than a permanent alliance based on principle'.[123]

The Board reaffirmed its commitment to a neutral political posture and the policy of non-involvement. This was not, however, an easy task. The question of where South African Jews stood on apartheid, not only individually but as a community, soon became the defining political question of South African Jewry in the latter half of the 20th century. The community's choices were closely scrutinised by Jews around the world, some of whom took the community's action or inaction as a reflection on Jewish values in general.[124]

The simplistic aphorism that is often used to summarise Jewish political behaviour during apartheid is that, while the vast majority of South African did not actively oppose it, and were happy to enjoy its benefits, Jews were tionately represented among whites who actively fought apartheid. In ere occasionally accused by the government and National Party eing among the government's chief political opponents. Letters aans press in the 1950s charging that Jews were prominent ited Party, as well as in the anti-apartheid movement.[125] portionately represented among those whites who were Treason Trial of the late 1950s, and all of the whites in early 1960s were Jews. In 1968, Minister of the Police Muller, published a list of students who had protested against the government and drew attention to the large number of Jewish surnames, asking the community to exercise greater control over its youth. Repeating its neutral stance, the Board protested that the community could not be held collectively responsible for the actions of individual members.[126]

The important role played by a minority of Jews in the anti-apartheid struggle has been closely scrutinised. Some, like Helen Suzman, were liberals, who generally expressed their opposition through the legal and parliamentary means afforded to whites in South Africa's truncated democracy. Others, like the late Joe Slovo, were radicals, who eschewed traditional politics for underground activism, mass action and even military confrontation with the state.

Attempts to ascribe the political convictions of these Jews to their religious values or cultural heritage generally founder when faced with the fact that they were a small minority within the community, and that few of them were particularly concerned with Judaism. More likely explanations focus on social factors. Many Jewish immigrants, for example, had brought with them to South Africa a tradition of involvement in radical politics. This inspired some of them, and their children, to continue their involvement in these causes—such as trade unionism, socialism and communism—on South African soil, in service not only of workers' rights and international socialist goals but of the rights of black people in South Africa.

Shimoni writes that Jewish radicals tended to share 'a situation of social marginality vis-à-vis both white society and the institutions of the Jewish community'.[127] He also notes the importance of 'some degree of ideological radicalism imbibed within the family or from the proximate social environment'.[128] Liberals, too, experienced some degree of alienation, though to a far lesser extent. They were more likely to maintain their involvement in the Jewish community. Shimoni also adds: 'There were also a few Jews whose response to marginal-outsider status was to seek acceptance into newly empowered Afrikaner circles by demonstrating their support of apartheid policy.'[129]

The strong and active presence of Zionism in the community was also a factor in shaping the political involvement of Jews. For many young Jews, including

---

126 Ibid, 296–7.
127 Shimoni 2003, 89.
128 Ibid.
129 Ibid, 103.

many future liberal and radical opponents of apartheid, Zionist youth movements provided exposure to the rhetoric of social justice and the practice of political organisation.[130] For others, Zionism was a new form of positive ethnic self-identification through which to explore and find common ground with Afrikaner nationalists. One case was that of the Zionist writer Henry Katzew, who expressed profound sympathy for Afrikaner national aspirations—while denouncing apartheid by drawing on his Zionist beliefs and his experiences on visits to Israel.

At a communal level, the Board insisted that there could be no collective political stance among South African Jews on issues beyond Zionism and matters directly affecting Jewish rights and interests. Practically, the Board sought to play the role of intercessor between the community and the government, and wished to avoid any political developments that would complicate its ability to do so. Consequently, the Board and the community in general were often at pains to distance themselves from political dissidents. Quietly and behind the scenes, the Board even attempted sometimes to convince outspoken Jews to tone down their criticisms of the government for the sake of the community's reputation.[131] Outspoken rabbis such as Chief Rabbi Louis I Rabinowitz, who was a vocal critic of apartheid as well as a staunch Zionist, came into conflict with the Board of Deputies. He eventually made *aliyah* and moved to Israel.[132] On several occasions, the Board departed from its policy of non-involvement—which theoretically upheld the rights of individual Jews to their own views—by failing to defend the political and civil rights of Jewish lay and religious leaders who fell afoul of the regime. Rabbi André Ungar, for instance, a Hungarian-born rabbi who was vocally opposed to apartheid, received no support from the Board when the government withdrew his residency permit.[133]

The strategy of Jewish leadership in this period, notwithstanding the oft-repeated policy of non-involvement, was to assert Jewish rights when necessary, but also to maintain a low political profile if possible and to cultivate good relations with the government. This strategy seemed to have the support of the bulk

---

130 Ibid, 89–90.
131 Shimoni 2003, 113–4.
132 Ibid, 40–3.
133 Ibid, 36–7.

of the community, notwithstanding occasional protests. Such behaviour was reinforced by still-fresh memories of the National Party's antisemitism, which were periodically revived by the abrasive rhetoric of government supporters or the outbursts of nationalist politicians. The community also carried the collective memory of the pogroms of Eastern Europe, as well as—indirectly for most, but directly for some—the suffering at the hands of the Nazis in the Holocaust. The echoes of Nazi ideology by the Afrikaner nationalist right wing of the 1930s and 1940s, and the trauma of the battles over immigration restrictions, were not easily forgotten.[134] Many Jews were simply relieved that the 'Jewish Question' had largely disappeared from national politics and that the focus of national attention was directed at some other group. As one critic observed rather unsympathetically, the goal of the political strategy of South African Jewry under apartheid was 'to be the last dog eaten'.[135]

The delicate political posture of the Board and other communal institutions came under constant pressure—not only from anti-apartheid Jews and outside observers but from the government itself. The greatest test was the Verwoerd affair of late 1961. Israel had begun to forge relations with the emerging postcolonial nations of Asia and especially Africa in an attempt to outmanoeuvre the stifling hostility of the Arab nations of the Middle East. This led Israel to join the Afro-Asian bloc in voting against apartheid in the United Nations in the early 1960s.

The South African government responded bitterly, and Prime Minister Verwoerd's full resentment was revealed in an infamous leaked letter to S A East. He described Israel's stance as a 'tragedy' for South African Jews, and suggested that it might have aroused antisemitic feeling in South Africa if the community had not acted so quickly to criticise Israel.[136] Verwoerd also said that the government had taken notice of Jewish support for the Progressive Party and lack of support for the National Party. In effect, he was indirectly questioning both the national and political loyalty of Jews.

Government supporters responded enthusiastically, often reverting to old antisemitic motifs about Jewish power and Jewish treachery. The pro-

---

[134] Shimoni 2003, 273–5; Shain 1994, 150–3; Kessler, S 1995. 'The South African rabbinate in the apartheid era'. *Jewish Affairs*, 31, Autumn.
[135] Weisbord, R G. 1967. 'The dilemma of South African Jewry'. *The Journal of Modern African Studies*, 5, 2, 236.
[136] Shimoni 1980, 310–1.

government newspaper *Die Transvaler* posed the question: 'Has the time not arrived for these Jews to do a little work of enlightenment in Jerusalem?', suggesting that South African Jews had enough influence to change Israeli government policy.[137] As the controversy over Israel's stance continued in subsequent years, the newspaper questioned the 'dual loyalty' of South African Jews: 'The Jews will thus now have to choose where they stand just as the Jews of Israel have chosen: with South Africa or with Israel. It can no longer be with both.'[138]

The crisis had a direct material consequence in that the government stopped South African Jews from transferring donated goods and funds to Israel, a measure that would only be repealed during the Six Day War in 1967.[139] This meant that the Verwoerd affair was not only a test of Jewish loyalty to South Africa but also a test of Jewish loyalty to Zionism. Debates within Israel about its stance towards South Africa revealed that Israel's leaders had believed that South African Jews would not be punished for the UN votes;[140] to the extent that they recognised the community's anxieties, they suggested that the best solution was for South African Jews to emigrate to Israel, a proposal the community's leaders found excessive.[141]

The strategy of the community's leaders in dealing with the Verwoerd affair revealed the reluctance of the Board and the SAZF to confront the government in public. Indeed, public statements by both organisations in the aftermath of Israel's vote to censure South African foreign minister Eric Louw criticised Israel and suggested that the Israeli government should have abstained, as other Western democracies had.[142] When Verwoerd's own views were made public, stern criticism came from individual Jews and from the Jewish press, but not from Jewish organisations or leaders. Instead, the communal leadership attempted to address the problem by holding discreet meetings with senior South African and Israeli government officials. In these meetings, Jewish leaders did not challenge the policies of either government but merely strove to make the feelings of the

---

137 *Die Transvaler*. Quoted in Shimoni 1980, 306.
138 Ibid, 332.
139 Shimoni 1980, 317, 353.
140 Ibid, 324–5.
141 Ibid, 347–8.
142 Ibid, 308–9.

community known.¹⁴³ These meetings were not particularly effective and failed to achieve their main objective of ending the freeze on funds transfers, which jeopardised the future of the Zionist Federation and the institutional strength of the community as a whole.¹⁴⁴

Eventually the Verwoerd affair and the difficulties South African Jews felt in relation to Israel's anti-apartheid stance were overtaken by events. Israel's lightning victory over hostile Arab neighbours in the 1967 war prompted new admiration from the South African establishment. In the early 1970s, Israel's Afro-Asian strategy failed when in the wake of the 1973 Yom Kippur War several African states broke off relations with Israel. The successful international campaigning of Yasser Arafat and the Palestine Liberation Organisation (PLO), backed by the Soviet Union, also brought many developing nations to adopt hostile anti-Israeli postures. Over time, Israel and South Africa, both pariahs in the developing world, were driven to closer cooperation by their shared isolation. From 1973 to 1975 the two signed a number of economic, technical and scientific agreements, and carried on a secret military relationship in spite of UN sanctions against South Africa.¹⁴⁵

As a consequence of the emergence of this Pretoria-Jerusalem relationship, the relationship between South African Jews and the apartheid government began to change as well. The Jewish community and its leadership were reassured by South Africa's new friendship with Israel, and began to enjoy better access to the government than ever before.¹⁴⁶ The early 1970s also marked the period of 'reformed' apartheid, which gave way to political and social unrest in the late 1970s, followed by violent confrontations and a state of emergency in the mid 1980s. These developments, too, had consequences for Jewish political behaviour. On the one hand, South Africa's improved relations with Israel meant that the Jewish community enjoyed better relations with the National Party regime. On the other hand, because of South Africa's own internal changes, the Jewish community felt greater freedom—and pressure—to criticise apartheid policies.

---

143 Ibid, 328, 345.
144 Ibid, 327–9.
145 See Chazan, N. 1987. 'Israeli perspectives on the Israel-South Africa relationship'. *Institute of Jewish Affairs, London: Research Report*, nos 9 &10, December.
146 Shimoni 2003, 160.

These two opposing tendencies were exemplified by events and episodes such as the banquet held by the Board in 1975 honouring Prime Minister B J Vorster—one of the foremost champions of apartheid and a former Nazi sympathizer—on his return from a state visit to Israel. Jewish opponents of apartheid criticised the Board for honouring Vorster. Dennis Davis, who was to serve as chairman of the Cape Council of the Board of Deputies three decades later, described Vorster as 'the leader of a political party whose politics, based so firmly on race, are the antithesis of the very body and soul of Jewish ethics'.[147] However, the banquet also featured an address by Board chairman David Mann declaring that South Africa 'must move away as quickly and effectively as is practicable from discrimination based on race or colour'.[148] It was the first time the communal leadership had been so bold and direct in its criticism.[149]

Additional pressure came from the anti-apartheid movement, which gathered momentum after the Soweto riots of 16 June 1976. Israel had once been viewed by the ANC as a source of inspiration. For example, ANC stalwart Walter Sisulu had included Israel on his historic 1953 voyage through the communist world,[150] and Jewish military organisations in Mandatory Palestine had partly inspired the ANC's armed wing, Umkhonto we Sizwe.[151] Now, however, Israel was viewed with suspicion. The alliance with the apartheid government was to cause lasting damage to perceptions of Israel and Zionism within the anti-apartheid movement.

Negative feelings towards Israel within the movement, and close identification with the Palestinians, were strengthened by the Israeli invasion of Lebanon in 1982. The war was unpopular within Israel itself. Massacres of Palestinian refugees in the Sabra and Shatila refugee camps in Beirut, carried out by Christian Phalangist militias as the Israel Defence Force looked on, aroused stern international condemnation. A wave of protests rocked South African university campuses, where the Palestinian cause was taken up by Muslim students and joined by anti-apartheid groups.

---

147 Davis, D. Quoted in Shimoni 2003, 186.
148 Mann, D. Quoted in Shimoni 2003, 136.
149 Shimoni 2003, 136.
150 Kapelianis, A. n.d. 'Who was Walter Sisulu?' *SABC news* [online article]. URL: http://www.sabcnews.com/features/walter_sisulu/bio.html
151 Mandela, N. 1995. *Long Walk to Freedom*. London: Abacus, 326, 334.

A new generation of politically conscious Jewish activists could not help but feel affected by the controversy. A small but vocal group of young Jews began to question the relationship between Israel and the apartheid government, and to insist that the community's commitment to Zionism ought not preclude criticism of Israel's policies. These were not messages that the communal leaders of the day found easy to accept. Most South African Jews had rallied behind Israel. Many were disturbed by the antisemitic rhetoric of some campus protests, which had provoked counter-demonstrations by Jewish student groups and had also led to several violent clashes. The community's solidarity with Israel remained firm, and Israel's critics within the community remained a small minority. But, for those who had challenged the community's position, the clashes would not soon be forgotten. Criticism of Israel within the anti-apartheid movement was sharpened by the first *intifada* (1987-1993), and the old analogy between Israel and apartheid was revived—this time by the political left instead of the right.[152]

Prodded by internal and external pressure, and emboldened by the government's willingness to consider reforms to apartheid legislation, the Board began to speak out more and more explicitly against racial discrimination in the early 1980s. In 1985 the long-awaited denunciation of apartheid was finally made in a resolution at the Board's 33rd national congress, and the condemnations of apartheid were even clearer at the 34th national congress in 1987.[153]

That same year saw the emergence of two independent Jewish activist groups formed specifically to oppose apartheid—Jews for Justice in Cape Town and Jews for Social Justice in Johannesburg. The groups attracted several hundred Jewish activists from such organisations as the United Democratic Front, which was in the forefront of anti-apartheid activism in South Africa at the time, and several rabbis were also drawn to the cause. These organisations defied the Board's policy of non-involvement by asserting that Jews should adopt a collective stance, grounded in Jewish ethics, in opposition to apartheid. They also criticised Israeli policies in the occupied territories, while at the same time offering explicit support for Zionism. Throughout the late 1980s, Jews for Justice and Jews for Social Justice succeeded in building bridges to anti-apartheid leaders in the country and in exile.[154]

---

152 Hoffman, T & Fischer, A. 1988. *The Jews of South Africa: What Future?* Johannesburg: Southern.
153 Shimoni 2003, 138.
154 Ibid, 196–200.

Despite these late shifts towards bolder criticism of the National Party government and its apartheid policy, the overall record of the South African Jewish community is a mixed one. It would be inaccurate to say that Jews collectively supported apartheid, but equally inaccurate to say that Jews collectively opposed it. There were many individual Jews who joined and led opposition movements, both liberal and radical, legal and illegal. Yet, though the role played by Jews in the anti-apartheid movement was considerable, many of these Jews—though certainly not all—were alienated from the cultural and religious mainstream of the community.

The early political struggles of the Jewish community around immigration rights cemented the role of the Board of Deputies as the political voice of Jews, but only on issues relating directly to Jewish interests. Jewish leaders dissociated the struggle for Jewish rights from broader struggles at a very early stage. In the 1930s and the 1940s, the Board broadened both the scope and scale of its political behaviour. Not only did it meet with important public officials and representatives but it also made use of Jewish MPs to argue its case in Parliament, sought alliances within the broad liberal democratic movement, and even attempted to intervene in particular elections by encouraging support for certain candidates and opposition to right-wing parties. After 1948, however, Jewish political behaviour was confined to a narrow range of issues and methods. With the 'Jewish Question' off the table, Jews began fully to enjoy the economic, social and political privileges shared by other whites in general. The fear of official antisemitism persisted for several decades, but gradually subsided.

Notwithstanding the Board's official policy of non-involvement and neutrality, in practice Jewish leaders began to act as intercessors between the government and the community. While they sometimes conveyed disagreement with government policies, they also tried to contain Jewish political dissent. Israel's Afro-Asian strategy of the 1960s led to tensions between the community and the government, but the 1967 war and the emergence of the Pretoria-Jerusalem axis in the 1970s led to closer and warmer relations. By the time Jewish political dissent emerged into the open in the 1980s and opposition to apartheid became communal policy, Jews were already integrated into the dominant caste of South African society.

But there was a cost, both moral and political. Not only did the community's leaders fail to take a clear moral and political position on apartheid for many decades but they also, on occasion, compromised the core priorities of the community in order to avoid antagonising the government. One such case was the Board's decision to criticise Israel in 1961 for its vote to censure the South African foreign minister at the United Nations. Viewed against a history of strong support for the State of Israel, this episode revealed the degree to which the Board felt pressure to mollify the government in order to protect the status of its Jewish constituents. Jewish voters continued to support opposition parties, and Jewish dissidents continued to protest against apartheid, but only in the waning years of apartheid did Jewish leaders feel bold enough to experiment with a more independent posture.

CHAPTER THREE

THE POST-APARTHEID JEWISH COMMUNITY

The end of apartheid and the transition to democracy brought sweeping and profound changes to South African politics and society. These changes affected the Jewish community together with other minority communities. Two new directions for communal political behaviour began to emerge. The first possibility was that the political behaviour of the Board and other Jewish institutions would become more open—more independent of the government, more outspoken on issues outside the narrow focus of Jewish affairs and more tolerant of dissent within the community. The second was that Jewish political behaviour would remain closed—that the community would isolate itself from a rapidly changing society, that internal debate within the community would be stifled, and that the Board would revert to its role as intercessor between the community and a government controlled by yet another powerful ruling party. In fact, both possibilities were realised. To understand these two directions and their implications for Jewish political behaviour, it is necessary to examine the history of the Jewish community in the post-apartheid era.

By the late 1980s, the apartheid government had largely overcome its radical opponents, jailing many leaders of the anti-apartheid movement and largely defeating its military wing abroad. Yet parts of the country had become ungovernable, and the state of emergency declared by the government in the mid 1980s had damaged morale among whites. The cumulative effect of years of international political and economic isolation had become severe. The PFP began to challenge the NP from the left and the Conservative Party (CP) from the right. Indeed, in the 1987 elections, the CP replaced the PFP as the official opposition. Change seemed unlikely and yet inevitable. The question was how long it would take and how violent it would be.

In late 1986 and early 1987, Israel began to re-examine its relations with South Africa. By the spring of 1987 Israel formally joined international sanctions against the apartheid regime, partly as a result of American pressure and partly due to internal opposition to apartheid within the Israeli government.[155] Israel began substantial contact with anti-apartheid leaders and organisations in 1992, following the arrival of new ambassador Alon Liel. Throughout the last years of the apartheid regime, Israel tended to relations with the government of F W de Klerk but began increasingly to expand contacts with the ANC leadership.[156]

Finally, in February 1990, President F W de Klerk announced Nelson Mandela's unconditional release from prison in an historic address to Parliament. Mandela's freedom broke the country's political deadlock and was welcomed enthusiastically by most South Africans, although some greeted it with trepidation, fear and hostility.

The next several years saw the removal of racial restrictions from the statute books, the holding of elections on a one-person, one-vote basis in 1994, and the negotiation and the adoption of a new liberal democratic constitution in 1993 (in interim form) and 1996 (in final form). South Africa basked in new hope and goodwill, and its internal efforts at reconciliation were accompanied by an end to its international isolation. The economy slowly began to recover from the stagnation of the apartheid era, and the new ANC government under Mandela and his successor Thabo Mbeki extended essential public services to millions who had been previously denied them.[157]

At the same time, new problems and new challenges arose. Political violence in the early 1990s was accompanied by a soaring wave of violent crime. The HIV/Aids pandemic, barely an issue in 1990, had reached staggering propor-

---

155 Shimoni 2003, 163.
156 Ibid, 164–5.
157 Shain, M. 2004. 'South Africa'. *American Jewish Year Book 2004*, eds D Singer & L Grossman, vol 104, 474. New York: American Jewish Committee.

tions 15 years later. By 2005, about six million South Africans—roughly 15 per cent of the population—were thought to be infected with HIV, according to the government.[158] Young adults were the worst affected, with more than one in three South Africans in their late twenties infected with HIV.[159] UNAIDS/ World Health Organization estimates of annual AIDS deaths in South Africa reached 370 000 in 2003.[160]

Despite moderate economic growth, unemployment continued to rise. New opportunities arose for black professionals, workers and entrepreneurs, but the majority of poor black people did not have access to these new possibilities. Service delivery in key areas such as health and education began to suffer serious breakdowns, particularly in local government, amidst renewed social unrest.

Jews in South Africa faced all of these developments, together with South Africans in general and white South Africans in particular. By and large, South African Jews and Jewish leaders welcomed the new political changes. When Mandela was released from prison, for example, the South African Jewish Board of Deputies applauded the government's decision. In a press statement following President F W de Klerk's watershed speech, the Board said that it hoped for 'an atmosphere for the establishment of genuine democracy for the benefit of the country and all its peoples'.[161]

As apartheid crumbled and democracy drew nearer, the Board of Deputies and other central Jewish institutions began to experiment with more vocal and active forms of political behaviour. For example, the Board began to meet publicly with figures involved in the anti-apartheid movement, such as Archbishop Desmond Tutu.[162] In 1992, the Board broke with its past opposition to a 'Jewish vote' and joined with the rabbinate in encouraging Jews to back F W de Klerk's referendum on constitutional reforms.[163] Following Mandela's release in 1990, political exiles began drifting home from abroad, and Jewish leaders began to welcome them back—sometimes

---

158 South African Department of Health 2005. 'National HIV and syphilis antenatal sero-prevalence survey in South Africa 2004'. 20 July [online report]. URL: http://www.doh.gov.za/docs/reports/2004/hiv-syphilis.pdf
159 Ibid.
160 UNAIDS/WHO. 'UNAIDS 2004 report on the global AIDS epidemic' [online report]. URL: http://www.unaids.org/bangkok2004/GAR2004_html/GAR2004_17_en.htm#TopOfPage
161 South African Jewish Board of Deputies 1990. *Press Items of Jewish Interest* (16 February). Quoted in Dubb, A A & Shain M. 1992. 'South Africa.' *American Jewish Year Book 1992*, eds D Singer & R R Seldin, vol 92, 416. New York: American Jewish Committee.
162 Ibid, 249, 256.
163 Ibid, 246–7.

encountering resistance from the community as they did so. The community had not yet come to terms with its dissidents, and old divisions would continue to haunt South African Jewry for several years, right through the Kasrils affair.

Some leading South African Jews, sensing the shifting ideological winds, were at pains to highlight points of intersection between Zionism and the anti-apartheid movement. These included referring to Zionism as the 'national liberation movement' of Jews, highlighting Nelson Mandela's claim that former Israeli Prime Minister Menachem Begin had been a source of inspiration,[164] and drawing positive analogies between Israel and a free South Africa. Such comparisons were often motivated by the desire to identify with South Africa's changes, and to overturn the malevolent comparisons to apartheid made by Israel's critics.[165] They were also, perhaps, a way of transcending the community's uneasy accommodation with apartheid, as well as an expression of anxiety about whether South African Jewry would be punished by a future ANC government for the Pretoria-Jerusalem axis of the 1970s and 1980s.

Tactically, the Board continued to position itself as an intercessor between the community and the government, keeping disagreements as quiet and calm as possible. While participating in many of the debates and discussions about the emerging social, economic and constitutional future of the nation, Jewish leaders also attempted to reassure the community about the country's new direction and to articulate the community's concerns.

There were many such concerns, some common to other minorities and some unique to the Jewish community. Like many other minority groups, South African Jews feared the loss of political power that would come with majority rule, as well as possible institutional and even military upheaval. Issy Pinshaw, the only Jewish member of the President's Council—a 60-member government advisory body—said in 1988: 'One man, one vote would spell chaos and destruction for the whole of South Africa ... We [Jews] are a minority group within a minority. The future of South African Jews is inextricably linked to the future of the white community in South Africa. Any threat facing the white community faces the Jewish community as well.'[166]

---

164 Mandela, N. 1995. *Long Walk to Freedom*. London: Abacus, 326.
165 Hurwitz, H. 1995. 'Menachem Begin and Nelson Mandela ...'. *SA Jewish Times* 27, Rosh Hashanah. Also Gordon, J. 1994. 'SA, Israel have much in common'. *SA Jewish Times*,10, 2 September.
166 Pinshaw, I. 1988. Quoted in Mufson, S. 'South African Jews'. *Tikkun*, 3, 1, 31.

There were two specifically Jewish anxieties. One was the prospect of a rise in antisemitism, whether from the political right or left. In the early 1990s, the major source of antisemitism was still the far-right wing. In addition to explicitly hard-line and militant Afrikaner nationalist groups such as the Afrikaner Weerstandsbeweging (AWB), right-wing political parties such as the Conservative Party also aroused concern among Jews. A series of antisemitic incidents reinforced these fears, including the desecration of cemeteries, the placing of pigs' heads outside synagogues and offices, and the appearance of antisemitic graffiti and rhetoric.[167] Many Jews feared they could be 'scapegoated' by groups unhappy with political change.[168] Soon, however, concern shifted to antisemitism among South Africa's Muslim population, numbering roughly 700 000.[169] Rallied by the Palestinian *intifada* of the late 1980s and by the Gulf War, Muslim radicals became increasingly militant and politically visible. They enjoyed some sympathy from and connection to the ANC, as well as more radical groups such as the Pan Africanist Congress (PAC).[170] Black antisemitism was also a feared prospect but one that was never realised, aside from the occasional use of antisemitic stereotypes in political rhetoric. (For example, in the 2004 general elections, the ANC spokesperson in KwaZulu-Natal province, Dumisani Makhaye, referred to Tony Leon as the 'DA Führer' in a statement that was slammed as antisemitic by Leon's party.[171])

The other major Jewish anxiety in the early 1990s was the possibility that the incoming democratic government would be hostile towards Israel and Zionism, given the recent memory of the Pretoria-Jerusalem axis. This suspicion was reinforced by the ANC's vocal support for, and alliance with, the Palestinian cause. In 1990, the community reacted with alarm when Mandela, two-and-a-half weeks after his release from prison, met with Yasser Arafat in Lusaka, Zambia—and in a photograph printed on the front page of several South African newspapers—was shown embracing him.[172] Jews were concerned not only about Mandela's solidarity with a man reviled by many as a terrorist and a mortal enemy of Israel but also at Mandela's

---

167 Dubb & Shain 1992, 417.
168 Shimoni 2003, 246.
169 Vahed & Jeppie 2004–5, 252.
170 See Bastos, M. 2002. 'Muslim Anti-Zionism and Antisemitism in South Africa since the Second World War, with Special Reference to Muslim News/Views.' Unpublished MA dissertation. University of Cape Town; and Akhalwaya, A. 1993 'A love-hate relationship: Jews and Muslims in South Africa'. *The Jewish Quarterly*, 17–9, Spring.
171 African National Congress 2004. 'Tony Leon challenged to resign'. Press statement, 23 February [online archive]. URL: http://www.anc.org.za/ancdocs/pr/2004/pr0223b.html
172 Dubb & Shain 1992, 415.

association of the South African struggle against apartheid with the Palestinian struggle against Israel, suggesting that a future ANC government might be hostile to the community's feelings. Adding to these worries were the remarks Mandela was reported to have made at a subsequent press conference: 'If the truth alienates the powerful Jewish community in South Africa,' he told reporters, 'that's too bad.'[173]

Subsequently, large communal meetings were held in Johannesburg and Cape Town at which religious and lay leaders attempted to reassure the community about their future in South Africa, while at the same time reaffirming support for Israel. Aside from assuaging Jewish fears, they were also implicitly charting a future political course: they would not accept Verwoerd's old bargain by trading away commitment to Zionism in return for full acceptance in South Africa. They would insist on having both. South African ambassador to the US and former Democratic Party politician Harry Schwarz made these conditions clear, but also told the gathering in Cape Town that 'we should not close the door' to the ANC.[174]

Not only did the community's leaders 'not close the door', they also began actively seeking ways to challenge and change the ANC's views. Jewish groups began holding meetings, discussions and debates with ANC leaders about the Middle East. In many ways, the Board was simply extending to new leaders its old practice of acting as the community's intercessor. At the same time, it had begun to experiment with a more open and even confrontational mode of political behaviour. Progress was tentative and fraught with fears and misunderstandings. In late 1992, for example, the South African Union of Jewish Students (SAUJS) joined a delegation from the ANC Youth League on a joint trip to Israel. The trip went well until the Youth League issued a press statement while still in Israel that was harshly critical of the Israeli government and its policies towards the Palestinians. This was viewed as a 'disaster' by the Jewish community and caused renewed controversy about the future of South Africa-Israel relations, as well as further anxiety about the ANC's understanding of the feelings of South African Jewry towards Israel.[175] The fears of many South African Jews were expressed by South African Zionist Federation President Julius Weinstein in August 1993

---

173 Mandela, N. 1993. Quoted in Dubb & Shain, 415.
174 Schwarz, H. 1990. Quoted in 'Capetonians flock to public meeting'. *Cape Jewish Chronicle*, 1, April.
175 'Israel's ambassador Alon Liel: No stranger among us' 1993. *Cape Jewish Chronicle*, 10, 3, 8, April.

when he said that '… in the new South Africa, it will be a different ball game: our friends will be in the minority and our enemies in the majority'.[176]

The ANC eventually tried to assuage these fears, with Mandela and other leaders repeatedly insisting on Israel's right to exist alongside a future Palestinian state. Mandela told the 37th national conference of the Board of Deputies in 1993:

> *The ANC's relations with the Palestinian Liberation Organisation have been a matter of concern for many Jews, not only here but also in other parts of the world. It was an issue we discussed when I recently met the American Jewish Committee. As a movement we recognise the legitimacy of Palestinian nationalism just as we recognise the legitimacy of the Zionism as a Jewish nationalism. We insist on the right of the state of Israel to exist within secure borders but with equal vigour support the Palestinian right to national self-determination. We are gratified to see that new possibilities of resolving the issue through negotiation have arisen since the election of a new government in Israel. We would wish to encourage that process, and if we have the opportunity, to assist.*[177]

As Mandela's comments indicated, ANC attitudes towards Israel remained frosty in the early 1990s, but improved with the election of a Labour government under Yitzchak Rabin in 1992. Attitudes warmed even more dramatically after September 1993, with the signing of the Oslo peace accords in Washington, DC by Israel and the Palestine Liberation Organisation. The ANC's reactions established a pattern that would hold well into the future, in which ANC postures towards Israel and Zionism responded positively to progress in the Middle East peace process.

At the same time that the Jewish community was grappling with change in the wider society, it was also undergoing dramatic internal changes. One of these

---

176 Weinstein, J. 1993. Quoted in 'Zionism in New SA: The experts debate'. *Zionist Record—and SA Jewish Chronicle*, 6, 6 August.
177 Mandela, N. 1993. Address at the opening of the 37th national conference of the South African Jewish Board of Deputies, Johannesburg, 21 August. [online text]. URL: http://www.anc.org.za/ancdocs/history/mandela/1993/sp930821.html

was the increased religiosity of the community, especially in Johannesburg, as more and more Jews chose to join the *ba'al teshuvah* movement and 'return to religion'.[178] This change was part of a small but significant trend of counter-assimilation in Jewish communities throughout the world, and was given extra impetus by the arrival in the 1970s of emissaries of the Hasidic Lubavitch Chabad movement in South Africa,[179] as well as by the arrival of Ohr Someach rabbis in the 1990s. It was also, some contended, a new form of insularity, of coping with—and to some extent escaping—the changing and uncertain world beyond. Thus, at the same time as the community encountered new opportunities to reach out beyond its borders it also faced new pressures to turn inward.

Emigration continued to take a demographic toll on the community, particularly among young South Africans, driven by the 'push' factors of crime and political change, and by the 'pull' factors of better economic opportunities abroad.[180] The median age of the community crept steadily upwards.[181] These demographic shifts and the shrinking size of the community—from roughly 120 000 people at its peak in the 1960s to about 80 000 in the 1990s—prompted new thinking about the financing and administration of communal organisations. Cutbacks within and mergers among organisations were envisioned in order to reduce costs and ensure the long-term financial viability of communal institutional life. The community's leaders also began to worry about the future of Jewish schools and homes for the aged, which it believed might no longer be subsidised by a new government primarily concerned with shifting resources to its largely black constituency.[182] The criterion that people using these institutions must be Jewish might also, it was thought, have to be reconsidered—a question that remained unresolved for several years into the new dispensation.[183]

Despite these challenges, Jewish leaders continued to encourage the community to embrace the new society unfolding around it, and to be part of the changes by

---

178 Shimoni 2003, 231.
179 Shimoni 2003, 230–1, and Dubb & Shain 1992, 425.
180 Kosmin 1999, 25.
181 Dubb, A A & Shain, M. 1993. 'South Africa'. *American Jewish Year Book 1993*, eds D Singer & R R Seldin, vol 93, 333. New York: American Jewish Committee.
182 Shain, M. 2002 in Encel & Shain.
183 Kessler, S. 2004. 'Should we open our institutions?' *South African Jewish Report*, 7, 16 January.

becoming involved politically and through community service or philanthropy. The late Chief Rabbi Cyril Harris, who is recognised as having provided crucial guidance to the community through this period, encouraged Jews not only to welcome those who had been part of the anti-apartheid struggle, Jewish and otherwise, but to begin reaching out to other communities and to contribute to the upliftment of the nation's poor. Many steps were taken in this direction, including the opening of South Africa's own branch of the Organisation for Rehabilitation and Training (ORT), a worldwide technical skills training organisation founded by Jews.[184]

The Board, too, wishing to build relations with South Africa's future leaders, met even more frequently with ANC leaders. It also met with the leaders of other parties representing black South Africans, including the Inkatha Freedom Party and others, preferring not to alienate them by focusing solely on the ANC.[185] For the first time in its history, the Board was reaching out to a broad range of leaders and groups from the country's racial majority. At the same time, the Board's behaviour was in keeping with its well-established tradition of seeking meetings with powerful figures as its primary mode of political activity. The ambivalence of its political posture was profound, and perhaps reflected the uncertainty of the times.

The years from 1994 to 1999 marked the formal beginning of South Africa's new democratic order. Jews and Jewish leadership generally developed positive feelings towards and relationships with the new government. The efforts of the Board to cultivate relations with Nelson Mandela seemed to bear fruit when the President-elect paid a visit to a Sabbath morning service at the Green and Sea Point Hebrew Congregation in May 1994, prior to his inauguration. In his address, Mandela praised the involvement of Jews in the anti-apartheid struggle and in the building of the country in general.[186] These warm relations continued between President Mandela and the Jewish community throughout Mandela's term in office.

There was, however, also occasional pushback from within the Jewish community against attempts by Jewish leaders to cultivate relationships with members of the

---

184 World ORT. 2008. 'How ORT began' [online article]. URL: http://www.ort.org/asp/article.asp?id=117
185 Shimoni 1993, 257.
186 Shain, M. 1996. 'South Africa'. *American Jewish Year Book 1996*, eds D Singer & R R Seldin, vol 96, 360. New York: American Jewish Committee.

new government. When Chief Rabbi Harris delivered the eulogy at the funeral of Joe Slovo, a steadfast atheist, some members of the Jewish community accused him of sacrificing principle for 'political expediency'.[187] There were also some disagreements between Jewish leaders and the new government, particularly over foreign policy. When the Palestine National Authority was permitted to open an embassy in Pretoria in 1995, many Jews reacted negatively. An editorial in the *South African Jewish Times* sharply criticised the move.[188] Many were also perturbed—not only in South Africa but also in Israel and around the world—when Arafat delivered his infamous 'jihad' speech in May 1994 in a Johannesburg mosque, vowing continued war against Israel in spite of the ongoing Oslo peace process.[189]

The Board reacted publicly to many of these events. For example, it criticised President Mandela for his 1996 meeting with American Nation of Islam leader Louis Farrakhan.[190] It also spoke out against South Africa's improving relations with Iran, Libya and Syria.[191] This was a new step: the Board had never been so vociferous in criticising or even commenting on the foreign policy of the previous regime. Indeed, when Israel had voted against South Africa at the UN, the Board had defended the South African government. However, it was also true that the apartheid government had never pursued a policy of friendship towards Israel's strategic enemies. Had the National Party government attempted to do so, the Board and the Jewish community may have felt the need to comment openly.

While the ANC government cultivated alliances in the Arab world it also maintained relations with Israel. These relations remained warm as long as the peace process moved forward. Relations grew distinctly colder after 1996, when Israeli voters elected Prime Minister Benjamin Netanyahu, who was viewed by South Africa (and the US) as obstructionist. However, the relationship had thawed during the latter years of the administration of Yitzchak Rabin, to the extent that senior ANC leaders attended memorial services for Rabin after his

---

187 Aggrieved Orthodox Jew (pseudonym) 1995. 'Chief Rabbi charged with political expediency'. *South African Jewish Times* Letter, 21, 24 February.
188 'The PLO in S Africa' 1995. *South African Jewish Times*,3, 10 March.
189 Arafat, Y. 1996. Quoted in Shain, *American Jewish Year Book 1996*, 356–7.
190 Shain, M. 1997 . 'South Africa'. *American Jewish Year Book 1997*, eds D Singer & R R Seldin, vol 97, 419–20. New York: American Jewish Committee.
191 Shain, M. 1998. 'South Africa'. *American Jewish Year Book 1998*, eds D Singer & R R Seldin, vol 98, 400–1. New York: American Jewish Committee.

assassination in 1995.[192] This seesaw pattern would continue in the years to follow, with the Jewish community and its leaders commenting frequently on the government's statements and actions, favourably or unfavourably.

Tactically, then, the Board had moved in two directions at once. On the one hand, it continued to pursue its role as the community's intercessor, mediating between Jews and powerful parties and figures, seeking high-level meetings and keeping disagreements hidden. At the same time, the Board had found a far stronger voice on issues relating to the Middle East. That more active approach may have been partly provoked by the particular stances taken by the ANC, but it also reflected a greater tolerance in South African society for political dissent.

The Board also began to reconsider the narrow boundaries of minority politics, and to explore the possibility of playing a broader political and social role than it had in the previous era. No longer simply defining itself as an organisation for protecting Jews and overseeing Jewish affairs, the Board adopted a new 'mission statement' that included the goal of working for the improvement of relations between Jews and other groups, and of participating in efforts to build the new South Africa.[193] As Shimoni noted, the Board had committed to moving from being a 'defence agency' to being an 'advocacy agency'.[194]

One of the most important and visible expressions of this new ethos was the formation of Tikkun (later MaAfrika Tikkun), a communal welfare organisation dedicated to helping South Africa's disadvantaged communities. With the support of the Board and other organisations, Tikkun became the face of Jewish philanthropy and service to the new South Africa. Another organisation,

---

192 Shain, M 1997. *American Jewish Year Book 1997*, 41, 8.
193 Shimoni 1993, 258; South African Jewish Board of Deputies Gauteng Council. '1994–1996 Conference issue'. Parktown: South African Jewish Board of Deputies, 1996. 3. The statement reads as follows: 'Mission Statement of the SAJBD: The South African Jewish Board of Deputies (SAJBD) works for the betterment of human relations between Jews and all other peoples of South Africa based on mutual respect, understanding and goodwill. It is committed to a new South Africa where everyone will enjoy freedom from the evils of prejudice, intolerance and discrimination. It will do all in its power to help ensure a safe and secure life for all the citizens of this country.'
Compare this to the old mission statement of 15 years before: 'Objects of the South African Jewish Board of Deputies: TO WATCH over and to safeguard the religious and civil rights and status and welfare of the Jews of the Republic of South Africa. TO ACT on behalf of the Jews of the Republic in all matters affecting their relationship with the Government of the Republic, provincial, municipal and all other authorities. TO PROMOTE the creative continuity and enhance the quality of Jewish life in the Republic of South Africa. TO MAINTAIN fraternal relations with Jewish communities and institutions in other lands. TO TAKE any lawful action which it may deem necessary in any matter affecting the Jewish community. TO COLLECT and to use funds for the carrying out of the above objects. IN PURSUANCE of the above objects to acquire and hold movable or immovable property and any interest therein; to mortgage or pledge any such property; to donate, sell, dispose of, or otherwise alienate such property and to enter into leases or other commitments in respect of any such property.' (South African Jewish Board of Deputies 1980. 'Report to South African Jewry: 1978–1980'.)
194 Ibid.

Gesher, was formed by left-wing Jews in 1996, and sought to articulate a Jewish intellectual and political approach to reconciliation and nation building, as well as to correct what it saw as backward and racist attitudes in the community itself.[195] Yet another new institution was the Cape Town Holocaust Centre, which opened its doors in 1999, presenting this critical era of Jewish history to other South Africans and placing it in the context of South Africa's own human rights struggles. These changes partly reflected a desire to overcome and atone for the community's near silence during the apartheid era. They were also an attempt to secure the future of the community by integrating it more thoroughly within an emerging multiracial and democratic society.

Old problems, however, persisted in the democratic era. The demographic changes in the community continued to result in the closure and merger of several Jewish organisations. Old synagogues that were once central to the community's life and identity, such as the Wolmarans Street synagogue in Hillbrow, shut their doors. Rural Jewish communities struggled to maintain their cultural and religious life. There was an increasing amount of intra-religious strife, both within the Orthodox community and between Orthodox and more liberal strains. In 1995, for example, angry men disrupted an Orthodox women's prayer service on Simchat Torah.[196] Rabbi Jack Steinhorn of the Green and Sea Point Hebrew Congregation—the largest in the Western Cape—was declared *persona non grata* by the Beth Din (ecclesiastical court) in 1998 in a dispute over conversions and other matters pertaining to Jewish law.[197] These developments tended to reinforce the insularity of the community, and held back the emergence of a more tolerant internal Jewish discourse.

The crime wave also had a heavy impact on the lives and morale of the Jewish community. Rather than simply appealing to the government, however, Jews began organising their own responses. Young people joined the Community Security Organisation (CSO), and rabbis and leaders organised prayer meetings and protests against crime. Predominantly Jewish neighbourhoods even organised self-defence initiatives such as the Glenhazel Active Patrol (GAP), a private

---

195 Shain 1997, 422.
196 Ibid, 425.
197 Shain, M. 1999. 'South Africa'. *American Jewish Year Book* eds D Singer & R R Seldin. New York: American Jewish Committee,. 424.

police force that became the subject of public controversy.[198] Aspiring Jewish professionals moving through the country's university system, especially doctors, continued to look for employment opportunities overseas. But Jewish schools continued to flourish, partly driven by an exodus of Jewish children from public schools but also because of the continued commitment of South African Jewry to maintaining the community's educational institutions.

The rise of militant Islam continued to cause a great deal of anxiety throughout the mid-to-late 1990s, particularly for Jews in Cape Town, where South Africa's Muslim community and its institutions are concentrated.[199] In 1996 a group of Muslim and Christian clerics and community leaders on the poverty-stricken and crime-ridden Cape Flats came together to form People Against Gangsterism and Drugs (PAGAD).[200] However noble PAGAD's initial intentions may have been, the group quickly became notorious for violent vigilante actions, and tended towards an increasingly militant Islamist political line. PAGAD was blamed for a series of bombings and bomb threats in the late 1990s and through 2000, targeting not only tourist attractions, restaurants and police stations but also Jewish institutions. Elsewhere in the Muslim community, anti-Israel protests acquired an increasingly antisemitic character, with verbal attacks against Jews launched on community radio stations and in other forums.

It fell to the Board of Deputies to respond, and it had to weigh its options carefully. Public confrontation, Board members worried, could lead to an escalation of violence. On the other hand, quiet meetings with Muslim leaders, while greatly desired, seemed fruitless. The Board opted for a series of legal challenges against antisemitism in the Muslim community, much as Jews had taken action in the courts against right-wing propaganda in the 1930s. In 1997, the Board began what would become a long series of legal confrontations with Islamic radio stations over the repeated broadcast of Holocaust denial and other antisemitic propaganda.[201] These carried on in the courts and in tribunals such as the Broadcasting Complaints Commission of South Africa for several years with varying degrees of success.

---

198 Kransdorff, M & Magid, S. 2007. 'GAP under fire'. *It's Almost Supernatural* (19 October) [weblog]. URL: http://supernatural.blogs.com/weblog/2007/10/gap-under-fire.html.
199 Large Muslim populations, predominantly of Indian and Pakistani origin, also live in Durban and Johannesburg.
200 US Navy 'People against Gangsterism and Drugs (PAGAD)'. From *Patterns of Global Terrorism, 2001* [online article]. URL: http://library.nps.navy.mil/home/tgp/pagad.htm; see also Vahed & Jeppie 2004–5.
201 Shain, M *American Jewish Year Book 1997*, 403.

As Jews and Jewish institutions grappled with the challenges of political change in South Africa, they felt increasing pressure to deal with difficult questions about the community's past behaviour. Throughout the early years of the new democratic dispensation, other South Africans also began to confront the realities, painful memories and enduring resentments of the apartheid past. The Truth and Reconciliation Commission (TRC), established to investigate human rights abuses committed by the apartheid government and its opponents between 1960 and 1994, conducted extensive hearings in 1996 and 1997, offering the prospect of individual amnesty in exchange for full disclosure. Many victims and many perpetrators testified, as did many political and religious organisations that sought to account for their behaviour.

Two official Jewish submissions to the TRC were made. One was by Chief Rabbi Cyril Harris in November 1997. He acknowledged that most Jews had benefited from apartheid as whites, and that the community's leaders had failed to speak out adequately—a failure not only in terms of human rights principles but also in terms of Jewish moral teachings. He spoke about mitigating factors, such as the fear of antisemitism and the large number of Jewish anti-apartheid activists, but did not use these as excuses. Instead he asked the TRC for forgiveness on behalf of the community and spoke of its ongoing commitment to uplifting the previously disadvantaged.[202] The other submission was made by Gesher, which attempted to explain Jewish religious views on reconciliation. Without directly implicating the community's leadership, it too acknowledged the past moral failures of the community.[203]

These submissions did not end debate on the matter. The community continued to examine whether, and to what extent, its members should feel a sense of shame or pride about their past behaviour, both individually and collectively. In 1997, the community's quarterly journal, *Jewish Affairs*, devoted an entire issue to considering the role played by Jews under apartheid, and included essays by contributors with vastly different views. Some, like the celebrated Jewish anti-apartheid activist Franz Auerbach, believed that 'Jewish communal leadership should have expressed stronger opposition to apartheid' and that the community should make a formal statement expressing its regret—as Chief

---

202 Shimoni 2003, 271–3.
203 Ibid, 255–6.

Rabbi Cyril Harris eventually did.[204] Others, such as Board of Deputies executive member Hanns Saenger, and the eminent Yiddish scholar and *Jewish Affairs* editor Dr Joseph Sherman, believed that, while the community ought to examine its past, its leaders had behaved with 'a measured sense of pragmatism' and that the calls of 'Jewish moral grandstanders' for the community to apologise should be rejected.[205]

Other retrospectives sought to explore the role played by Jewish anti-apartheid activists. In December 2000, the Isaac and Jesse Kaplan Centre for Jewish Studies at the University of Cape Town organised a colloquium that examined the Jewish past, and the papers presented were later published in an anthology.[206] At roughly the same time, the Kaplan Centre held an exhibition—later to appear at the new South African Jewish Museum—chronicling and celebrating the contribution of South African Jews to the anti-apartheid struggle. Entitled 'Looking Back: Jews in the struggle for democracy and human rights in South Africa', it received a great deal of media attention and attracted the interest of many of the veteran activists themselves.[207]

Some members of the community were vociferous in their criticism of the past actions (or inaction) of South African Jewry. A young Jewish journalist, Claudia Braude, wrote a scathing article accusing Jewish lay and religious leaders of complicity in apartheid and of sacrificing Jewish ethics in favour of a moral compromise with Afrikaans nationalism. Braude described the community's strong Zionism as 'one collusional tool in Jewish consciousness under apartheid. It functioned to dissuade South African Jews from opposing the racist policies of the National Party and the government'.[208] Braude's views were published in the *Mail & Guardian*, a national weekly newspaper after *Jewish Affairs*, on whose board Braude sat, refused to print her article. The internal communal debate about the past was thus made rather uncomfortably public. The debate continued for another several years in public forums and newspapers, Jewish and general, and reverberated later in the Kasrils affair as well (as the next chapter shall show).

Debates over the Jewish community's political behaviour under apartheid had

---

204 Auerbach, F. 1997. 'Should we apologise? South African Jewish community responses to apartheid'. *Jewish Affairs*, Autumn.
205 Saenger, H & Sherman, J. 1997. 'Shouting from the grandstand: By way of an afterword'. *Jewish Affairs*, Autumn.
206 Shain, M & Mendelsohn, R (eds) 2000. *Memories, Realities and Dreams: Aspects of the South African Jewish Experience*. Johannesburg: Jonathan Ball.
207 Shain, M et al. 2001. *Looking Back: Jews in the Struggle for Democracy and Human Rights in South Africa*. Cape Town: Isaac and Jesse Kaplan Centre for Jewish Studies and Research, University of Cape Town.
208 Shimoni 2003, 266–8.

direct implications for questions and debates about how it should behave in the post-apartheid era, both towards the government and towards dissidents within the community itself. In 1999, in an article in the *South African Jewish Report* entitled 'Jewish leadership during and after apartheid: Double standards?', policy analyst and Gesher co-founder Steven Friedman hit out at 'the Jewish mainstream's failure to welcome' former Jewish anti-apartheid activists the community once shunned.[209]

Friedman's article was a response to an article the week before by the Board's senior researcher, David Saks, who had attacked the idea that the community had 'expediently embraced former Jewish leftists, whereas it had pointedly ignored them during the apartheid years'.[210] 'This,' Saks wrote, 'was neither fair nor accurate. For one thing, it was the Jewish left that first turned its back on the Jewish mainstream and not the other way around. For another, ordinary Jews have on the whole remained lukewarm towards their activist brethren, notwithstanding the fall of apartheid.' He cited the reluctance of the community to warm to SACP stalwarts Slovo and Kasrils as examples.

In his response, Friedman disputed that the Jewish left had 'first turned its back', arguing that few rabbis or lay leaders had shown concern for Jewish anti-apartheid activists or detainees. When they did turn away, Friedman argued, the leftists were not rejecting Judaism as such but 'shtetl Judaism,' which was insular and conformist, and which sought to appease the government of the day.

Friedman then accused the community's current leaders, including Chief Rabbi Harris, of continuing the tradition of 'shtadlanut', of cultivating political connections for reasons of expediency, not values or morality:

> *Is Saks not aware of the assiduous attempts by the Board of Deputies to court left wing Jews?... There is nothing new about this. Again the spirit of the shtetl lives. The leadership is reviving the galut custom of shtadlanut in which a well-placed Jew is found to intercede for the community. Here, by Saks's standards, the people concerned are more well placed than Jewish. Like the customs of the shtetl, shtadlanut was understandable when our people were powerless. As a strategy for citizens in democracy, it is expedient and counter-productive.*[211]

---

[209] Friedman, S. 1999. 'Jewish leadership during and after apartheid: Double standards?' *South African Jewish Report*, 6, 6 August.
[210] Saks, D. 1999. 'Jewish leftists: SA Jewry's lost tribes?' *South African Jewish Report*, 7, 30 July.
[211] Friedman, S. 1999. 'Jewish leadership during and after apartheid: Double standards?' *South African Jewish Report*, 6, 6 August.

In a rebuttal two weeks later under the title 'No shame in Jewish lobbying', Saks hit back, arguing that Jews, like other 'special interest groups', had the right to lobby government. 'It is not a case of 'special pleading' or 'looking for favours',' Saks wrote. Rather, he argued, Jewish lobbying was 'part and parcel of any healthy democracy'.[212] As Saks's reply indicated, the Board was still exploring quiet avenues of achieving its aims—despite its move towards an advocacy role, and despite its increased willingness to criticise the government on foreign policy. To Friedman, behind-the-scenes tactics smacked of inauthenticity. They were, moreover, inappropriate in the context of an open, democratic society. To Saks, the Board's behaviour was legitimate and fully in line with normal democratic practice.

The most comprehensive evaluation of Jewish political behaviour under apartheid was that of Prof. Gideon Shimoni, undertaken in his masterful survey *Community and Conscience: The Jews in Apartheid South Africa* (2003). Shimoni explored the Board's official position of neutrality and non-involvement, which was viewed by members and supporters of the government as evidence of Jewish dissent, and was viewed by those who opposed the apartheid regime as a form of tacit acquiescence. Overall, Shimoni concluded:

> *[T]his was characteristic minority-group behaviour—a phenomenon of self-preservation, performed at the cost of moral righteousness ... although there is nothing in this record deserving of moral pride, neither does it warrant utter self-reproach. The record also shows that on the whole the community's leaders, lay and religious, acted consciously but with deep pangs of conscience, although whether this at all qualifies as a morally redeeming factor will no doubt remain a point of contention.*[213]

Shimoni noted that the Board's shift to an 'advocacy' role represented an important break with the apartheid past, both tactically and ideologically.

In 1999 South Africa saw a peaceful and confident transfer of power from President Mandela to President Mbeki. The latter had addressed both the Union

---

212 Saks, D. 1999. 'No shame in Jewish lobbying'. *South African Jewish Report*, 6, 20 August.
213 Ibid, 276.

of Orthodox Synagogues and the Board respectively, before and after the 1999 general elections. The government's relations with Israel improved following the election of Labour Prime Minister Ehud Barak, and trade with Israel soared.[214]

Locally, new Jewish political leaders came to the fore as Tony Leon, leader of the Democratic Party, became South Africa's first Jewish Leader of the Opposition after the 1999 elections. Jewish ANC MP Andrew Feinstein moved from the Gauteng legislature to the National Assembly, where he played a prominent role on Parliament's standing committee on public accounts (Scopa) and led South Africa's first-ever parliamentary debate on the Holocaust.[215]

Crime was still high, and news of an Israeli crime syndicate operating in Johannesburg embarrassed the community. The CSO had proved effective, however, in protecting most Jewish institutions. Nelson Mandela was appointed patron-in-chief of Tikkun in 2000, cementing the organisation's national prominence.[216] The new Great Park Synagogue opened in Hyde Park, Johannesburg, a near-replica of the abandoned Wolmarans Street synagogue, symbolising the community's renewal in an era of change.

At the same time, however, the community continued to struggle—as it had during apartheid—with internal dissent, particularly over religious matters. Reform Rabbi David Hoffman of Cape Town was shunned by Orthodox rabbis at a communal Holocaust Remembrance Day ceremony, and tensions between the Green and Sea Point Congregation and the UOS continued after the former considered a motion to break away from the Orthodox movement.[217]

In June 2000, a debate erupted in the pages of the *South African Jewish Report* over Steven Friedman's regular columns, after he challenged various aspects of Orthodox Judaism. Friedman had supporters among the readers and staff of the paper, but the Orthodox rabbinate, including Chief Rabbi Harris, felt highly offended by his views. Friedman defended his opinions, and challenged what he saw as the Orthodox establishment's monopoly on Jewish identity. Ultimately, Friedman's column was removed from the newspaper after the Board of Directors of the *South African Jewish Report* decided to discontinue it. This decision was made in spite of

---

214 Shain, M. *American Jewish Year Book 2001*, 458.
215 Ibid, 463.
216 Ibid, 468.
217 Ibid, 470–1.

support from editor Geoff Sifrin for both Friedman's column and for the general principle of presenting a diversity of views. The axing of the column prompted a flurry of letters in protest against 'censorship', to little avail. Friedman described himself has having been 'banned' in the old apartheid style.[218]

Overall, then, on the eve of the outbreak of the *intifada* in 2000, the Jewish community in South Africa was flourishing, with many new institutions growing even as old ones consolidated or closed. But the community was still one in transition, struggling with internal and external change. Politically, the Board and other Jewish institutions were experimenting with more open and active forms of behaviour, while at the same time attempting to create back channels to the new government. Inside the community itself, debates were sometimes acrimonious and Jewish leaders, particularly the rabbinate, were slow to show tolerance towards unconventional views.

On 28 September 2000, the new Palestinian *intifada* was launched. Tensions had been rising in the Middle East since the breakdown of Israeli–Palestinian peace talks at Camp David in July. The visit of right-wing Israeli politician and former general (later Prime Minister) Ariel Sharon to the Temple Mount in Jerusalem—known to Muslims as the Haram Al-Sharif or Noble Sanctuary—became a pretext for violent Palestinian demonstrations in the days thereafter. Palestinian leaders gave their full weight to the demonstrations, later claiming that they had planned and organised them. Israeli responses were often viewed as disproportionately harsh, and the violence escalated.

In South Africa, reaction was immediate. Muslims demonstrated outside American and Israeli embassies and marched in street protests. A McDonald's restaurant was attacked in Cape Town, and students marched on the Kaplan Centre for Jewish Studies and Research at UCT, which marchers linked to Israel.[219] Almost overnight, ANC goodwill towards Israel evaporated and was replaced by outright hostility. ANC leaders organised street demonstrations against Israel, and ANC MPs held a special parliamentary debate on the Middle East, which was used to blame Israel for the new eruption of violence.[220]

---

218 Friedman, S. 2001. 'Kasrils' statement a cause for hope'. *South African Jewish Report*, 9, 9 November.
219 Shain 2001, 459–60.
220 Ibid, 459–61.

The Board's response was both sharp and public. Board officials publicly accused the ANC of abandoning its 'even-handed' approach to the Israeli–Palestinian conflict,[221] and the national president of the Board, Marlene Bethlehem, accused the ANC of playing a 'cheap political game' by using the Middle East to drum up support among Muslim voters ahead of the local government elections only two months away.[222] One example of this ANC tactic, and of anti-Zionism crossing the line into antisemitism, was a poster reading 'A vote for the DA is a vote for Israel' above a bloodied Israeli flag. The poster appeared in Muslim neighbourhoods in Cape Town and was linked to the ANC after the *Mail & Guardian* established that the brother of ANC provincial leader Ebrahim Rasool had been involved.[223]

As the rhetoric escalated, the Board also tried the old back channel methods. It requested a meeting with the Department of Foreign Affairs in late 2000, at which the two sides agreed to maintain daily contact, and after which a joint statement was issued, appealing to Jews and Muslims 'not to let the Middle East conflict lead to disturbances of the public peace in South Africa'.[224] The Board's national chairman, Russell Gaddin, announced that the Board was 'given a wonderfully warm reception and left with a feeling of reassurance'.[225]

However, the government's statements on the conflict continued to disturb many in the Jewish community. After a speech by President Mbeki at an Organisation of the Islamic Conference summit meeting in Doha, Qatar, in which he called for a Palestinian state with Jerusalem as its capital and the right of return for Palestinian refugees, the Board and the Chief Rabbi, among others, objected publicly to what was seen as a one-sided and biased approach by the South African government.[226]

Public debate continued in much the same vein throughout 2001, with continued frustration in the Jewish community about the government's perceived pro-Palestinian bias. That frustration became fear in August 2001, with the arrival of the United Nations World Conference against Racism, Xenophobia and

---

221 Ibid, 459–61.
222 Bethlehem, M. 2001. Quoted in Shain , 460.
223 Barrell, H. 2000. 'Rasool's brothers linked to anti-Semitic poster'. *Mail & Guardian*, 24 November [online article]. URL: http://www.mg.co.za/articledirect.aspx?articleid=162924&area=%2farchives__print_edition%2f
224 Shain 2001, 460–1.
225 Gaddin, R. 2001. Quoted in Shain, 461.
226 Shain 2001, 461–2.

Other Related Forms of Intolerance in Durban. The conference agenda, particularly in the non-governmental organisation (NGO) forum running alongside, was dominated by organisations and activists demanding a hard line against Israel. Israel was singled out among all countries as a unique abuser of human rights, and anti-Israel demonstrations continued throughout the conference.

Often, anti-Israel protests blended seamlessly into outright antisemitism, a fact that was acknowledged at the time by conference chair and UN Commissioner for Human Rights Mary Robinson—and, much later, by the South African government. The US and Israel had sent low-level delegations that eventually walked out of the conference; the Board and most other worldwide Jewish organisations boycotted it. This left a handful of activists, mostly students, to make the case for Israel and to resist the conference's antisemitic rhetoric. They confronted anti-Israel protestors with flowers and distributed T-shirts and leaflets stating their case. But the damage had been done. A conference intended to fight racism had ended up promoting it.

This left Jews around the world feeling uneasy, and South African Jews most of all. Though they offered few outright criticisms of the government, many South African Jews felt they had been abandoned by it, a feeling that was reinforced when the ANC referred to 'racist practices of the Israeli state against the Palestinian people' in an issue of its weekly newsletter timed to coincide with the racism conference.[227] Both directions that the Board and the communal leadership had pursued—cultivating relationships with the new government, while at the same time speaking out more forcefully on a broader range of issues—seemed to have reached a dead end. Meetings with government officials had failed to produce results, and the community was losing badly in the arena of public opinion.

Some had tried to engage the participants in the conference in debate. Rabbi Hoffman had invited the anti-Zionist, Israeli-born Uri Davis, who was on a tour of South Africa sponsored by the Congress of South African Trade Unions (Cosatu) prior to the racism conference, to address a panel discussion at his congregation. For the Board's part, it continued to try to influence the government and public opinion by holding meetings and distributing information to policymakers. But

---

227 'World cannot ignore the plight of the Palestinian people' 2004. *ANC Today*, 1, 31, 24 August [online newsletter]. URL: http://www.anc.org.za/ancdocs/anctoday/2001/at31.htm#art1

these efforts could not stem the tide of demonisation. The situation became even worse after the terror attacks of 11 September 2001, which further raised Jewish fears of antisemitism and intensified public debates about the Middle East.

A staff member at the Board interviewed for this book recalled that the feeling at the Board at the time was 'like being on a treadmill going too fast'. Not only did the Board have to react to the events in the Middle East themselves, which touched the sentiments of the Jewish community deeply, but also to increasingly hostile anti-Israel and sometimes antisemitic street demonstrations, as well as strong criticism of Israel by the government and pressure from within the Jewish community to take action.

At this crucial moment, the South African Zionist Federation, the oldest national Jewish institution and the community's voice on Middle East affairs, was in a state of administrative and financial disarray. There was talk of closing the SAZF entirely. At a Board meeting held shortly after the Kasrils declaration, Board members expressed concern at the 'startling silence' of the SAZF.[228] The Board, and other Jewish institutions, also felt cut off from the new administration of President Thabo Mbeki. Despite frequent contacts with cabinet ministers, the Board had not met formally with the new president since he began his term of office in June 1999. The close and warm relations the community had enjoyed with the government under President Nelson Mandela had faded into cold silence. The political crisis of the new *intifada* had become an institutional crisis as well, as Jewish organisations struggled both to represent the views of the community in the public realm and to communicate directly with the government.

The government itself faced trying political circumstances. The ANC was confronted in August 2001 with national strikes organised by Cosatu, its major governing ally in the Tripartite Alliance together with the SACP. Cosatu was protesting against President Mbeki's market-oriented economic policies and his centralised leadership style, grievances that would continue to surface in the years that followed. President Mbeki was also the target of national and international criticism over his controversial views on the HIV/Aids pandemic and his refusal to condemn the ongoing human rights violations and dictatorial behaviour of

---

228 'Minutes of the meeting of the management committee of the South African Jewish Board of Deputies held on Thursday, 25 October 2001, at 15.00 pm'. Provided by South African Jewish Board of Deputies, Johannesburg. Unpublished.

President Robert Mugabe in neighbouring Zimbabwe. Allegations of corruption surrounding the government's multibillion-rand arms purchases—which had been largely managed by Mbeki in his previous role as deputy president—also dogged the ANC and the presidency.

Making matters worse for the ruling party was the emergence of a new opposition force in the form of Tony Leon's Democratic Alliance, which had won over 20 per cent of the vote in the nationwide municipal elections of December 2000. By the latter half of 2001, political tensions between the two main partners in the DA, the Democratic Party and the New National Party, had become serious, and the ANC hoped to exploit them. But even a weakened and divided DA was seen as a potent threat to the ANC's hegemonic ambitions.

The new *intifada* provided the Mbeki government with a new way to rally the ruling party and to project an image of political strength by playing a larger role on the international stage. In local elections, ANC propaganda projected the DA as the party of Israel by exploiting Tony Leon's religious affiliation and the fact he had recently married an Israeli woman. In international forums, such as the Non-Aligned Movement, which South Africa chaired from 1998 to 2003, the government articulated the Palestinian position while at the same time insisting on a two-state solution to the conflict. It sent fact-finding missions to the region and offered its assistance in mediating between the two sides.

As the South African government staked its position, the Jewish community was struggling to find a way forward. The old methods of intercession had broken down, and the communal leadership was faltering in the new public debate that had emerged. It was in this context that Ronnie Kasrils introduced his declaration on the Israeli–Palestinian conflict. In doing so, he ignited a controversy that raged for months—one that further tested the institutional foundations of South African Jewry and challenged the direction and nature of Jewish political behaviour in the new South Africa.

CHAPTER FOUR

THE KASRILS AFFAIR

The Kasrils affair was not the first confrontation between the South African Jewish community and the government over Israel, nor was it the first time that dissent had been expressed by a group of South African Jews over Israeli policies. But it was the first time that both had happened at once—that a South African Jew, in a prominent government position, had questioned the community's support for Israel.

In the Verwoerd affair of the early 1960s, the government had challenged the community to oppose Israel's stance against apartheid, and sought to pressure Jews into supporting the National Party and its worldview. In the Lebanon crisis of the 1980s, the community's support for Israel was contested by a small group of young dissidents, many of whom had become involved in campus activism and the broader struggle against apartheid. Jewish leaders had been able to contain both these crises. The behind-the-scenes meetings of Jewish leaders with government officials, and the Board's attempts to officially distance the community from Israel's voting behaviour at the UN, helped mend bridges in the Verwoerd affair. Moreover, the short-lived nature of the protests over Sabra and Shatila in 1982 meant that the challenge to mainstream Jewish opinion over Israeli policies dissipated fairly quickly. Shimoni, describing a brief period in 1973 when a group of anti-apartheid Jewish students openly challenged the community's stance towards the government, notes: 'It was in the nature of student activism that it fluctuated in intensity owing to the short span of time that students spent within the university's walls.'[229] And so, too, with the Lebanon crisis.

The Kasrils affair, however, combined Lebanon and Verwoerd—the challenge of internal dissent with the challenge of external pressure from the government. Moreover, it took place in a political context that had changed radically. A left-wing party with ties to Israel's historic and strategic enemies was now in power, rather than a right-wing party that—despite its history of antisemitism—was connected to Israel's allies in the West. Although the ANC had long held a strong stance against antisemitism, it also had a recent history of anti-Israel rhetoric and military cooperation with the PLO.

Furthermore, since the release of Mandela and the transition to democracy, South Africa had become a far more open society—more open, at least, than it had been under apartheid. Many people whose views might have been ignored or suppressed before now had access to the mainstream media. And contests between different views could not simply be resolved by arranging a meeting with the appropriate minister or newspaper editor. Ideas and arguments had to be confronted with opposing ideas and counter-arguments. The Board and the Jewish community had indeed become more outspoken and more involved in public debates. New attempts at outreach had taken the Board beyond the confines of narrow minority politics. Yet the vigorous contest of ideas over the Middle East, which was greatly intensified by the Kasrils affair, was a public clash for which Jewish institutions were not yet well prepared.

The Kasrils affair began on 23 October 2001, when Minister Kasrils read a prepared statement in the National Assembly during a debate over the report of a parliamentary fact-finding mission that had travelled to Israel and the Palestinian territories to gather information on the ongoing conflict and make policy recommendations.

Kasrils and his ANC colleague Max Ozinsky, a member of the provincial legislature in the Western Cape, then circulated that statement as a petition to be signed by 'South Africans of Jewish descent'.[230] The statement, later entitled the

---

229 Shimoni 2003, 185.
230 Kasrils, R & Ozinsky, M. 2001. 'Statement on the Israeli–Palestinian conflict'. Address by Kasrils to the National Assembly, Cape Town. 23 October. See Appendix.

'Declaration of conscience on the Israeli–Palestinian conflict by South Africans of Jewish descent',[231] caused an immediate uproar, both within the Jewish community and beyond.

Critics would later charge that Kasrils was being opportunistic, seizing the moment to raise his public profile by speaking out on an issue that he had never taken up before. Several of the Jewish leaders interviewed for this book claimed that Kasrils had admitted being told by President Mbeki to take this stand, though at least one other interviewee contested that claim. Certainly, Kasrils had been somewhat subdued in expressing whatever objections to Israeli policy he had had up to that point. In a 1994 interview with the community's in-house journal, *Jewish Affairs*, Kasrils noted:

> *Let's hope that the future is going to see closer ties between a democratic South Africa and Israel. I think this is possible … I have had discussion with representatives of the Israeli government. We want to see a warm development of these relations … we can learn a great deal from Israel in this country, in terms of agriculture, reclaiming the scrubland, the Karoo, a whole range of possibilities. I think that Israel has got to deal with the Palestinian problem more sensitively, and hopefully with Labour now in power, there will be greater progress.*[232]

In a wide-ranging interview published in 1997, Kasrils candidly described his feelings about Israel. He spoke of a boyhood in which news from Israel was followed closely, when 'I read *The Star* religiously every single evening, searching for every bit of information concerning the War of Independence'.[233] He related that he had become disillusioned with Israel over time: '… [I]t wasn't a question of breaking off a romance, it was more a question of the romance having subsided.' He recalled protesting against the Six Day War, and drew connections between what he believed was Zionism's concept of the 'chosen people' and the racial exclusivity of Afrikaner nationalism in South Africa. He spoke of a

---

231 Kasrils, R & Ozinsky, M. 2001. 'Declaration of conscience on the Israeli–Palestinian conflict by South Africans of Jewish descent'. Final draft of declaration. 19 November. See Appendix.
232 Kasrils, R. 1994. Quoted in 'Talking to Jews in the ANC'. *Jewish Affairs*, 17–24, Autumn.
233 Kasrils, R. 1997. Quoted in Suttner, I (ed.) *Cutting Through the Mountain: Interviews with South African Jewish Activists*. Johannesburg: Penguin, 275.

Jewish upbringing that had 'no relevance to the life around me in South Africa', and spoke of his ability to identify with Jews and Israelis who had 'made the passage from having both minds and hearts squarely in a Jewish exclusivity, from having strong emotional connections with Zionism that you could never rationally challenge'. Yet he also noted: 'I have never denied my Jewish origin … I am also looking forward to visiting Israel at some stage … although I'm not happy about the status of the Palestinians, and even the status of Arabs within the State of Israel.' He also related that the 'sting' of his criticism of Israel had been 'drawn' by meeting Israelis on the political left: '… and I think when I look back, some of my criticism of Israeli foreign policy, of the wars that were fought, was too one-sided.'[234]

By October 2001 Kasrils seemed to have found his 'sting' again. In defending his declaration, he cited strong and growing personal convictions that Israel was abusing Palestinian rights. He had been affected, he said, by his meeting with radical Israeli and pro-Palestinian activist Uri Davis, as well as the pro-Palestinian 'documentary' *Judgment Day* by John Pilger which drew connections between the Israeli–Palestinian conflict and the South African struggle, and which had been shown on South African television.[235] However, it would appear that Kasrils's negative feelings towards Israel were not recent, and that contemporary events had pushed him from curious ambivalence back into a more critical posture.

Whatever his personal motives or feelings, Kasrils did not write his declaration entirely by himself. A preliminary draft was apparently prepared by Laurie Nathan, then chairperson of the Centre for Conflict Resolution. Indeed, several passages appear to have been taken directly from Nathan's address to Parliament's portfolio committee on foreign affairs on 10 October 2001, in which Nathan discussed 'the agenda for peace and justice', including the issue of Palestine, in the aftermath of the 9/11 attacks in the US.[236]

The Kasrils declaration also closely resembled the 'Home for All' declaration of December 2000, also written by Nathan. The preliminary draft of the Kasrils declaration was then edited, amended and added to by Ozinsky, whom Kasrils

---

234 Ibid, 279–82.
235 Gordin, J. 2001. 'Kasrils defends call for "Jews to raise their voices". *Sunday Independent*, 3, 28 October.
236 Nathan, L. 2001. Presentation to portfolio committee on foreign affairs, Parliament of South Africa. 10 October. URL: http://www.pmg.org.za/viewminute.php?id=1010

would acknowledge as co-author. After its initial release in the National Assembly, the declaration was amended again (including some revisions by this author) until the final draft was circulated to its signatories and to the media on 19 November 2001.

Both the initial (23 October) and final (19 November) drafts of the declaration included six sections: 1. 'The Fundamental Causes of the Conflict'; 2. 'The Holocaust Compels Us to Speak Out' (in the final draft, 'Our History Compels Us to Speak Out'); 3. 'Repression Intensifies Resistance'; 4. 'The Security of Israelis and Palestinians is Inseparable'; 5. 'A Call for Peace and Security'; 6. 'As an Immediate Step Toward Peace, We Call on the Government of Israel'.

The October version stated:

> *Successive Israeli governments and the world Zionist movement have consistently denounced their critics as anti-Semites and blamed the Palestinians for the failure to reach a negotiated settlement. We emphatically reject those assertions. We do not dispute that sectors of the Palestinian population have resorted to terror ...*
>
> *Yet this is not the root cause of the ongoing violence. The fundamental cause of the conflict is Israel's occupation of Palestine, and the suppression of the Palestinian struggle for national self-determination ... The establishment of the State of Israel in 1948 inflicted a great injustice on the Palestinian people, compounded by the subsequent Israeli rule of the Occupied Territories and denial of the legitimate claims of the Palestinian refugees.*
>
> *A recognition of the fundamental causes of the ongoing violence does not constitute antisemitism. Nor does it amount to a denial of Israel's right to exist. Rather, it constitutes an urgent call to the Israeli government to redress injustice and satisfy legitimate claims, without which peace negotiations will fail.*
>
> *All Jews live in the shadow of the Holocaust. For some, the overriding lesson is that survival is the highest morality ... Other Jews believe that the Holocaust compels them to support justice and freedom from persecution for all people, regardless of their nationality, ethnicity or religion. We stand firmly in this camp.*

> *After the suffering experienced by Jews in Europe during Nazism we are utterly appalled at the ruthless security methods employed by the Israeli government against Palestinians ... The notion that security can be achieved through reliance on force is demonstrably false as the struggle against Apartheid testified.*
>
> *We understand the fears of Jews in Israel and their longing for security. The security of Israelis and Palestinians, however, is inseparably intertwined ... There is consequently no viable alternative to a negotiated settlement that is just, that recognises both Palestine and Israel as fully independent sovereign states, and that provides for peaceful coexistence and cooperation ...*
>
> *... [I]t is incumbent on Israel, the dominant force and power over the Palestinians to demonstrate its serious intent in this respect ... by recognising the legitimate rights of the Palestinian people and creating the basis for peace and stability ... We call on South Africans of Jewish descent, and Jews everywhere, to raise their voices ...*
>
> *As an immediate step toward peace we call on the Government of Israel: To resume and sustain negotiations with the Palestinian authority in good faith. To conduct negotiations within the framework of the relevant resolutions of the United Nations Security Council ... To conduct its security operations with restraint and in accordance with international law. To work in partnership with the Palestinian leadership to build a lasting peace on the basis of reconciliation.*[237]

After this version (reproduced in full in Appendix A) was read in the National Assembly, suggestions for changes were made by numerous contributors, including Nobel literature laureate Nadine Gordimer and myself. Some of these changes were reflected in the final version of the declaration. These included recognition that Israel 'was founded as a homeland for the persecuted Jews of Europe'—a proviso insisted upon by Gordimer[238]—and a call on Palestinian leader Yasser Arafat, suggested by myself, 'to pursue every effort to end terrorist acts committed by some sectors of the Palestinian population'.

The final declaration was 'launched' on 7 December 2001 in parallel ceremonies in Johannesburg and in Cape Town.[239] The second event was held

---

237 [Online text]. URL: http://www.dwaf.gov.za/Communications/MinisterSpeeches/Kasrils/2001/Address%20to%20 National%20Assembly%20about%20Israeli%20Government%20on%2023%20Oct%2001.doc
238 Roberts, Ronald Suresh. *No Cold Kitchen: A Biography of Nadine Gordimer*. Johannesburg: STE Publishers, 2005. 585.
239 Battersby, J & Gordin, J 2001. 'Ronnie Kasrils launches declaration of conscience'. *Sunday Independent*, 1–2, 9 December.

at the District Six Museum in Cape Town, a venue chosen for its symbolism as a monument to coexistence in the era before apartheid's forced removals. Jewish blessings were recited, Muslim leaders in attendance were acknowledged and messages of support from Israeli peace activists were read out.[240]

A group of supporters and signatories of the declaration, members of whom were present at the launch, had already formed an organisation to back the Kasrils declaration. They began referring to themselves as 'Not In My Name', borrowing the title from a group of left-wing Jews in Chicago that had been started in November 2000 to organise protest among Diaspora Jews against Israeli government policies.[241] The South African 'Not In My Name' campaign soon enjoyed national and international media coverage. In the weeks and months of controversy that followed, the group organised demonstrations and vigils, participated in public debates and wrote articles and letters in local newspapers in support of Kasrils and the declaration.

Reaction to the Kasrils declaration was immediate and intense. It was welcomed enthusiastically by the ANC, by pro-Palestinian activists and by Muslim leaders.[242] An article in the *Muslim Views* of Cape Town proclaimed: 'October 23 will be recorded in the annals of contemporary history as the day a new threshold was crossed when Ronnie Kasrils, MP, Minister of Water Affairs who is of Jewish descent, opened the door for a new critical discourse on Israeli oppression.'[243] In a statement quoted in the weekly ANC newsletter, the party noted:

At this moment of increased terror and heightened violence and tension, it is essential that voices such as these are heard throughout the world. It is essential that in such a climate of anger, suspicion, accusation and counter-accusation, there are people who are able to throw off the blinkers of prejudice and hate and honestly seek workable solutions to this problem.[244]

---

240 Brodovcky, N. 2001. 'Not In My Name: Ronnie Kasrils launch of declaration'. Transcript and notes of presentation, District Six Museum, Cape Town, 7 December.
241 Feuerstein, S. 2001. 'Re: Not In My Name'. E-mail to Bradley Bordiss, 20 September. Provided by Ebrahim Fakir.
242 Jassat, I. 2001. 'Kasrils slams Israel'. *Muslim Views*, 13, November; Sawant, G. 2001. 'SA takes stand against Israeli oppression'. *Muslim Views* 13, November.
243 Jassat, ibid.
244 'Declaration of conscience challenges roots of mistrust' 2001. *ANC Today,* 7 December [online newsletter]. URL: http://www.anc.org.za/ancdocs/anctoday/2001/at46.htm#art1 (The word 'Israel' is consistently misspelled as 'Isreal' throughout the document.)

Support also came from Archbishop Emeritus Desmond Tutu. Tutu celebrated the stance taken by Kasrils and Ozinsky, 'two heroes of the anti-apartheid struggle', who had drawn 'an explicit analogy between apartheid and current Israeli policies' and who had, he said, bolstered the case for disinvestment from Israel.[245]

Many journalists and media outlets supported Kasrils, implicitly and explicitly. The *Sunday Independent*, whose editor John Battersby took a special interest in the debate, called the declaration 'an historic and courageous commitment that could, in time, play a significant role in persuading the government of Israel to sue for peace'.[246] Some journalists, however, were more critical. John Patten, a columnist for the *Cape Times*, took Kasrils to task for glossing over the challenge that Palestinian terror posed to a resolution of the conflict, and concluded: 'South Africa's emotional contribution is adding little to the solution.'[247]

The declaration was dismissed by several opposition parties, including the DA. Retired liberal anti-apartheid politician Helen Suzman distanced herself publicly from the declaration, as did a few former radical activists such as former South African Communist Party member Pauline Podbrey. Others, such as Jewish crossover Zulu-rock singer Johnny Clegg, quietly declined Kasrils's entreaties to join his campaign.[248] *The Citizen*, one of the few opposition-leaning newspapers, criticised Kasrils, Deputy Foreign Minister Aziz Pahad and the government 'for taking sides in an extreme manner'.[249]

The Board of Deputies rejected the Kasrils declaration outright. In a press release, national chairman Russell Gaddin said the Board 'regarded Mr Kasrils as a friend' but that he 'was not properly informed', and accused him of 'using his Jewish background to give credibility to the pro-Palestinian stance of the ANC'. Gaddin added that he was 'not prepared to debate these issues with Mr Kasrils in the media and would seek a meeting with him'.[250] The rabbinical establishment,

---

245 Tutu, D & Urbina, I. 2002. 'Against Israeli apartheid'. July. [online article]. URL: http://www.merip.org/newspaper_op-eds/Tutu_IU_Israeli_Apartheid.html. The article was printed in several international newspapers. Tutu co-wrote a series of such articles with Urbina, including 'Confronting Iraq: Might doesn't make right' (14 March 2003), and 'Anti-war thinking: Acknowledge Despair, highlight progress on moral preemption' (20 March 2003). The 'Against Israeli apartheid' article often appeared under Tutu's byline alone, though Urbina was not shy to take credit on the web page of the Middle East Research and Information Project.URL: http://iticwebarchives.ssrc.org/Middle%20East%20Research%20and%20 Information%20Project/www.merip.org/newspaper_op-eds/newspaper_op-eds.html
246 'Declaration of conscience giant step to dialogue' 2001. Editorial, *Sunday Independent*, 9 December.
247 Patten, J. 2001. 'Are Kasrils and co helping to solve the Middle East problem?' *Cape Times*, 8, 13 December.
248 Clegg, J. 2003. Personal communication with the author, 31 October.
249 'Pahad, Kasrils stirring it up' 2001. Editorial, *The Citizen*, 12, 25 October.
250 South African Jewish Board of Deputies, 2001. Press release, October.

including Chief Rabbi Cyril Harris and the Beth Din (ecclesiastical court), also rejected the Kasrils declaration and described it as 'a fault-ridden and unbalanced document emanating from Jews who have left the fold of the Jewish community'.[251] Many members of the Jewish community responded as well, in a barrage of letters and articles published in community and general newspapers.

One of the most frequent criticisms of the Kasrils initiative was that it was 'one-sided', placing most of the blame and the burden of responsibility on Israel and little on the Palestinians. Mike Berger, for example, a former professor of chemical pathology at the University of Natal and a frequent commentator on the Middle East in local newspapers, wrote disparagingly of Kasrils's approach:

> *The Palestinians are victims and they are thus excluded as contributors to and participants in the evolution of the conflict ... Israel is defined as a settler colonialist state. All reality is filtered through this ideological prism and the actors emerge in their assigned and permanent roles of oppressed and oppressor, victim and racist.*[252]

Felicia Levy, a member of the Johannesburg Jewish community who carried on a running debate with Kasrils in the letters pages of several newspapers, wrote on one occasion: 'You attribute the cause of the Middle East conflict solely to Israel; hold Israel solely responsible for the Palestinians not having obtained statehood; and demand that Israel take sole responsibility for the establishment of peace.'[253]

In a more invitational style, anti-apartheid activist and author Colin Legum wrote:

> *I welcome Ronnie Kasrils's appeal to South African Jews to raise their voices 'in support for justice for Palestine'. But why not justice for both Palestinians and Israelis? Much as I esteem my friendship with him [Kasrils] and respect his political courage, I feel that by taking a one-sided view as shown in the quote above, he is not promoting the cause of peace in the Middle East, which I know is as close to his heart as it is to mine ... To blame only one side—the common mistake in the present controversy—reflects prejudices against one side or the other.*[254]

---

251 Harris, C et al. 2001. 'What about the truth?: Rabbis respond to Ronnie Kasrils's. Press release, 20 December.
252 Berger, M. 2001. 'Of rhetoric and resistance'. *Mail & Guardian* 21,14 December.
253 Levy, F. 2001. 'Israel is not to blame ...' *Sowetan*, 14 December.
254 Legum, C. 2001. 'No peace until both sides forgo victory by force'. *Sunday Independent*, 4 November.

Another common criticism of Kasrils and his supporters was that they made factual errors and seemed ill-informed about current events and history in the Middle East. Professor Milton Shain, Director of the Isaac and Jesse Kaplan Centre for Jewish Studies and Research at the University of Cape Town, for example, described the declaration's account of the conflict as 'at best a simplistic reading of contemporary history'.[255] Kasrils dismissed such criticism as 'a typical attempt to wish away an unpalatable point of view',[256] but the claim appeared rather well founded on several occasions.

One of these was a debate on the letters pages of the *South African Jewish Report* between Kasrils and Rabbi Ben Isaacson, who had been one of the few rabbis to oppose apartheid at its nadir. Isaacson had written a scathing criticism of the Kasrils declaration in which he had referred to the collaboration of the mid 20th century Palestinian national leader Haj Amin Al-Husseini with the Nazis in Berlin.[257] Kasrils struck back, accusing Isaacson of descending to a 'low intellectual level' and dismissing Al-Husseini as 'an obscure Palestinian who sided with Hitler during the war'.[258] Isaacson retorted: '[Kasrils] has at last demonstrated the abysmal ignorance that is his only weapon. Haj Amin Al-Husseini obscure? This was the moulder and leader of Palestinian-Arab sentiment …'[259]

Kasrils and his supporters defended their views as the only reasonable response to the conflict. In response to *The Citizen*'s charge that he and the government had taken sides in the Israeli–Palestinian conflict, Kasrils, in a letter co-signed by Pahad, wrote: 'Only those who regard Israel as beyond reproach could describe our interventions in the way you have. Our call is in line with that of the European Union, the UN, and now, at this time of global crisis, that of President Bush.'[260] Sheilagh Gastrow, acting director of Development at UCT, agreed: '… The government's position as outlined by Kasrils will prove to be the only functional outcome to the crisis. That position recognises both Israel and Palestine's right to safety and security.'[261] Kasrils also insisted that his position was well founded: 'Far from being uninformed,' he wrote, 'what I have done is

---

255 Shain, M 2001. 'Please, Ronnie Kasrils, not in my name' *Sunday Independent*, 16 December.
256 Kasrils, R 2001. 'Speaking out against Israel'. *Sowetan*, 1 November.
257 Isaacson, B 2001. 'Isaacson's challenge to Ronnie Kasrils's. *South African Jewish Report*, 6, 16 November.
258 Kasrils, R 2001. 'Low intellectual level of Jewish soothsayers'. *South African Jewish Report* 6, 23 November …
259 Isaacson, B 2001. 'Give me a worthy opponent'. *South African Jewish Report*, 8, 30 November.
260 Kasrils, R & Pahad, A 2001. 'We're trying to help settle M-E conflict'. *The Citizen*, 31 October.
261 Gastrow, S 2001. 'Kasrils recognises both sides' right to safety'. *Sunday Independent*, 4 November.

bring to the debate an important perspective on the Israel and Palestine conflict which supporters of Israel would prefer to ignore ... I base my position on well-documented facts concerning Israel's repression of Palestinian rights ...'[262]

His supporters agreed that claims to the contrary were motivated by ideological bias. In a letter co-signed by the leading members of Not In My Name, they hit back: 'Claims that he is ignorant appear to arise from the fact that, as a born and Bar Mitzvah'd Jew, he has the courage to speak out against the human rights abuses suffered by the Palestinian people.'[263] Kasrils responded in like fashion to Gaddin's accusation that he was 'not properly informed': 'Had I lauded Israel he would, no doubt, have praised my intelligence.'[264]

But these responses did not satisfy many critics, some of whom accused Kasrils not only of distorting facts but of drawing false parallels between Israel and hated regimes around the world. A group of five former Soviet Jews co-signed a letter accusing Kasrils of comparing 'Israel's legitimate protection of her citizens' with Nazism in his initial remarks to the National Assembly.[265] Kasrils denied having done so. Indeed the transcript of his remarks revealed that he said: '... I am not using the icon of the concentration camps ... I am not making that comparison.'[266] He also said, however, that Israeli policy 'smacks of the way Fascism in Europe dealt with people they considered to be nonpeople', leaving his intentions somewhat unclear in this regard.

One parallel that Kasrils drew clearly and repeatedly was between the Israeli–Palestinian conflict and the struggle against apartheid. He and his supporters also argued, on occasion, that Israel was actually worse than the apartheid regime. Max Ozinsky, comparing the destruction of District Six with house demolitions in Gaza, remarked: '... [T]he one difference ... is the fact that here, houses were torn down with bulldozers and shovels whereas in Gaza, houses are being torn down by rockets and bombs.'[267] Here, the old debates over the community's stance in the 1950s and 1960s found their echo, nearly half a century later.

---

262 Kasrils, R. 2001. 'Speaking out against Israel'. *Sowetan*, 1 November.
263 Bordiss, B et al. 2001. 'Kasrils: We stand by him'. *The Citizen*, 21 November.
264 Kasrils. 2001.
265 Rabiner, AP et al. 2001. 'An open letter to Minister Ronnie Kasrils by five former Soviet Jews'. *South African Jewish Report*, 1, 2 November.
266 Kasrils, R. 2001. Speech in the National Assembly, Parliament of South Africa, Cape Town. 23 October. *Debates of the National Assembly* no 19 (23 to 26 October 2001): 6845–6.
267 Ozinsky, M. 2001. Speech at launch of Kasrils declaration, District Six Museum, Cape Town, 7 December.

References to apartheid, are a frequent refrain in many contemporary South African political debates, where a politician's or party's stance on apartheid is still seen as an indicator of legitimacy or otherwise. But for Kasrils and many other Jewish former anti-apartheid activists, such references were also about old grievances—whether over the community's passivity in the 1950s and 1960s, or its embrace of the Pretoria-Jerusalem relationship in the 1970s and 1980s.

The Israel-apartheid analogy provoked criticism from Helen Suzman, among others, who wrote: '[Kasrils] obviously identifies Palestine with the victims of apartheid and Israel with the apartheid regime—the same ludicrous identification that almost derailed the UN Conference against Racism held in Durban last August, and which turned it into the expensive farce it became.'[268]

By imposing the template of the South African experience on the Middle East, critics charged, Kasrils was polarising opinions in the Jewish community and caricaturing the views of those who disagreed with him. This claim was reinforced by Kasrils's references to his critics in public appearances where he claimed to represent Jews who were 'more democratic-minded and tolerant'[269] and characterised Jews who disagreed with him as 'narrow-minded'.[270]

Kasrils often emphasised the point by highlighting the anti-apartheid credentials of many who had supported his declaration, and by comparing the dissent of Jews opposed to Israeli policy with the dissent of whites who had opposed the apartheid government. 'I ... have no fears of constituting a minority,' he wrote. 'That, after all, was what the tiny fraction of whites constituted in their brave opposition to apartheid ... It is interesting to note that almost all the signatories were involved in the struggle against apartheid.'[271] Here Kasrils ignored the small but sometimes vocal group of former anti-apartheid activists, both liberal and radical—including Isaacson, Podbrey, Legum and Suzman—who had refused to sign the declaration and who spoke out against it on occasion.

Israeli ambassador Tova Herzl, too, weighed in. In an essay printed in several newspapers, she strongly opposed the attempt of Kasrils and his supporters to propose a parallel between apartheid South Africa and Israel: 'While perpetrating

---

268 Suzman, H. 2001. 'Israel as apartheid state is ludicrous'. *Sunday Independent*, 5 January.
269 Kasrils, R. 2001. *Tim Modise Show*, SAfm, 23 November.
270 Kasrils, R. 2001. *Newsmakers*, SABC, 27 October.
271 Kasrils, R. 2001. 'Don't condemn the rape victim'. *The Citizen*, 19 December.

an injustice on the memory of apartheid, they also cloud an understanding of the current situation, essential if one wants to help solve it ... Any democracy must do its utmost to redress inequalities created by accident of birth. But to call them apartheid is sheer nonsense, and reflects either malice or ignorance.'[272]

Defenders of Kasrils and supporters of the declaration were equally vociferous in putting forth their case. The most important fact about the Kasrils declaration, many argued, was that Kasrils had spoken up in the first place, allowing greater opportunity for those who dissented from the pro-Israel sentiments of most other Jews to express themselves. Gastrow wrote: 'There are a number of Jews in South Africa who agree with the government that there can be no peace without justice in the Middle East. Unfortunately our voices are not being heard and Kasrils's statement has offered essential leadership to this group.'[273]

Steven Robins of the University of the Western Cape agreed and offered an optimistic outlook on the future of Jewish dissent:

> *For decades, the South African Jewish establishment stuck to a conservative, insular and parochial acceptance of the official Israeli line: to be a 'proper Jew' meant to be unquestioningly loyal to the Israeli government. Now, at least there appears to be some attempt to engage with Jewish and non-Jewish critics of the Israeli government ... This political openness could help Jews recover the democratic traditions of dialogue and contestation that characterised the vibrant Jewish political cultures of the pre-second world war era.*[274]

The *South African Jewish Report*, which did not take an editorial stance in favour of or against the Kasrils initiative, nevertheless took a view similar to that of Robins: 'Whether one agrees or not with what Kasrils said about the Israeli issue itself, he may have done the community a service simply by speaking out and showing that not all Jews have to follow the 'party line' as specified by the mainstream Jewish organisations.'[275]

Several 'Not In My Name' members took this argument even further, and claimed that by showing the political diversity of South African Jews, Kasrils was helping to fight antisemitism. Ozinsky declared:

---

272 Herzl, T. 2001. 'To call the inequalities apartheid is sheer nonsense'. *Cape Argus* 14, 5 December.
273 Gastrow, S. 2001. 'Kasrils recognises both sides' right to safety'. *Sunday Independent*, 4 November.
274 Robins, S. 2001. 'Voices of reason older than Israel'. *Sunday Independent*, 7, 25 November.
275 'Open debate in troubled times' 2001. *South African Jewish Report*, 2 November.

> *The problem with public silence from the Jewish community on human rights abuses in Israel is that the message goes out to the rest of South Africans that Jewish support for Israel is unconditional, a blank cheque regardless of the human cost ... The public stand by those SA Jews who support the declaration serves to decrease antisemitism. Just as the presence of whites within the struggle against apartheid served to support the non-racialism of the ANC, so the public support of SA Jews for human rights and a just peace in the Middle East acts to reduce the power of anti-Semites.[276]*

The same logic was invoked by Kasrils, who recalled:

> *After my statement I was approached by a Muslim leader who told me that my views had reminded him that he must stop thinking in stereotypes about Jews—that there are Jews who think differently about the Middle East situation than what is generally presented as the Jewish community viewpoint. This, it seems to me, is suggestive that a proper bridge can be set up between the local communities. At the moment they are starting to bare their teeth at one another on the issue.[277]*

This approach seemed, to some, a latter-day version of the thinking of Henry Katzew, who advocated a rapprochement between Jews and Afrikaner nationalists. Some even compared Kasrils and Ozinsky's stance to that of Percy Yutar, suggesting that they were proponents of a kind of appeasement that would give *carte blanche* to antisemites. The former Soviet Jews who had complained of Kasrils's reference to Nazism wrote in one letter: 'When a public figure, in the course of an official presentation, demonstrates open partiality and bias, he does not promote peace, but rather fuels hatred and incites the unending cycle of violence.'[278] Kasrils's stand, wrote another correspondent, 'must indeed be causing the anti-Israel lobby, and the antisemites among them, a great deal of satisfaction'.

Furthermore, by encouraging antisemites to make distinctions between different kinds of Jew based on their willingness or refusal to condemn Israel, Kasrils and

---

276 Ozinsky, M. 2001. 'Jewish debate on Mid-East crisis a healthy sign'. *Cape Times*, 12, 30 November.
277 Kasrils, quoted in Gordin, J. 2001. 'Kasrils defends call for "Jews to raise their voices". *Sunday Independent*, 3, 28 October 2001.
278 Rabiner, A P et al. 2001. 'Minister fuels violence cycle'. *The Citizen*, 20 November.

his supporters were, some argued, failing to challenge the underlying antisemitic attitudes at issue. This point was underscored, unwittingly, by responses such as those of prominent black businessman Solly Moeng, who wrote that Kasrils and Ozinsky had shown 'that not all Jews are bad people', implying (perhaps unintentionally) that those who disagreed with them might be considered 'bad', or that acceptance of Jews was conditional on Jewish rejection of Israel or Israeli policies.[279]

At the same time that critics were concerned about rising antisemitism, Kasrils and the members of 'Not In My Name' complained that they had been vilified by the Jewish community—that they had been referred to as 'Jewish anti-Semites',[280] 'self-hating Jews', and 'traitors'.[281] Kasrils even reported that he had received death threats.[282] The very Jewishness of the dissidents had been questioned. Ken Katz of the South African Zionist Federation, for example, ridiculing the term 'South Africans of Jewish descent', wrote: 'I do not believe Mr Kasrils is a pivotal member (or for that matter a member at all) of our community; is he really in a position to talk as a Jew who is committed to the values that our community cherish?'[283]

The same point was put by a few observers who sympathised with Kasrils's cause but questioned what they saw as his opportunistic use of his Jewish identity. Justice Dennis Davis, while describing the signatories of the declaration as 'the guts of the Jewish intellectual community', added: 'I don't think you can say 'not in my name' when you've never revealed that your own world is dictated in some way by something Jewish.'[284] Freelance writer Pat Schwartz added:

> *I will not sign a statement supporting Israel right or wrong nor will I sign a statement based on fundamental fallacies and drawn up and endorsed by people like Ronnie Kasrils and others of his ilk who have spent their lifetimes eschewing their Jewishness and now, in their striving for political correctness and advancement, cynically claim it only in order to denounce it.*[285]

---

279 Moeng, S. 2001. 'Declaration shows 'not all Jews are bad people'.' *Sunday Independent*, 16 December.
280 Apfel, S. 2001. 'Can there be Jewish anti-Semites?' *South African Jewish Report*, 7, 9 November.
281 Barron, C. 2002. 'Not In My Name'. *Fairlady*, 37, 22 May.
282 Kasrils, R. 2002. Quoted in Freedom of Expression Institute. 'Minister receives death threats on his stand on Palestinian/Israeli conflict'. Press release 28 May. [online text]. URL: http://fxi.org.za/archives/press/2002/28-5-2002.0.htm
283 Katz, K. 2001. 'I will not be joining you, Mr Kasrils…'. *South African Jewish Report*, 7, 2 November.
284 Davis, D. 2002. Quoted in Barron, C. 'Not In My Name'. *Fairlady*, 38, 22 May.
285 Schwartz, P. 2002. 'There is no moral high ground'. *Mail & Guardian*, 19, 26 April.

Kasrils and Ozinsky replied to these criticisms, addressing their detractors with no small degree of irony: 'In our case we are both Marxists and atheists ... But we both have Jewish antecedents.[286] In the case of Ronnie Kasrils this was recognised as such by the Jewish Board of Deputies, the Israeli government and the Jewish community who since the ANC became 'kosher' have sought to invite him into their fold—as long as he remained uncritical of Israel!'[287]

The members of Not In My Name wrote that Kasrils's treatment by fellow Jews was 'similar to the rejection that an Afrikaner like Bram Fischer felt when he took his stand against the injustices of the apartheid government. All the contempt and rejection of the Afrikaner establishment came raining down on him because he dared to speak against the crimes of fellow members of his tribe'.[288] Here, once again, they invoked the apartheid (and anti-apartheid) past to lend legitimacy to present claims. They also attacked the Jewish community's apparent inability to accommodate diverse views, a grievance that at least some of Kasrils's supporters had nurtured since the Lebanon crisis.

However, some critics accused Kasrils and his supporters of exaggeration. Psychologist Theo Schkolne, who contributed frequently to the debate, wrote that the comparison between Kasrils and Bram Fischer was 'disingenuous':

> *While a lone and courageous Bram Fischer felt compelled to stand up to apartheid's evil empire, at great cost to his personal freedom, who is Kasrils standing up to? A tiny community of 80 000 souls, which is falsely caricatured as intransigent and reactionary? The 'contempt and rejection' by the Jewish 'tribe' is largely in the programmed heads and alienated hearts of Kasrils and fellow dissenters.*[289]

Schkolne noted that the community had in recent months held many open dialogues with critics of Israel, including anti-Zionist Uri Davis, which Kasrils had ignored. 'Is it because they lack the courage to directly engage the community,' Schkolne wondered, 'that they have convinced themselves that it

---

286 In Ozinsky's case, the claim to have 'Jewish antecedents' was a matter of some public dispute. His father was Jewish, but his mother was not, leading critics to question his authenticity.
287 Kasrils, R & Ozinsky, M. 2001. 'In a propaganda war, truth is the victim'. *South African Jewish Report*, 7, 9 November.
288 Bordiss, B et al. 2001. 'Support for Kasrils's stand'. *South African Jewish Report*, 8, 23 November.
289 Schkolne, T. 2001. 'A Jewish Uncle Tom'. *South African Jewish Report*, 8, 23 November.

is the community's intransigence that prevents them from doing so? Are they afraid to face the challenge of recognizing that the Israeli–Palestinian conflict is not one of 'wrong versus right', but of 'right versus right', of finding dual justice in a conflict of profound archetypal dimensions?'[290]

Others agreed, saying that the angry response from the Jewish community was not because Jews opposed a two-state solution or because Kasrils had criticised Israel, but because of the way in which he had done so. In the words of one letter writer:

> ... Israelis and Jews generally are often Israel's harshest critics. No, it is the manner in which Kasrils has criticised Israel that has upset people. Seldom has there been a more biased, one-eyed and factually incorrect criticism of Israel ... in comparing Israel to Apartheid SA, all Kasrils has done is show his bias, lack of understanding of the issues, and his unwillingness to deviate from the party line ... It is little wonder that the Jewish community is up in arms over his statement.[291]

Other correspondents observed that Kasrils and Ozinsky, too, indulged in personal attacks against their opponents, 'replete with sweeping and frequently scurrilous accusations that border on character assassination', in the words of David Saks, senior researcher at the Board.[292] Ozinsky had, for example, written of Schkolne: 'Perhaps, just as Schkolne believes that he can be a "leftist" whilst supporting the right wing, so he believes he is working for peace whilst supporting a policy of war, military occupation and assassination?'[293] These claims were unfounded, as Schkolne had taken no such positions.

Other critics of the Kasrils declaration speculated about Kasrils's possible personal and political motives. '... [O]ne has to stop, analyse and wonder what is the whole issue really about and what is Minister Kasrils's real motive and agenda?', one correspondent wrote. 'Could it be that there are other issues and pressures taking place within the ANC that threaten the minister's position within his party? ... Does Minister Kasrils regard his portfolio as minister of water affairs and forestry as not being quite as exciting as he would like and not as high in profile as being in the ministry of defence?'[294]

---

290 Ibid.
291 Joffe, H. 2001. 'Biased, one-eyed criticism'. *South African Jewish Report*, 7, 23 November.
292 Saks, D. 2002. 'Personal attack'. *Cape Times*, 11 February.
293 Ozinsky, M. 2002. 'Left out'. *Cape Times*, 6 February.
294 Tanner, J. 2001. 'Stop, analyse and wonder'. *South African Jewish Report*, 8, 14 December.

Supporters sprang to Kasrils' defence. Veteran anti-apartheid activist Franz Auerbach protested against the harsh response to Kasrils from many members of the community: 'I find it regrettable that some of those who replied find it necessary to attack Mr Kasrils' credibility and knowledge, essentially because his perspective on the conflict differs from theirs.' He added: 'I believe Mr Kasrils' appeal has much merit, and deserves careful consideration, which I hope it will get when the Board and Mr Kasrils talk to each other.'[295]

Professor Jocelyn Hellig of the University of the Witwatersrand, while distancing herself from Kasrils's attempt to create a parallel between apartheid South Africa and Israel—a comparison that she said 'made sense only with regard to the occupied territories'—also questioned those who attacked Kasrils's motives. She observed:

> *As I see it, he is asking South African Jews, in the light of their own experience—both of the Holocaust and South Africa—to listen to the voice of the Palestinian people, to help put pressure on Israel to restart negotiations, and to withdraw from the occupied territories. He may have been guilty of over-simplifying the background to the conflict and careless about pinpointing its fundamental causes, but is what he is asking so terrible?*[296]

Supporters of the declaration sometimes acknowledged its flaws, but argued that it had succeeded in generating debate. Robins agreed that the comparison between Kasrils and Bram Fischer may have been far-fetched, since Kasrils at least enjoyed the privileges of high office. 'Nevertheless,' he concluded, 'progressive Jews need courage and *chutzpah* to break ranks with conservative Jewish opinion.'[297] Ozinsky acknowledged that debates within the Jewish community had existed before the declaration had been launched. But while these had taken place only inside the community, he argued, the Kasrils initiative had taken the 'important step' of making these debates public.[298]

Steven Friedman, who had earlier criticised the Board's political behaviour and whose column in the *South African Jewish Report* had been cancelled the

---

295 Auerbach, F. 2001. 'Demonising the other side'. *South African Jewish Report*, 6, 16 November.
296 Hellig, J. 2001. 'Why impugn Ronnie Kasrils' motives?' *South African Jewish Report*, 6, 9 November.
297 Robins, S. 2001. 'Voices of reason older than Israel'. *Sunday Independent*, 7, 25 November.
298 Ozinsky, M. 2001. 'Jewish debate on Mid-East crisis a healthy sign'. Letter, *Cape Times*, 12, 30 November.

year before, argued that the Kasrils affair had exposed the weakness of the community's leadership and its failure to adjust to the democratic era. '… [N]ot only does Kasrils deserve support,' he wrote, 'but … the saga illustrates the sickness at the heart of the mainstream of our community … it marks the failure of the communal leadership's bankrupt policy of *shtatlanut*—of pinning the Jewish future here on courting any Jew in a high position.' He argued further that '[i]n the early 1990s, Jewish leadership here had the opportunity to reposition our community so that it could face the challenges of the new South Africa,' but that communal leaders had preferred 'the strategy of trying to get politically prominent Jews to think with their blood'—which, he said, had 'failed'.[299]

The intensity of the debate in the Jewish community about the Kasrils affair not only revealed the passionate differences in feeling about Israel but shed light on the continued and bitter divisions about the community's past attitude toward the apartheid government and its political behaviour in contemporary South Africa. As Kasrils noted in a bitter interview with the Cairo-based *Al-Ahram*: 'We have been described as an insignificant minority whose views should not be taken seriously. The irony is: this is the same accusation senior Jewish figures levelled at the members of the Jewish community who fought against apartheid. Once apartheid collapsed, the same figures hailed us as heroes.'[300] Again, the raw wounds of the apartheid era were exposed.

The apartheid analogy here may have been appropriate in one sense, that the Kasrils affair closely resembled the Verwoerd affair of the 1960s. Once again, a prominent government official was calling for South African Jews to criticise Israeli policy and to adopt the worldview of the ruling party. Once again, the threat of antisemitism hung in the background. However, there were some important differences. This time, the pressure came from a government official who was himself Jewish. And the danger of antisemitism was not one that Kasrils threatened, as Verwoerd had, to use against the community; rather, he claimed that he was helping to contain it. He also did not directly take issue with the fact that most Jews voted for the opposition, whereas Verwoerd had explicitly noted Jewish support for the Progressive Party. However, Kasrils did refer to his

---

299 Friedman, S. 2001. 'Kasrils' statement a cause for hope'. *South African Jewish Report*, 9, 23 November.
300 Kasrils, R. 2002. Quoted in Ghanem, Y. 'Insulted by Israel'. *Al-Ahram Online*, 28 March.

opponents as 'conservative' and his supporters as 'democratic'. He associated opposition to Israel with support for the new South Africa, and support for Israel with the bygone apartheid era. In this sense he had re-imposed the dilemma that Verwoerd had once thrust upon the community—namely that to achieve fuller political inclusion in South Africa Jews would have to abandon, or radically change, their connection to Israel.

In addition, for many South African Jews—both supporters and opponents of the Kasrils declaration—who had been involved in or sympathetic to the anti-apartheid struggle, the tumult of the Kasrils affair recalled the painful confrontations in the community over the Lebanon War in the early 1980s. At the time, a cohort of young Jews whose consciences had been roused by the Soweto uprisings and their aftermath viewed the community's solidarity with Israel with disappointment and frustration. Justice Davis recalled his experiences in speaking out at the time against Israel's role in the Sabra and Shatila massacres in Beirut in 1982: 'I got more phone calls at 2 am and 3 am from Jews threatening to kill me than I ever got from the security police,' he said.[301] Twenty years later, in a completely different political environment, the community was still struggling with the question of how to deal with external challenges and internal dissent, not only on Israel but on broader political issues.

There was, however, one critical difference between the Kasrils affair and the Lebanon controversy: this time, the dissenters were represented and supported by senior figures in the national government. Whatever marginality Kasrils and his supporters felt in relation to the Jewish community and its leaders, Jews in turn felt it in relation to South Africa as a whole. This was not just a confrontation between a small group of dissenters and their institutional opponents; this was also a confrontation between a small minority community and a government that actively supported the dissenters' viewpoint.

The feelings of many Jews were reflected in a letter that Gaddin had sent on behalf of the Board to all MPs prior to the debate on the parliamentary fact-finding mission. Gaddin implored the MPs to uphold the Constitution's ban on hate speech, and added, ominously: 'The past few months has [sic] witnessed a number of disturbing developments, which have seriously undermined the confidence of

---

301 Davis, D. 2002. Quoted in Barron, C. 'Not In My Name'. *Fairlady*, 38, 22 May.

South African Jewry in the future of the country and of their place within it.'[302]

The *South African Jewish Report* had expressed similar views in an editorial published during the World Conference Against Racism in Durban in August, when it said that the government's attitude had become 'genuine cause for concern' for the future of Jews in South Africa.[303]

In at least one respect, Friedman's analysis was correct: Jewish institutions were under-prepared for the Kasrils initiative and failed to respond effectively for many months. On top of the administrative and financial troubles at the SAZF, the Board of Deputies was confused and divided over how to answer Kasrils and his supporters in a way that would satisfy the majority of Jews without alienating the government.

At a management committee meeting held at short notice in Johannesburg two days after Kasrils made his address in the National Assembly, the national leadership of the Board discussed the way forward.[304] Yehuda Kay, then the national director of the Board, who had been present in the parliamentary gallery, noted that the Board's attempts to influence the debate by distributing materials to all MPs had backfired. (These materials had included Gaddin's letter; a five-page critique of the report of Parliament's fact-finding mission; and a Kaplan Centre photographic booklet on the exhibition, 'Looking Back: Jews in the struggle for democracy and human rights in South Africa', which the Board had purchased for a planned reception for parliamentarians that had been cancelled because of the 9/11 attacks.)[305] At least one opposition MP who opposed the fact-finding mission's report was accused in the debate of 'paraphrasing' the Board's text.

Board member Solly Kessler, who had also been in the gallery, noted at the meeting that Kasrils in particular had used the booklet to argue that all of the anti-apartheid activists mentioned in it had been anti-Zionists. Indeed, Kasrils had argued, '[t]his honourable group of anti-apartheid fighters … were in fact anti-Zionists and rejected Zionism because they believed in a common humanity and that there should not be an exclusive state …'.[306] In a later comment to the

---

302 Gaddin, R. 2001. Quoted in 'Kasrils incenses with ME remarks'. *South African Jewish Report*, 2, 26 October.
303 'Hijacking of a grand idea' 2001. *South African Jewish Report*, 6, 31 August.
304 'Minutes of the meeting of the management committee of the South African Jewish Board of Deputies held on Thursday, 25 October 2001, at 15.00 pm.' Provided by South African Jewish Board of Deputies, Johannesburg. Unpublished.
305 Shain, M. 2006. Personal communication with the author. February.
306 Kasrils, R. 2001. 23 October, 6852.

media, Kasrils elaborated: 'Ninety-nine per cent of those people would dissociate themselves from Israel's position vis-à-vis the Palestinians. It's outrageous to try and gather support for Israel in this way.'[307]

The Board meeting then considered what action to take—and, specifically, whether to seek a meeting with Kasrils. Kessler argued that the Board should not meet with Kasrils because it should not attempt to defend every single Israeli action. Michael Bagraim took a different view, arguing that the Board should seek a meeting with Kasrils 'because he [Kasrils] had been a useful connection for the Board in the past and also because he [Bagraim] believed he [Kasrils] could be convinced there were more pressing international problems closer to home to deal with'.[308]

Other Board members agreed, believing that 'the Government should not be continuously confronted until it turned against the Board since the Board, in order to fulfil its role, had to maintain channels of communication'. This was especially true, it was argued, in the case of the CSO, which had to work with police and security services to protect synagogues and other Jewish institutions. If the Board could not change Kasrils's views, one Board member argued, 'it could at least moderate them'. National chair Russell Gaddin had the final word, and argued that while it was important 'not to alienate government', the Board 'had to communicate what their views on Israel were and stand up for them'. The Board then agreed to seek a meeting with Kasrils.

By the time of the next management committee meeting in December, the day before Kasrils re-launched the declaration, the Board had yet to meet with Kasrils, even though he had written to express his willingness to meet. The Board, noting the potential for division in the community as well as between Jews and Muslims, resolved to continue to pursue a meeting.[309]

Meanwhile, the Board resolved at the management committee meeting to set up a committee that would deal with the media and appoint 'the right kind of person' to run a public relations department—a sign of a growing consciousness at the Board that it had been struggling to respond effectively to public debate.

---

307 Kasrils, R. 2001. Quoted in 'Kasrils incenses with ME remarks'. *South African Jewish Report*, 1, 26 October.
308 South African Jewish Board of Deputies, 'Minutes', ibid.
309 'Minutes of the meeting of the management committee of the South African Jewish Board of Deputies held on Thursday, 6 December 2001, at 15.00 pm'. Provided by South African Jewish Board of Deputies, Johannesburg. Unpublished.

A 'Media Response Team', including two paid staff members, was soon started and run out of the revived SAZF in Johannesburg. It was complemented by volunteer efforts throughout the country. Essentially, the Board had decided to continue its dual strategy of the past several years—seeking meetings on the one hand; speaking out publicly on the other. However, it now sought to sharpen and to institutionalise its media efforts.

Adding to the Board's difficulties in defending the community's views in the media was a growing tide of internal dissent. The Cape Council of the Board, which considered itself somewhat more politically flexible than the National Board in Johannesburg, disagreed with the way in which the National Board had dealt with Kasrils. Cape Board member and former national chairman Mervyn Smith, for example, told a meeting of the Cape Council in November that he believed the debate about the Kasrils declaration was a healthy one because there were different views within the community about Israel.[310] He added that he believed the National Board should not have attacked the Minister himself.

Later, in 2003, a debate emerged in the pages of the *South African Jewish Report* between Gaddin and members of the community who felt the Board's response to Kasrils had been ineffective. One correspondent wrote that the Board was 'not seen to be doing anything'[311] about anti-Israel propaganda, an accusation that Gaddin disputed. When *Palestine is Still the Issue*, a propaganda film by John Pilger attacking Israel, was screened several times on the television channel e.tv, several members of the community took matters into their own hands and took the channel to the Broadcasting Complaints Commission of South Africa, against the advice of Gaddin, who urged the public to leave such actions to the Board itself.[312] The complaint failed, but the complainants wrote a letter in response to Gaddin's criticisms, saying that they were 'unashamed' to have stood up on their own.[313]

Several formal, independent media organisations were started outside the Board by members of the community. These included the Truth In The Middle East (TIME) group in Johannesburg, and the Jewish Media Network (JMN) founded by community radio host and businessman David Hersch in Cape Town.

---
310 'South African Jewish Board of Deputies (Cape Council) Cape Committee Meeting: Tuesday, 27 November 2001'. Minutes of meeting.
311 Josselowitz, B. 2003. 'React to biased letters, programmes'. *South African Jewish Report*, 14, 18 July
312 Gaddin, R. 2003. 'Above Board.' *South African Jewish Report*, 2, 25 April.
313 Rosenberg, A et al. 2003. 'Above Board and 'below the belt". *South African Jewish Report*, 16, 2 May.

These distributed news and information about the Middle East to members of the community and responded to articles and stories in the mainstream media. These initiatives were often effective, where the Board had not been, in rallying the community and encouraging informed debate, internally and externally. Eventually the Board, rather than competing with such initiatives, decided to co-opt them. The work of the JMN, for example, was soon linked to and later subsumed by the Cape Council's media subcommittee after Hersch was appointed subcommittee chair in late 2003.

One independent suggestion that was eventually taken up by the Board and the SAZF was a counter-petition to rival the Kasrils declaration—a 'pledge of support' for Israel and for a peaceful resolution to the conflict. Originally proposed by Saul Behr, a member of the community, the central Jewish leadership took up the idea and circulated the petition through communal organisations. Eventually 13 000 signatures—comprising roughly 20 per cent of the total South African Jewish population—were collected, and the petition was presented to Israeli President Moshe Katsav by a SAZF delegation.

The Board continued to seek meetings with the government over the course of the Kasrils affair and its aftermath, usually holding discussions with Deputy Minister Pahad, but not with Kasrils or President Mbeki. After many of these meetings, the Board would announce—usually through the 'Above Board' column of the National Chairman in the *South African Jewish Report*—that it had been reassured that the government was committed to an 'even-handed' approach to the Middle East, only to be disappointed by the next government condemnation of Israeli actions. In March 2002, for example, Gaddin wrote: 'Despite the Government's past failure to be even-handed on the conflict, our recent meetings with senior ministers and officials has [sic] persuaded us that there has been a definite shift in Government's thinking on the matter.'[314] These assurances were quickly undermined a few weeks later by President Mbeki's call on Israel to withdraw its forces from their siege positions around Arafat's headquarters in the Muqata in Ramallah—a call that did not include any criticism or condemnation of ongoing Palestinian suicide bombings. Gaddin reacted:

---

314 Gaddin, R. 2002. 'Above Board.' *South African Jewish Report*, 2, 15 March.

We are appalled at this one-sided call. We believe that, unaccompanied by a similar call by the president to end the unbridled acts of terror against the Israeli civilian population, Mr Mbeki compromises South Africa's officially-stated policy of even-handedness in the Israeli–Palestinian conflict.[315]

This cycle of events—meetings, assurances, disappointment and subsequent meetings—recurred several times in the following months.

For nearly two years, according to members of the Board interviewed for this book, the Board was unable to effectively lobby senior government ministers on issues of concern to the Jewish community. "Go make your peace with Kasrils first,' we were told,' said one interviewee, whose account of frustrating meetings with ministers was corroborated by the recollections of others.

The conflict with Kasrils left the Board in a difficult position. As the Board's Cape Council Chairman, Philip Krawitz, complained in November 2001: 'We no longer have the ear of government.' Some members of the Board, including Bagraim, publicly declared that they would pursue more aggressive 'in your face' tactics. In Board meetings, however, he argued in favour of seeking a meeting with Kasrils. In the event, no meeting was held until Bagraim took over as national chairman nearly two years later. By then, the Board's political strategy had begun to undergo significant changes.

---

315 Gaddin, R. 2002. Quoted in 'Mbeki disappoints'. *South African Jewish Report*, 3, 5 April.

CHAPTER FIVE

THE AFTERMATH

The overall effect of the Kasrils affair on South African policy debates on the Middle East would prove to be somewhat limited. Few people's views appeared to have shifted, though the Kasrils declaration had certainly brought differences of opinion into sharp focus. The effect on the Jewish community's political posture, however, would prove to be profound and lasting. The Board managed to revive the SAZF and to invest in more effective media responses. At the same time, troubled by its isolation in the Kasrils affair, it adopted a new strategy of 'lobbying' that brought it into far closer political contact with the ruling party.

Kasrils continued speaking out in late 2001 and the early months of 2002, not just in the media but at rallies and demonstrations throughout the country. Most of these were small gatherings, supported by Anglican and muslim clergy. They included, for example, a demonstration in support of Israeli 'war resisters' (soldiers who refused to serve in the occupied territories) and a vigil outside the Cape Town City Hall.[316]

Some of these demonstrations, however, included alarming and extremist rhetoric. At a Palestinian solidarity rally in 2002, Kasrils addressed a crowd of 10 000 predominantly Muslim anti-Israel demonstrators in Athlone, Cape Town. Amidst shouts of 'Free, free Palestine', Kasrils condemned 'this butcher

---

316 Van Hees, B. 2001. 'Ministers hold Middle East vigil'. *The Citizen*, 1–2, 29 December.

Sharon'.³¹⁷ Sharing the podium with him were speakers who spoke in favour of terror attacks ('martyrdom operations') against Israelis, among other radical views.³¹⁸ The rally adopted a resolution calling for, among other things, 'the expulsion of the Israeli ambassador from South Africa, and the imposition of sanctions against Israel'.³¹⁹

Kasrils was among the guests invited to a meeting of Israeli opposition politicians and Palestinian leaders held by the South African government at the Spier wine estate in January 2002. It was the most determined effort by President Mbeki at mediating between the two sides, though Israeli government representatives were not invited. Kasrils appeared to play a subdued role at the meeting.

However, Kasrils remained outspoken, and his rhetoric became more radical over the next few months. In an interview in March 2002, Kasrils expressed support, in principle, for a single-state solution to the Israeli–Palestinian conflict; claimed that Israeli repression of Palestinians was worse than the apartheid regime's repression of black South Africans; and attacked his critics, referring to Chief Rabbi Harris as 'a man known for his antiquated views and profound bitterness'.³²⁰ In May, the Chief Rabbi struck back, excoriating Kasrils for his participation in a rally on Holocaust Remembrance Day in April in Durban, at which Kasrils was seen standing near a banner reading 'Zionism is Nazism'.³²¹

The debates reached a climax in April 2002, when Israel launched Operation Defensive Shield, aimed at responding to a wave of Palestinian terror attacks in March by destroying Palestinian terror organisations in the West Bank. Israeli forces encountered heavy fighting in refugee camps in Jenin. Palestinian spokesman Saeb Erekat claimed that there had been a 'massacre' of civilians in Jenin by Israeli soldiers, but failed to ever substantiate these claims.³²²

The Jenin controversy marked a turning point in the debate over the Israeli–Palestinian conflict, both in South Africa and around the world. Wildly exaggerated Palestinian claims of civilian deaths undermined the credibility of Palestinian

---

317 Kasrils, R. 2002. Speech at Vygieskraal stadium, Athlone, Cape Town, South Africa. 21 April 2002.
318 Brother Mangash 2002. Speech at Vygieskraal stadium, Athlone, Cape Town, South Africa, 21 April.
319 Smetheram, J-A. 2002. '10 000 turn up at Palestinian solidarity rally'. *The Star* 22 April.
320 Kasrils, R. 2002. Quoted in Ghanem, Y. 'Insulted by Israel'. *Al-Ahram Online*, 28 March.
321 Belling, M. 2002. 'S. African rabbi blasts pro-Palestinian Jewish politico'. *Jewish Bulletin News of Northern California*, 3 May [web article]. URL: http://www.jewishsf.com/bk020503/ip17a.shtml
322 Associated Press 2002. 'U.N. report: No massacre in Jenin'. *USA Today*, 1 August. [web article].
  URL: http://www.usatoday.com/news/world/2002-08-01-unreport-jenin_x.htm

representatives, and Israel's successes against Palestinian terror groups severely damaged these groups' ability to carry out future attacks. Jews around the world, stirred by anger at Palestinian false claims of mass murder by Israeli soldiers, rallied in support of Israel in the subsequent weeks.

In May 2002, the South African Zionist Federation (SAZF) organised a 10 000-strong Israel solidarity rally in Johannesburg. The comprehensive show of Jewish communal unity sent a signal to the government that the community had largely rejected the government's position, despite Kasrils's attempt to garner Jewish support. The rally marked one of the first major media successes of the Jewish community since the start of the *intifada*—though coverage of the event on e.tv, whose reporters had been pursuing an anti-Israel angle for months, was widely perceived by Jews to be slanted against the community. The rally also marked the beginning of the reversal of the fortunes of the SAZF, which had until then been fairly dormant in the debate. Indeed, one of the greatest ironies of the Kasrils affair was that the SAZF, teetering on the edge of dissolution when the declaration was launched, recovered and was reorganised during the controversy. It would emerge stronger than before, buttressed by new staff, new leadership and new activists.

At that point, Kasrils seemed to withdraw temporarily from public debate over the Israeli–Palestinian conflict. Many people speculated as to the precise reason. Some members of the Board interviewed expressed the conviction that he had been reined in by President Thabo Mbeki or the ANC. Others suggested that he had achieved his objectives—whether raising awareness of Jewish opposition to the Israeli government, or raising his personal political profile—and could afford to rest. He was appointed Minister of Intelligence after the ANC's victory in the 2004 elections, cementing his place in Mbeki's cabinet, which some felt had been his primary goal. A few suggested the opposite—that he had failed decisively to convince the Jewish community of his point of view.

But Kasrils did not disappear entirely. He gave a speech attacking Israel at the Justice in Palestine Conference in Johannesburg, one month prior to the World Summit on Sustainable Development in Johannesburg in 2002. In his address he acknowledged the research provided by the Media Review Network, a radical Islamist pressure group.[323] He was the keynote speaker at a London conference on divestment and sanctions against Israel in December 2002.[324] He also debated with British academic Hagai Segal on e.tv in 2003 following the screening of *Palestine is Still the Issue*.

In 2004, shortly before the general elections, Kasrils took up the case against Israel's security barrier in and along the West Bank in a series of articles. 'It is an apartheid wall of dispossession and a prison by any name,' he wrote in one article, continuing to draw parallels between apartheid and Israel.[325] In opposing the barrier so vehemently, he was merely stating the official position of the South African government, which was one of the few democratic countries to submit testimony against Israel's security barrier in the proceedings in the International Court of Justice (ICJ) at The Hague in February of that year. But, once again, strong personal convictions seemed to underlie his actions.

Also in March 2004, Kasrils wrote about his recent visit to ailing Palestinian leader Yasser Arafat, and attempted to deny accusations that Arafat was 'fixated on amassing the personal fortune and luxury attributed to him by his enemies'.[326] In May 2005 Kasrils joined British journalist Victoria Brittain in endorsing an abortive boycott of Israel's University of Haifa and Bar-Ilan University by the British Association of University Teachers (AUT).[327] And, in January 2006, Kasrils published an article in Britain and South Africa attacking the 'Myths of Zionism'.[328]

The Second Lebanon War in mid 2006 inspired Kasrils to return to the fray in full cry. In a two-part series in the ANC's official online journal, *Umrabulo*, Kasrils compared Jews and Israelis to Nazis.[329] In an op-ed in the *Mail & Guardian*, he repeated the Nazi parallel and referred to Israelis as 'baby-killers'.[330] These statements eventually led the Goethe Institute in Johannesburg, an official

---

323 Kasrils, R. 2002. 'Inequity of distribution of Resources in Palestine—Apartheid in the Holy Land'. Speech at Justice in Palestine Conference, Sandton, Johannesburg. 20 July. URL: http://www.dwaf.gov.za/Communications/Articles/Israel/2002/Justice%20in%20Palestine%20Conference%2020%20July%2002.doc
324 Kasrils, R & Brittain, V. 2002. 'No room for justice'. *Guardian*, 21 December [online article]. URL: http://www.guardian.co.uk/israel/comment/0,10551,864049,00.html
325 Kasrils, R. 2004. 'Israel's wall a prison by any name'. *Business Day*, 9 March
326 Kasrils, R. 2004. 'My lunch with Arafat'. *This Day*, 8 March.
327 Kasrils, R & Brittain, V. 2005. 'Silence from academe'. *Mail & Guardian*, 29, 27 May.
328 Kasrils, R. 2006. 'Myths of Zionism'. *Mail & Guardian*, 21, 27 January. See also Kasrils, R. 2006. 'Land and Peace'. *Socialist Worker Online*, 21 January [online article]. URL: http://www.socialistworker.co.uk/article.php?article_id=8113
329 Kasrils, R. 2006. 'David and Goliath: Who is who in the Middle East'. *Umrabulo* 27, November [online article]. URL: http://www.anc.org.za/ancdocs/pubs/umrabulo/umrabulo27/art11.html; Kasrils, R. 2007. 'David and Goliath: Who is who in the Middle East / Part 2'. *Umrabulo* 28, March [online article]. URL: http://www.anc.org.za/ancdocs/pubs/umrabulo/umrabulo28/art12.html.
330 Kasrils, R. 2006. 'Rage of the elephant'. *Mail & Guardian*, 2 September [online version]. URL: http://www.mg.co.za/articlePage.aspx?articleid=282802&area=/insight/insight__comment_and_analysis/.

German cultural organisation, to withdraw a speaking invitation to Kasrils.[331] There was also hostile reaction in the *South African Jewish Report*, including an op-ed by Anthony Posner entitled 'Some Pertinent Questions to Kasrils's. When Kasrils responded, editor Geoff Sifrin declined to publish his article on the grounds that many readers would consider it 'hate speech'.[332] This provoked a stern rebuke from South Africa's Freedom of Expression Institute (FXI), which accused Sifrin of 'censoring' Ronnie Kasrils.[333] The Board responded, accusing the FXI of pursuing 'a very definite political agenda', pointing out that former FXI chairman Salim Vally had attempted to disrupt pro-Israel events in the past and that senior FXI staffer Na'eem Jeenah was also a pro-Palestinian activist.[334] Kasrils received support from the Media Review Network, which published his article in full.[335]

The debate carried over into the mainstream media. In a letter to the *Business Day: Weekender Edition*, journalist Rehana Roussouw criticised the Goethe Institute for uninviting Kasrils.[336] Anti-apartheid veteran Helen Suzman responded in a letter a week later, pointing out that the South African Constitution did not protect hate speech, 'into which category Kasrils's allegations clearly fall'.[337] Kasrils then approached the South African Human Rights Commission (SAHRC) to determine whether his remarks about Israel had, indeed, constituted 'hate speech'. In a controversial decision, the SAHRC supported Kasrils, interpreting the constitutional ban on hate speech narrowly, ruling that hate speech must be actual 'advocacy of hatred' and declaring: 'The robust debate of ideas, the lifeblood of any constitutional democracy, must be safeguarded.'[338] The SAHRC also thanked Sifrin and Suzman for making 'further representations', although there was no sign that they had in fact made further input or that such input had been considered. Kasrils considered the decision a vindication of his 'critique of Israel', and released a press statement from the Ministry of Intelligence challenging 'his detractors, including the

---

331 Fabricius, P. 2006. 'Kasrils triggers seminar flutter.' *The Star*, 12 October.
332 Mizroch, A. 2006. 'S. African Jewish paper causes storm'. *Jerusalem Post*, 22 November.
333 Freedom of Expression Institute. 'On Jewish Report's censoring of Ronnie Kasrils' [online statement]. URL: http://www.fxi.org.za/index.php?option=com_content&task=view&id=38&Itemid=1
334 Saks, D. 2006. 'Letter to Jane Duncan, Director: Freedom of Expression Institute', 29 November.
335 Jassat, I. 2001. 'Jewish weekly slaps ban on Kasrils's [online statement]. URL: http://www.mediareviewnet.com/newnote_new.asp?ID=1856
336 Rousouw, R. 2006. 'Using religion to muzzle society'. *Business Day: Weekender Edition*, 6, 14 October.
337 Suzman, H. 2006. 'Antisemitism the issue.' *Business Day: Weekender Edition*, 5, 21 October.
338 South African Human Rights Commission 2007. 'In re: Referral by Mr. Ronnie Kasrils's. 23 March 2007 [available online]. URL: http://www.sahrc.org.za/sahrc_cms/publish/article_247.shtml

Goethe Institute who refused to allow him to address a meeting at their Johannesburg premises, to accept the HRC findings'.[339]

Kasrils continued to provoke controversy in the months that followed. On a visit to Iran in April 2007, he was reported by Iranian state news as having endorsed that country's nuclear programme, calling it 'wise'—which Kasrils later denied.[340, 341] In May 2007, he visited Palestinian Prime Minister and Hamas leader Ismail Haniyeh in Gaza. Kasrils invited Haniyeh to visit South Africa: 'We in South Africa look forward to you being able to lead a delegation to our country.'[342] Despite some controversy over whether Kasrils had the authority to issue such an invitation, and whether he had done so formally or in his personal capacity, Hamas itself confirmed the invitation.[343] On the same visit, he delivered a speech at Birzeit University in the West Bank, in which he attempted to impart lessons from the South African struggle. Israel's ambassador to South Africa, Ilan Baruch, complained to the South African government, and later wrote in the South African media that Kasrils 'was quoted by the Palestinian media as having encouraged rival parties in Gaza to stop their infighting and direct their weapons toward their enemy'.[344] When Kasrils denied this, accusing Baruch of 'a cynical smear tactic',[345] Baruch provided a quote from the Palestinian daily *Al-Ayam* of 6 May 2007 in which Kasrils was reported to have 'called for national unity, as the only road to success, particularly because the enemy conspires to divide and control', and to have 'emphasised that the guns should be pointed towards the enemy, to better serve the struggle for liberation and independence'.[346] Kasrils claimed that he had been quoted out of context,[347] and provided an (edited) video of his speech on the Ministry of Intelligence website.[348] Though Kasrils' videotaped speech includes several remarks distancing himself from attacks

---

339 South African Ministry of Intelligence 2007. 'Ruling from the Human Rights Commission on 'Ronnie Kasrils and his critique of Israel''. Press statement, 23 March [available online]. URL: http://www.intelligence.gov.za/MediaStatements/SAHR%20Media%2023%20Mar%2007.doc
340 Press TV 2007. 'S. Africa says Iran visit positive'. 18 April [online article]. URL: http://www.presstv.ir/detail.aspx?id=6515&sectionid=351020101
341 South African Press Association 2007. 'Kasrils refutes Iranian media claim'. 20 April [Online article]. URL: http://iafrica.com/news/sa/792748.htm
342 South African Press Association and Associated Press 2007. 'Palestinian leader invited to visit SA'. 3 May.
343 South African Broadcasting Corporation. 'Hamas has 'no problem with Jews'', 16 May [available online]. URL: http://www.sabcnews.com/politics/government/0,2172,149239,00.html
344 Baruch, I. 2007. 'Economic and diplomatic boycotts of Israel are destructive and misguided.' *Cape Times*, 9, 25 June.
345 Kasrils, R. 2007. 'Solidarity with Palestinians is not a call to murder Israelis'. *Cape Times*, 8, 28 June.
346 Baruch, I. 2007. 'SA needs to know too'. *Cape Times*, 10, 3 July.
347 Kasrils, R. 2007. 'Contents of my lecture misquoted and spun out of context.' *Cape Times*, 8, 9 July.
348 Kasrils, R. 2007. Speech at Birzeit University, Ramallah, Palestinian Authority, 5 May [available online]. http://www.intelligence.gov.za/MediaStatements/Birzeit2.wmv.

against civilians—'we must not descend to the indiscriminate terror of the enemy'—the tone of the speech was confrontational.

Despite Kasrils's occasional public contributions—often from abroad—the 'Not In My Name' campaign became less and less active. Its members reunited for a one-year anniversary, observed on the Jewish holiday of Chanukah at the District Six Museum in December 2002. Ozinsky and Kasrils released a press statement in which they declared: 'The demands we made in our Declaration are as relevant today as a year ago …'[349] However, the group made few statements and held few activities thereafter. A letter co-signed by several members mourning the death of Yasser Arafat in late 2004[350] was ridiculed in the Jewish communal press.[351] Still, dissent continued. A new group called Jewish Voices SA was founded in Johannesburg in 2002,[352] and participated in demonstrations with pro-Palestinian groups. Other similar efforts followed.

As the Kasrils affair faded, the South African Jewish community was both politically stronger and weaker than it had been before. Stronger, because it had begun to grapple with both internal and external debate; had begun to build and restore its institutional strength, particularly the SAZF; and had mustered an impressive show of unity on issues related to Israel and Zionism. But the community was weaker, too. It had failed to shift government policy in the Middle East, and had suffered significant public relations damage. Old fault lines within the community over its stance towards apartheid, and over its support for Israel during the era of the Pretoria-Jerusalem alliance and the first Lebanon War, had been exposed. Most of all, the community felt increasingly isolated from the government and was haunted by renewed anxiety about its collective future in South Africa.

The leaders of the Jewish community felt their vulnerability especially keenly. Their mandate had been shaken by new criticism from community members frustrated at the Board's poor performance in public debate. Even more acutely, the Board felt that the rift with Kasrils had driven a wedge between them and the government officials with whom they wished to interact. Kasrils had also challenged the very legitimacy of the Board as the representative voice of South African Jews, and damaged its credibility.

---

349 Kasrils, R & Ozinsky, M. 2002. "Not In My Name'—One year on'. Press release, 28 November.
350 Bordiss, B et al. 2004. 'Tribute to Yasser Arafat'. *South African Jewish Report*, 14, 19 November.
351 See *South African Jewish Report*, 17 26 November 2004; and 38, 3 December 2004.
352 Isaacs, D. 2004. 'Finding a liberal voice in Jewish community.' *South African Jewish Report*, 5, 12 March.

In the course of my research for this book, in order to understand the Kasrils affair from the perspective of Jewish communal leadership, I conducted a number of interviews with members and staff of the Board of Deputies. Eight interviews were conducted in all, four in Cape Town and four in Johannesburg, during September and October 2005. The interviews were conducted informally, though a common set of questions was used to guide interviews, and the participants were assured of anonymity.

The interviewees' overall views of the Kasrils affair showed several similarities. All agreed that Kasrils had failed to divide the community, with one describing the 'split' as '99 to one' against Kasrils. Yet most were in agreement that the Kasrils affair had been a serious test—'the community's first major crisis in the post-apartheid era', in the words of one staff member—and that it had placed the leadership of the community under severe stress in what had already been a difficult period. 'We never slept,' one interviewee recalled.

All agreed that the Board had struggled to respond appropriately. One regretted the Board's 'blunder' at distributing copies of the 'Looking Back' booklet to MPs ahead of the fateful parliamentary debate; another judged the community's response to Kasrils as 'an overreaction, because the community was feeling shell-shocked'. Yet all agreed that a response had been necessary. One even described the debate as 'a sobering, maturing process'.

There was wide disagreement among the interviewees on other issues, however. For example, many different explanations were offered as to the imagined motives of Kasrils. Some suggested that he had been motivated by personal political gain, or that he had acted on Mbeki's orders. One described Kasrils as an 'archetypal self-hating Jew'. Another, however, argued that Kasrils 'was pushed into taking his stance by the community', because he had been 'left out' of relationships with it. Another considered that it was simply 'difficult to evaluate Kasrils's motives'.

Similarly, Board members disagreed about the merits of Kasrils's stance. All agreed he had taken his campaign to an extreme, but some felt that it had at least some intrinsic merit. 'Very few people looked at what he was saying,' one told me. 'He was simply saying: 'I don't blindly support Israel'.' Others, however, disagreed. 'There was nothing constructive in Kasrils's stance,' one interviewee said. Another remarked: 'I was sympathetic to Kasrils—a lot of things he said were true about Israel's human rights violations.' But he felt Kasrils had let him down. 'Kasrils didn't represent criticism [of Israel]—he hijacked, or tried to hijack, that viewpoint.'

Despite Kasrils's temporary withdrawal from the debate in 2002, the South African government continued to follow a critical line towards Israel. It did so while attempting to play a role in mediating in the conflict by continuing to hold meetings with Israeli opposition figures, while at the same time shunning the Sharon government. In early 2003, for example, the South African government held a meeting with retired Israeli military officials who were critical of the Sharon government's policies in the occupied territories.[353]

In March 2004 the ANC condemned the killing by Israel of Hamas spiritual leader Ahmed Yassin, associating the operation with various other perceived acts of oppression against the developing world. In a speech delivered at the memorial service for Minister of Transport Dullah Omar, President Mbeki said:

> *We live and work in a world in which the dominant are determined to use their power to determine the shape and direction of the modern world, regardless of the desires and aspirations of the billions who are poor and weak. It is as a result of this reality that we have witnessed a Sheik Ahmed Yassin of Palestine assassinated in cold blood, a Jean-Bertrand Aristide of Haiti removed from office, and a mercenary operation mounted to overthrow the government of Equatorial Guinea.*[354]

In February 2004, the South African government testified at the ICJ at The Hague in opposition to Israel's security barrier in and along the West Bank.[355] Israeli officials, including Prime Minister Ariel Sharon, would later describe this step as the low point in South Africa–Israel relations.[356] In an oral submission presented on behalf of the government, Deputy Minister of Foreign Affairs Aziz Pahad said:

---

353 Shain 2004.
354 Mbeki, T. 2004. Speech at the Memorial Meeting for Minister Dullah Omar, 24 March.
355 International Court of Justice 2004. 'Legal consequences of the construction of a wall in the Occupied Palestinian Territory (request for advisory opinion)'. Press release, 25 June [online text]. URL: http://www.icj-cij.org/icjwww/ipresscom/ipresscom2004/ipresscom2004-23_mwp_20040625.htm
356 Sharon, A. 2005. Personal communication with the author, Jerusalem, Israel. 12 January.

The legal consequences arising from the construction of the Separation Wall is [sic] an issue that this Court cannot ignore. The Separation Wall is not a security wall. It is a wall to enforce Occupation, a wall that has separated hundreds of thousands of Palestinians from their families, homes, lands, and religious sites ... The Separation Wall is an anathema to the peace process as envisaged in the Roadmap as it eliminates the prospect of the two-State solution.[357]

South Africa's critical stance culminated in its hosting, in June 2004 in Cape Town, of the UN African Meeting in Support of the Inalienable Rights of the Palestinian People (CEIRP). In his opening remarks to the conference, President Mbeki linked the Palestinian and South African struggles, and struck a moderate yet determined tone:

I think we owe it to [the Palestinian people] to communicate a message that however long that struggle has taken; the fact of its length does not mean it will not succeed. I think we need to communicate the message that even for Israel its own future and the future of its own people lies in an independent Palestinian state, consistent with all of the decisions that have been taken by the international community in this regard to communicate to Israel the understanding that no amount of force is going to force the Palestinians to give up their struggle for their rights.[358]

The Israeli government responded discreetly but firmly. In 2003, it sent the director-general of its foreign ministry, Yoav Biran, to meet with government officials to issue a veiled warning about South Africa's treatment of the Sharon administration. Expressing a desire for closer ties, Biran noted that 'not always did we feel that the government of Israel, which was elected democratically in very free elections, was treated likewise by some of our friends here'. He warned that South Africa's efforts to mediate in the Israeli–Palestinian conflict were not being taken seriously because they left out the Israeli government: 'If we do

---

[357] Pahad, A. 2004. Statement at International Court of Justice, The Hague, Netherlands. 23 February [online text]. URL: http://www.dfa.gov.za/docs/2004/icj0223.htm
[358] Mbeki, T. 2004. Statement at the opening of the United Nations African Meeting in Support of the Inalienable Rights of the Palestinian People, Cape Town. 29 June [online text]. URL: http://www.dfa.gov.za/docs/speeches/2004/mbek0701.htm

not succeed to develop such political dialogue it would be regrettable, but the result would be that South Africa will remain a bystander, a distant observer, to what is happening in the Middle East.'[359] The Israeli government underlined this message by delaying the appointment of a new ambassador to South Africa following the return home of Tova Herzl at the end of 2003.

Following South Africa's participation in the proceedings at The Hague, Israel took more deliberate steps. In May 2004, Israel announced that it would be closing its trade mission in Pretoria. The reasons given were budgetary, but the departure of the trade representatives of South Africa's largest export destination in the Middle East sent a clear diplomatic signal, and was seen as such by many observers.

At the same time, however, Israel's own policies towards the occupied territories began to shift. In June 2004, the Israeli Cabinet approved Prime Minister Sharon's plan for a 'disengagement' from the Gaza Strip and several settlements in the West Bank. This marked a dramatic about-face for Sharon. During his term as Minister of Agriculture in the late 1970s, Sharon had been one of the foremost advocates of settlement, and continued to be so through the late 1990s. 'Everybody has to move, run and grab as many [Palestinian] hilltops as they can,' he was reported to have said, 'to enlarge the [Jewish] settlements because everything we take now will stay ours ... Everything we don't grab will go to them.'[360] Even as late as April 2002, Sharon had refused to consider the uprooting of settlements, telling the Knesset's Foreign Affairs and Defence Committee: 'The fate of Netzarim [a settlement in Gaza] is the fate of Tel Aviv.'[361] Now, Sharon was proposing to withdraw Israeli settlers from Netzarim—and to destroy it, along with all other settlements in Gaza and several in the West Bank.

Within a few months, South Africa began to change its posture towards Israel. The ANC government hosted a delegation of Members of Knesset from Israel's governing Likud Party in September 2004. This visit was followed by that of Israeli Deputy Prime Minister Ehud Olmert in October to discuss trade and investment

---

359 South African Press Association 2003. 'Israel wants better relations with SA: D-G'. 27 June.
360 Agence France-Presse 1998. 'With Sharon's encouragement, settlers seize another West Bank hill.' 16 November.
361 Hirschberg, P. 2002. 'Sharon talks regional peace to American Jews'. *Ha'aretz*, 24 April [online article]. URL: http://news.haaretz.co.il/hasen/pages/ShArt.jhtml?itemNo=155134

issues, and to sign related agreements. The following year, after the execution of the disengagement policy, President Mbeki sent a letter to Ariel Sharon commending him on its success: 'We salute your courage and assure you of our support as you dismantle the Jewish settlements in Gaza and the West Bank, and thus make an unprecedented contribution towards the just solution of the protracted and deadly Israel-Palestine conflict.'[362] The two also met briefly at the UN in September 2005. In November, the South African government sent an official business delegation, headed by Minister of Trade and Industry Mandisi Mpahlwa, to meet with Olmert and explore investment opportunities.[363]

Interviews for this book revealed that Board members actually had markedly different views on what had caused the government's shift in policy towards Israel. They also disagreed about what had caused Kasrils to withdraw from the debate. Some Board members believed that their intercession had led indirectly or even directly to a change in policy. One, for example, claimed that he personally had asked President Mbeki to have Kasrils 'tone it down'. Another explained that because the Board had 'coached' the members of the visiting Israeli Likud delegation on how to talk to the South African government, they had been able to help change the government's position.

Publicly, Bagraim claimed credit for the Board's behind-the-scenes tactics. In his column in the *South African Jewish Report*, he lauded the 'politics of engagement' practised by the ANC, and thanked the government on behalf of the Board for its meeting with Deputy Prime Minister Olmert in October 2004 and holding other such meetings.[364]

Others, however, tended to emphasise the pressure applied by the Israeli government itself. The fact that Israel had announced the closure of its trade office, and that it had taken more than a year to appoint a new ambassador after Tova Herzl's return to Israel, 'sent a signal' to the government, according to one interviewee.

Two Board members, however, spoke of a third explanation. They described meetings between the visiting American Jewish Committee and President Mbeki in August 2003, during the celebrations of the Board's centenary, as the turning point.

---

362 Mbeki, T. 2005. Letter to Israeli Prime Minister Ariel Sharon. Provided by Israeli Ministry of Foreign Affairs, August. [online text]. URL: http://www.mfa.gov.il/MFA/Government/Communiques/2005/PM+Sharon+receives+letters+from+Moroccan+King+and+South+African+President+17-Aug-2005.htm
363 'Mpahlwa, business delegation on three-day visit to Israel'. 2005 *Business Day*, 3, 12 November.
364 Bagraim, M. 2004. ''Politics of engagement' lauded'. *South African Jewish Report*, 2, 29 October.

'They promised they'd work wonders for him in America,' one said, in exchange for a more moderate stance on the Middle East. However, he added, he believed that the repeated failures of Yasser Arafat had also damaged the government's prior enthusiasm for the Palestinian cause, and had led to an 'unravelling' of ANC-PLO relations.

Meanwhile, the Jewish community, which had struggled at first to deal with the crisis that Kasrils had precipitated, had begun to regroup. The Board and the SAZF began to take a far more active role in not only responding to but also anticipating anti-Israel demonstrations such as those experienced in Durban. Throughout 2002, the Board prepared for the World Summit on Sustainable Development (WSSD) in Johannesburg in August, working with international Jewish organisations and the South African government to ensure that the conference agenda was not once again sidetracked by Israel-bashing and antisemitic rhetoric. Yehuda Kay, National Director of the Board, secured a seat on the Executive Committee for the Global (NGO) Forum of the WSSD.[365] Attempts by Palestinian activists to disrupt Israeli sessions, such as a presentation by the Jewish National Fund, were unsuccessful.

The only serious attacks against Israel occurred beyond the conference at the University of the Witwatersrand, where Israeli Foreign Minister Shimon Peres gave a speech and where violent protestors threw bottles and provoked a confrontation with police in which one officer was stabbed and more than a dozen people were arrested. Sensationalised reports by the *Mail & Guardian* charged, 'Israeli forces take over Wits', referring to security personnel outside the venue, but the controversy soon faded.[366] 'From being a potential threat to Israel and world Jewry,' Saks would later write, 'the WSSD was ultimately turned into a successful public relations event on behalf of Israel. While there was an active and vocal pro-Palestinian presence, the Middle East issue ultimately had a relatively low profile.'[367]

By mid 2003, the community had begun to recover a sense of equilibrium, but relations with the government remained strained. The South African

---

[365] Saks 2003, 27–8.
[366] Macfarlane, D. 2002. 'Israeli forces take over Wits'. *Mail and Guardian*, 5 September [online article]. URL: http://www.mg.co.za/Content/l3.jsp?a=59&o=8607
[367] Saks 2003, 28.

government was still avoiding official contacts with the Israeli government, and reacting to events in the Middle East in a way that prompted criticism from within the Jewish community. Jewish leaders met with government ministers for 'reassurance' but continued to feel cut off, as President Mbeki had refused to meet with the Board since 1999.

Soon, however, relations between the Jewish community and the government began to thaw. The turning point appeared to come at the Board's centenary conference in 2003, at which President Mbeki gave the keynote address. It was his first formal interaction with the Board in four years. The President gave a well-received speech in which he pledged the government's commitment to fight antisemitism and gave assurances that the government was open to the community:

> ... I would like to say firmly and without equivocation that our government would be pleased to spend as much time as may be required to discuss the concerns of our Jewish community with its representatives, so that both the government and all other South Africans are empowered to act decisively to address the concerns of the Jewish section of our population.[368]

At the conference, the Board elected Bagraim as its new national chairman. Under Bagraim's leadership, the Board appeared to adopt a new political strategy. It began to cultivate closer and closer relations with the ruling ANC in the hope that this would help it influence government policy towards Israel and other issues relevant to the community, particularly antisemitism and security.

The first sign of the new strategy was Bagraim's decision to meet privately with Kasrils shortly after taking office as national chairman. He did so, according to interviewees for this book, against the advice of the rest of the Board and despite likely opposition within the community if the meeting had been publicised. Though controversial, the meeting helped re-establish the relationship between the Board and Kasrils, and appeared to improve relations with the government in general.

---

368 Mbeki, T. 2003. Address at the Centenary Conference of the South African Jewish Board of Deputies. Johannesburg, 7 September.

In the months that followed, the Board focused on building its relationships with senior ANC leaders. It did so not only in private meetings but at public events as well. In April 2004, for example, shortly before that year's general elections, the Board held a special Passover *seder* at Liliesleaf Farm, the old headquarters of the ANC's armed wing Umkhonto we Sizwe, now converted into a conference centre. The ceremony commemorated the Freedom Charter, the ANC's watershed 1955 manifesto, and honoured the contributions of Jews to the liberation struggle.[369] The event, so soon before a national election, was viewed by some opposition parties as overtly partisan, and a tacit endorsement of the ANC. Ruth Rabinowitz, an IFP MP, and Anthony Grinder, an IFP member of the Gauteng provincial legislature, wrote a letter to the *South African Jewish Report* claiming that the Board's *seder* was 'inappropriate'.[370] Rabinowitz withdrew her objections after she and IFP leader Mangosuthu Buthelezi were invited, later calling the *seder* a 'memorable and tasteful event,'[371] but criticised the Board again six months later for 'tagging onto the ANC.'[372] Bagraim responded:

> ... [I]t should be noted that the Board of Deputies' real business is to keep South African Jewry safe and well catered for. So when it is stated that our invitation database is stacked with names from the ANC, and this may be good for business, they are in fact correct. However, it must be noted that our database is far from exclusive and we will certainly look for friends anywhere they can be found. Furthermore, an unfortunate fact of life is that when the business is the safety of Jewry, you have to engage even with those who are not friends but could be converted into our friends of the future.[373]

More than simply explaining Jewish concerns to the ANC, at times the Board found itself in the unusual role of explaining the ANC and its policies to the Jewish community, as well as to Israeli guests. In one edition of 'Above Board',

---

369 'SAJBD to celebrate adoption of Freedom Charter' 2005. *South African Jewish Report*, 3, 6 May; Saks, D. 2005. 'Activists commemorate Charter anniversary'. *South African Jewish Report*, 3, 17 June.
370 Rabinowitz, R & Grinker, A. 2004. 'Liliesleaf Freedom Seder 'inappropriate''. *South African Jewish Report*, 14, 2 April.
371 Rabinowitz, R. 2004. 'A memorable and tasteful event'. *South African Jewish Report*, 14, 23 April.
372 Rabinowitz, R. 2004. 'SAJDB 'tagging onto ANC''. *South African Jewish Report*, 14, 11 October.
373 Bagraim, M. 2004. 'Friends wherever they can be found'. *South African Jewish Report*, 14, 22 October.

Bagraim's weekly column in the *South African Jewish Report*, he recounted how he had explained the African concepts of *lekgotla* and *ubuntu* to the visiting members of the Likud Party:

> ... [W]e concentrated on debriefing our visitors on the South African political situation, and on how the process of negotiations worked in the African context. This meant explaining at length the lekhotla [sic] concept,[374] something our government very much employs in the decision-making process in this country. Traditional African democracy operates in the form of discussions. While there are leaders, everyone gets a chance to speak, building consensus. Briefly explained, the lekhotla [sic] involved a round table format in which each individual expresses his view, at the end of which the leader makes his decision. Also focused on was the African concept of ubuntu, defined as 'a person is a person through other persons' and in which a person's worth is inextricably linked with his interaction with others as part of a greater whole.[375]

In the Cape, the Cape Council of the Board of Deputies pursued a similar approach to the ANC. It paid particular attention to cultivating its relationship with Premier Ebrahim Rasool. Rasool was viewed by many Jewish leaders as a 'moderate' Muslim voice, able to control religious extremism in his community. This view of Rasool persisted in spite of his occasional links to anti-Israel activism. Rasool himself struck a conciliatory tone in meetings with the Board, both public and private, and as Premier he was a keynote speaker at many Board events and functions, including the Cape Board centenary in 2004 and a communal observance of the 50th anniversary of the liberation of Auschwitz in 2005.

At the same time, the Board continued to criticise the government over its policies towards Israel, actively and publicly. In March 2004, for example, Bagraim used his column to protest against the government's stance at the ICJ against the Israeli security barrier.[376]

---

374 The generally accepted spelling is *lekgotla*.
375 Bagraim, M. 2004. 'All about lekhotla and ubuntu'. *South African Jewish Report*, 2, 24 September.
376 Bagraim, M. 2004. 'Govt misses point'. *South African Jewish Report*, 2, 5 March.

Increasingly, such duties were delegated to the SAZF, which became more vocal in its objections to the government's policies towards Israel. When Kasrils visited Yasser Arafat in Ramallah in 2004, for example, Avrom Krengel, the new chairman of the SAZF, used his weekly column in the *South African Jewish Report* to complain about Kasrils's views and to accuse the minister of acting to boost his personal political fortunes: 'To secure his position in the Cabinet, the minister desperately needs to raise his visibility, profile and popularity.'[377]

The Board, however, did not leave such criticism entirely to the SAZF. It responded harshly, for example, to comment that suggested that South African Jews were in some way responsible for Israel's behaviour. Shortly after the Yassin killing, for example, the *Mail & Guardian* used an editorial

> to throw down a challenge to South Africa's Jewish community—or at least the many members of the community who uncritically back the government of Ariel Sharon ... Though relatively small in number, South Africa's Jews have historically been an important source of financial and moral support for the state of Israel. If their representatives begin to speak out against Sharon's policy of mindless reprisal, and to press for peaceful solutions—beginning with formal Israeli recognition of the 1967 borders—they might have some beneficial influence.[378]

Similarly, in early 2006, following the incapacitation of Ariel Sharon due to a cerebral haemorrhage, the *Sunday Times* editorialised: '... South African Jewry should examine how it can share with Israel the lessons learnt from our negotiated settlement, which resulted in this country's peaceful transition from a racial powder keg to a paragon of reason and tolerance.'[379]

The Board's response to the *Sunday Times* was defensive. In a letter to the newspaper, Bagraim objected to its 'assumption of collective responsibility on the part of the South African Jewish community. This has distinctly sinister

---

377 Krengel, A. 2002. 'No! Mr Minister'. *South African Jewish Report*, 16, 5 March.
378 'Time to reject Sharon' 2004. Editorial, *Mail & Guardian*, 25 March.
379 'Israel has window of opportunity' 2006. *Sunday Times*, 8 January; for a fuller exploration of such potential lessons see Adam, H & Moodley, K. 2005. *Seeking Mandela: Peacemaking between Israelis and Palestinians*. Johannesburg: Wits University Press.

overtones…'.³⁸⁰ The Board also joined the SAZF in reacting to public comment that questioned Israel's right to exist or raised the spectre of 'dual loyalty' among South African Jews. Such comments had actually been rare during the Kasrils affair; despite their harsh views of Israel and Zionism, neither Kasrils nor his supporters called for the banning or suppression of Zionist organisations in South Africa. Though Kasrils had argued that opposition to Israeli policies was a responsibility for anyone of Jewish descent to speak out against Israel's ruthless measures of repression against the Palestinian people who are striving for their national and human rights,³⁸¹ he never suggested that the South African Zionist Federation therefore had no right to exist.

In later years, however, a few critics attacked the SAZF directly. Commentator Allister Sparks, who began calling for a one-state solution to the Israeli–Palestinian conflict in a series of articles in September and October 2005, dismissed criticism of the SAZF by accusing it of being an institutional arm of the Israeli government. The SAZF, he claimed, 'is an affiliate of the World Zionist Federation [sic], which in turn is an arm of the Israeli government [sic], and so … bears the stamp of state approval'.³⁸²

Anthony Holiday, a former anti-apartheid activist and frequent contributor to the *Cape Times*, suggested that the SAZF should be banned in the aftermath of the Yassin killing. In an article entitled 'Local Federation Promotes Zionism: Patriotism of SA Jews Undermined', he wrote: 'Prior to the killing [of Yassin] we might possibly have gone on viewing the agitation of the federation with weary tolerance. That time is not now.' Holiday argued further that the SAZF—a 'foreign organisation', in his view—was damaging patriotism among the South African middle classes through its programmes of actively encouraging Jews to emigrate to Israel, thus 'sapping the nourishment' of a nascent African nationalism.³⁸³

The Board's official response was co-signed by the SAZF and the rabbinate. Claiming that 'South African Jews are overwhelming[ly] Zionist and born Zionist', they called Holiday's article 'a vile slur on the many thousands of Jews over the past century who have successfully combined being loyal, productive

---

380 Bagraim, M. 2006. 'The Palestinians have no Freedom Charter'. *Sunday Times*, 16, 15 January.
381 Kasrils, R. 2001. 'Speaking out against Israel'. *Sowetan*. 1 November.
382 Sparks, A. 2005. 'The boys who cried "anti-Semite". *The Star*, 5 October.
383 Holiday, A. 2004. 'Local federation promotes Zionism: Patriotism of SA Jews undermined'. *Cape Times,* 30 March.

citizens of South Africa with full-blooded commitment to the millennia-old Zionist cause'. They accused Holiday of 'contempt for liberal democracy', and attacked what they saw as an attempt to question Jewish patriotism: 'What is truly intolerable, and unpatriotic, is the kind of naked prejudice as epitomized in Holiday's disgraceful article. It is an assault on the loyalty and integrity not just of the Zionist Federation but of the entire Jewish community. For the future wellbeing of our young democracy, we can only hope that such venomous viewpoints are firmly confined to the fringes of public discourse.'[384]

Another less vitriolic but perhaps more accurate response was published by Pauline Podbrey, whose credentials as a former anti-apartheid activist and SACP member made her status in left-wing circles unassailable. 'There is nothing in Zionism that prevents Jews from being patriotic citizens of SA', Podbrey declared. [385] She compared Holiday's description of the SAZF to the Nazis' description of Jews as 'a bourgeois fifth column, a foreign presence that prevented the German folk from rising'. 'As a secular SA Jew', Podbrey wrote, 'I have never been a member of the federation but I would resist its banning and the banning of any other organisation, just as I resisted the banning of the ANC and the SACP in the past.' This proved to be the final word on the subject, as the essay drew no rebuttal from Holiday or any other correspondent.

Though it continued to criticise views it regarded as hostile to Israel, the Board also began to moderate its responses, and to seek meetings with members of government even if their anti-Israel views were known to be strident. As Bagraim noted in his column in the *South African Jewish Report* in late April 2004, the Board had decided to meet even with those who were known to have strong anti-Israel opinions. The important thing, he argued, was to '[g]uard against being sidelined'.[386] Bagraim and his colleagues apparently wished to avoid returning to the position that the Board had been in at the height of the Kasrils affair, when it had lost 'the ear of government.'

The Board's new approach was tested in June 2004 with the arrival of the UN African Meeting in Support of the Inalienable Rights of the Palestinian

---

384 Harris, C et al. 2004. 'Insidious assault on democratic ideals that underpin our society.' *Cape Times*, (2 April [online article]. URL: http://www.capetimes.co.za/index.php?fSectionId=273&fArticleId=390549
385 Podbrey, P. 2004. 'Holiday's article is a dangerous diatribe, based on prejudice'. *Cape Times*, 8 April.
386 Bagraim, M. 2004. 'Guard against being sidelined'. *South African Jewish Report*, 2, 30 April.

People (CEIRP) in Cape Town. The Board declined a government invitation to attend the conference, but instead of withdrawing completely, as it had from the Durban racism conference of 2001, the Board organised volunteers to monitor the proceedings, and to monitor media coverage of the event. At the same time, the Board decided that it would not react to criticism of Israel at the conference, whether from delegates inside the venue or protestors on the streets outside. It would confine its reactions to signs of antisemitism, should any arise. To this end, it held meetings with government officials to ensure that anti-Israel rhetoric and rallies did not become antisemitic.

In effect, this approach meant that the Jewish leadership was prepared to countenance strong criticism of Israel, including criticism by members of the South African government, in exchange for the government's help in restraining antisemitism. This strategy, and rainy weather outside, helped restrain the tone of the conference and the rhetoric of local protests. Bagraim would later claim that the Board's 'networking' with the government helped prevent the Palestinian rights conference from turning into a reprise of the Durban racism conference:[387]

> *The encouraging lesson the CEIRP taught us is that lobbying, conducted sensibly and responsibly, bears fruit. In the weeks leading up to the conference, the Board met constantly with senior members of government, civil society and the UN officials responsible for organising it, making known the community's concerns and urging that every step be taken to avoid a repetition of the Durban fiasco ... The Board is often criticised within the community for not speaking out strongly enough when Government is perceived as overly biased on the Middle East issue. We have, in fact, on occasion been very forthright in our criticism of Government, but by far our preferred course of action is to engage in dialogue rather than in public confrontations. It is all very well to vent one's outrage in the public realm, but it makes it considerably more difficult to establish relationships afterwards.*[388]

Reviewing the events from 2002 to 2004, it would seem that the Board could justifiably take some credit for projecting a stronger presence for the

---

387 Bagraim, M. 2004. 'Above Board: Board ready to meet CEIRP issues'. *South African Jewish Report*, 2, 2 July.
388 Bagraim, M. 2004. 'Above Board: Moderation prevails at CT UN conference'. *South African Jewish Report*, 2, 9 July.

Jewish community and its views in the media, while at the same time mending and improving relations with the government. At the same time, the Board's greatest successes tended to occur when it was not directly involved. Many of the community's major media successes had been scored by independent voices, such as the JMN and Podbrey; the government's policy shift on Israel had as much to do with the American Jewish Committee as it had with the Board; and the SAZF had begun to play a far greater role than the Board in speaking out and organising community activism on Middle East issues. It was with a multiplicity and diversity of voices that the Jewish community had begun to restore its self-confidence.

Yet the Board still struggled to encourage tolerance for diversity and dissent within the community. Arguments erupted, for example, at the centenary conference of the Cape Council of the Board in August 2004 when Nathan Geffen, the national director of the Treatment Action Campaign (TAC), a prominent HIV/Aids lobby, used his address to the gathering to attack the community's solidarity with Israel and to criticise Israel's isolation of Palestinian leader Yasser Arafat. In late 2005, a new debate was sparked over the refusal of Chief Rabbi Goldstein to attend a memorial marking the 10th anniversary of the assassination of Yitzhak Rabin due to the participation of a Reform rabbi. Justice Davis, writing in the *South African Jewish Report*, exhorted the community to accept a multiplicity of voices:

> ... [T]he demand for respect must be mutual. It is equally important to acknowledge that there are many different Jewish voices ... By insisting on the importance of a community which embraces every Jew, on truly adhering to the principle that each Jew is responsible one for the other, we must be able to achieve a balance of the promotion of our own conception of Judaism in our own way and constructing a simultaneous sense of a community unified in its respect for, among other things, Jewish diversity.[389]

Board members interviewed for this book disagreed strongly about whether the Kasrils affair had changed internal debates within the community. Some argued that the community had become even less open to criticism of Israel than it had been before, that the Board's position had not shifted towards greater tolerance

---

[389] Davis, D. 2005. 'Listen to the many Jewish voices'. *South African Jewish Report*, 8, 9 December.

and that Kasrils's stance 'didn't make it less difficult' to speak out. One Board member, who had been in favour of meeting with Kasrils, claimed that Kasrils had made the community more 'right wing' than it had been before. 'We're not yet tolerant of different points of view,' he said, citing examples such as the visit of a gay American Orthodox rabbi in 2005 that had led to controversy within the community.

Other Board members, however, saw a definite change of attitudes among South African Jews. One, who had opposed the Kasrils declaration, acknowledged that '[h]e opened up the question of debate, of freedom of expression, of criticism of Israel ... There is greater openness in the community and more tolerance than there used to be'. A theme repeated by the Cape Town interviewees was that they felt the Cape Town community was more open to debate and criticism of Israel than the community in Johannesburg. This perception—though not necessarily its validity—was acknowledged by one interviewee in Johannesburg, who attributed the Johannesburg community's more conservative views on Israel to its deeper religiosity.

The Board's new and more conciliatory approach to the ANC and the government was reinforced by the emergence of a new generation of young community leaders in their early 30s, each determined to demonstrate the commitment of Jews to the new South Africa. One such was Warren Goldstein, who was named in 2004 and inducted in 2005 as South Africa's new Chief Rabbi. Rabbi Goldstein was not only young, at 32 years of age, but also South African-born, unlike his predecessor. Though his views on religious matters and on Zionism remained quite conservative, Goldstein was also outspoken in his enthusiasm for the new South Africa. He had co-authored a book, *African Soul Talk*, with Nelson Mandela's grandson Dumani Mandela.[390] He defended affirmative action as a means of 'levelling the playing field', an unusual position for a leader from a minority community, and blamed complaints about falling university standards due to affirmative action on 'latent racism'.[391]

Other newly appointed young Jewish leaders included Gauteng Board chairman Zev Krengel, SAZF chairman Avrom Krengel and South African Board

---

390 Goldstein, W & Mandela, D. 2005. *African Soul Talk: When Politics is Not Enough*. Johannesburg: Jacana Media.
391 Derfner, L. 2005. 'New Jews in a new South Africa'. *Jerusalem Post*, 22 September.

of Jewish Education acting director Rabbi Craig Kacev, all in their early 30s. They believed strongly in identifying with the new South Africa and asserting a patriotic Jewish identity within it. Goldstein referred to the Krengel brothers as 'the Jewish young lions, the new South African Jewish leadership that has a vision for the entire country, not just their own community'.[392] They saw South Africa with optimistic eyes, and viewed themselves as a bridge between the community and the ANC government.

Often, these leaders expressed their enthusiasm for South Africa by praising the achievements of the ANC government, highlighting its successes and downplaying its failures. Zev Krengel, for example, praised the government in a 'letter from a South African Jewish community leader' that was included in a special four-page advertising insert placed by the South African government in the Israeli daily *Ha'aretz* in 2005 to commemorate the 11th anniversary of South Africa's first democratic elections. Krengel wrote:

> *Let me declare unequivocally that from my perspective, South African Jews have never had it so good. I will take it further, and say that we South Africans have entered a golden age in our country's history. Never before have all the peoples of our country been freer, more hopeful and more prosperous.*

While acknowledging the challenges that the country faced, and some of the political difficulties that the Jewish community had encountered after the collapse of the Oslo peace process, Krengel concluded: 'South African Jews are well organised and secure and looking to the future with increasing confidence ... there is no reason to believe that these challenges, too, will not be triumphantly overcome.'[393]

The young leadership of the community drew confidence from two encouraging empirical signs. One was the slowdown in Jewish emigration. New survey data released in 2005 indicated that emigration, though still a challenge, had slowed significantly among Jewish South Africans.[394] Though the community was still aging, the prospect of large numbers of people leaving in the near future began to seem more and more remote. 'Mass emigration has ceased to be a

---

392 Derfner 2005, ibid.
393 Krengel, Z. 2005 'A letter from a South African Jewish community leader'. *Ha'aretz*, 27 April.
394 'Emigration drops dramatically'. *South African Jewish Report*, 1, 2 September.

significant phenomenon in the South African Jewish community', the Chief Rabbi Goldstein told the *Jerusalem Post*. 'It's down to a trickle, and at the same time we're also getting reverse movement—of people coming back,' he said.[395]

The other positive sign was the low incidence of violent antisemitic attacks during the period of the Kasrils affair. Krengel wrote in his 2005 'letter':

> *Today's South Africa vigorously promotes the ideals of tolerance and non-discrimination. One important indication of the success it is enjoying in this regard is the significantly lower rates of antisemitism that exist in comparison with other Diaspora countries. Last year, a mere 37 anti-Semitic incidents were recorded, few of them being of a serious nature. When one compares this with the 532 incidents in the UK and the whopping 837 recorded in Canada for the same period, one realizes how safe a haven South Africa is for Jews.*[396]

A year later, antisemitism would reach record levels in South Africa.[397] Crime, too, rose alarmingly in several violent categories, particularly armed robbery.[398] Some reports indicated that the murder rate rose 2.4 per cent between April 2006 and March 2007.[399] The brutal murder of young comedian Brett Goldin and his friend, fashion designer Richard Bloom, both Jewish, in April 2006, sent a shiver of fear through the community.[400] Prior to these events, however, Krengel's sentiments were shared by many members of the Board. One Board member from Johannesburg interviewed for this book remarked: 'This is the most comfortable period in South African history for Jews. There's a healthy economy … emigration has tailed off … There are no real *issues* today.' Board members in Cape Town agreed, although they expressed concern about the deterioration in relations with the Muslim community and the perceived hostility of Muslim leaders. All agreed that relations with Kasrils had improved,

---

395 Goldstein, W. 2005. Quoted in Derfner, ibid.
396 Krengel 2005, ibid.
397 The Stephen Roth Institute for the Study of Antisemitism and Racism at Tel Aviv University. 'South Africa 2006' [online article]. URL: http://www.tau.ac.il/Antisemitism/asw2006/sth-africa.htm
398 Baldauf, S. 2007. 'Murder of a reggae star spurs reflection in South Africa'. *Christian Science Monitor*, 26 October [online article]. URL: http://www.csmonitor.com/2007/1026/p04s01-woaf.html
399 Botha, S. 2007. Quoted in Bosch, M. 'S. African reggae star's murder puts focus on crime'. Reuters, 19 October [online article]. URL: http://www.canada.com/ottawacitizen/news/arts/story.html?id=b152651f-7702-4270-af37-7dedc98a04e3&k=80440
400 Maughan, K & Dolley, C. 2006. 'Double murder leaves arts community in tears'. *The Star*, 1, 17 April.

especially since his appointment as Minister of Intelligence. The Board had met with him repeatedly to discuss security matters and the threat of antisemitism, I was told. 'The man who was an enemy has become an ally,' one interviewee said, even though he acknowledged Kasrils's enduring unpopularity in the Jewish community.

The Board continued its broader advocacy role. It formed formal links in 2001 with the TAC, backing its attempts to lobby the government to provide antiretroviral drugs and take stronger action in the fight against the HIV/Aids pandemic. The Tikkun organisation, renamed MaAfrica Tikkun, continued to expand its work in disadvantaged communities throughout South Africa. Jewish day schools partnered with schools in former black townships, and Jewish organisations lent their efforts to relief work throughout South Africa and the continent. The Board even offered special assistance in emergencies. During the Asian tsunami disaster of December 2004 and January 2005, the Board led South African relief efforts, chartering a flight with medical personnel to treat victims, recover bodies and bring South African survivors home.[401]

The emergence of a young leadership committed to the new South Africa, as well as the slow emergence of a greater number of diverse, independent voices, helped the Board to respond more effectively to the challenges of democratic debate—not just on Middle East issues, but on many others as well. Yet the Board's focus narrowed as the leadership of the Jewish community continued to nurture relations with the ANC. Increasingly, this meant not only that Jewish leaders represented the interests and views of South African Jews to the government but that they frequently found themselves defending the views of the government in the Jewish community and beyond.

This was the case in January 2006, when Holiday wrote an article in the *Cape Times* attacking the government's shift towards a friendlier relationship with the Sharon government, in Israel, he noted that, in President Mbeki's message of sympathy for Sharon after the Israeli leader's massive and debilitating stroke that month, he had not only wished Sharon well but had expressed hope that Sharon would return to lead his government. This, Holiday argued, heralded a shift in the

---

[401] Saks, D & Romain, M (eds) 2005. 'Helping hands across the ocean: South African Jewry and the Tsunami Disaster'. Johannesburg: South African Jewish Board of Deputies.

Mbeki 'line' towards Israel—a shift that had not necessarily been endorsed by the rank and file of the ANC. The President, he wrote, had 'an obligation to dispel the fog of ambiguity' surrounding the government's approach to the Israeli–Palestinian conflict. Holiday also took a swipe at the Board, claiming that it boasted of having influence with the Israeli government.[402]

In his reply, Bagraim was not simply content to defend the Board and the Sharon government but also stood up for President Mbeki and his policy towards Israel. The South African government, Bagraim claimed,

> ... has always recognised the legitimacy of Israel and its right to exist within secure borders, while being equally firmly committed to the achievement of a viable independent Palestinian state coexisting peacefully alongside it. Hence, South Africa has consistently been supportive of Israeli governments that take positive steps towards the achievement of Palestinian statehood.[403]

This was a somewhat disingenuous argument, since it downplayed both the shifts in the government's attitude towards Israel and the severe disagreements between the Board and the government during and after the Kasrils affair. Bagraim's reply was all the more remarkable given that the government itself had not responded to Holiday's critique; the Board was now stepping in pre-emptively to protect the government 'from criticism'.

Board members disagreed widely about how the organisation should best interact with the government. Some openly supported the Board's new rapprochement with the ANC government, and the use of behind-the-scenes meetings with Kasrils and other government officials. One Board member, who said he had supported attempts to 'engage' with Kasrils, advised: 'Keep your friends close and your enemies even closer.' He claimed that more had been achieved behind the scenes than in public interaction, and even claimed that Jewish survival throughout history had depended 'on our ability to be the chameleon—to blend in'.

For its part, the government seemed eager to respond to the Jewish community's new overtures. In November 2004, the government released a press release on

---
402 Holiday, A. 2006. 'Has Mbeki changed line on Israel?' *Cape Times*, 10 January.
403 Bagraim, M. 2006. 'Mbeki and Israel'. *Cape Times*, 13 January.

behalf of the Cabinet that commented on a successful meeting between the Presidential Working Group and the Board: '… Cabinet noted and welcomed the assessment of the Board that the Jewish community in South Africa had never in its history felt as safe, appreciated, at home and unthreatened in our diverse society.'[404]

Some government officials appeared openly to encourage Jewish leaders to adopt a quiet, behind-the-scenes approach. South Africa's ambassador to Israel, Major General Fumanekile Gqiba, told me about the advice he gave Jewish leaders when Kasrils reportedly invited the leader of Hamas to South Africa:

> *Zev Krengel [then-national vice-chairman of the Board], he phoned me, and also here the South African Jewish Board of Deputies. I told them, I said, 'Guys, just shut up. Don't go to the papers. This thing is a small thing. You go to the papers, you set [an] agenda for somebody, it doesn't work like that. Strategists don't do that.' I said, 'Just shut up, you'll see this thing is going to die.' But what they did, was to write papers, to this, I said, 'You are promoting the whole thing', you see? You know, sometimes, if you're a strategist, you look at this and then you keep quiet (snaps). It's going to die tomorrow.*[405]

In support of the Board's strategy, several Board members mentioned the powerful American Israel Public Affairs Committee (AIPAC), a pro-Israel lobby in the US, as a new model for the Board's political behaviour. The Board should, they said, lobby powerful people—as well as their 'underlings', the people who would one day rise to prominent positions in the ruling party. One who held this view said that one of the reasons the Board had had difficulty relating to President Mbeki during the first years of his term and throughout the Kasrils affair was that it had spent the 1990s meeting with President Mandela and virtually ignoring his deputy.

A few interviewees, however, regretted the Board's new approach. 'We are, in fact, in a ghetto Jew position,' one lamented, 'but that's the way it is.' Another

---

404 Government Communication and Information System 2004. 'Statement on cabinet meeting'. 3 November [online press release]. URL: http://www.info.gov.za/speeches/2004/04110318001001.htm
405 Gqiba, F. 2007. Interview by the author. Tel Aviv, Israel, 13 August.

described the approach as 'back door' and 'obsequious': 'The contact with the government is no longer from the standing of Jews, as Jews. It's all about exposure, and the notion that Jews can deliver the business community.'

Even Board members who strongly supported a behind-the-scenes approach to the government acknowledged that it sometimes had limitations. One interviewee in Cape Town, for example, said: 'We need to get the government to take action about the letter we received from the [Muslim Judicial Council]', referring to inflammatory correspondence sent in 2005 after the MJC had attempted to lead anti-Israel marchers to the Jewish communal offices.[406] He said he had tried to obtain help from Deputy Minister Pahad, to no avail. 'I need to speak to Mbeki ... If we're not getting anywhere, we will go public.'

The Board's shifting approach towards the government was never formally discussed at any of its annual meetings, nor was it ever placed before the community for affirmation or rejection. Few protests were raised from within South African Jewry, suggesting that most Jews backed the Board's new tactics. Soon, however, the Board found it necessary to defend its political behaviour against tough criticism from the political opposition and from leading Jewish intellectuals—and to rethink its approach towards the government.

---

[406] Davis, D. 2005. 'SA Jewish Board of Deputies (Cape Council) Chairman's report: 2004–2005'. Presented at the annual conference of the Cape Council of the South African Jewish Board of Deputies, Cape Town, 18 September; see also Bagraim, M. 2005. 'This memorandum wrongly addressed'. *South African Jewish Report*, 2, 27 May; Bagraim, M. 2005. 'Don't incite a lone wolf'. *South African Jewish Report*, 2, 3 June; Bagraim, M. 2005. 'MJC vitriol an eye-opener'. *South African Jewish Report*, 2,10 June; Belling, S. 2005. 'MJC picks fight on spurious grounds'. *South African Jewish Report* 8, 27 May; Speeches at MJC March, Cape Town, 25 May 2005. Radio 7886 broadcast. Unpublished transcript. On 25 May 2005, the MJC led a march of roughly 10 000 demonstrators who were protesting against what they alleged was Israel's plan to destroy the Al-Aqsa Mosque in Jerusalem. They attempted to deliver a memorandum to the Jewish communal offices but were stopped by police. Cape Council Chairman Dennis Davis issued a response in which he emphasised that South African Jews did not speak for Israel, while at the same time debunking the MJC's accusations. He invited the MJC to meet with the Board at any time to discuss the issues. The response from the MJC shocked the Board and the community: it accused the Board of being 'liars and fabricators of untruths' and claimed that Jews were 'killers and murderers of prophets', including Jesus.

CHAPTER SIX

CHALLENGING THE BOARD'S STRATEGY

In navigating their approach to the government, Jewish leaders were operating within the peculiar context of minority politics in South Africa. In the 1990s, the Board's movement towards an 'advocacy' role broke out of the strictures of minority politics that had confined it during the apartheid era. The Kasrils affair, however, seemed to prod the Board back towards a narrow approach as the community's intercessor with the government, even though it had become more outspoken than it had been during apartheid. Verwoerd's trade-off—that the Jews would have to abandon support for Israel in order to be more secure in South Africa—had reappeared, albeit in a somewhat less threatening form. The punishment for failure to pay homage to the ruling party and its ideological worldview would not be antisemitic violence, as Verwoerd had threatened, but rather political isolation. The Jewish community was not the only minority community to face this dilemma, but the shifts in its posture were perhaps the most dramatic.

The Board's changing approach was, for example, signalled by the change in the rhetoric used by its executive. In November 2001, Bagraim had declared: 'No longer can we say as we did in the '60s, '70s and '80s that 'we must not rock the boat', and no longer can we say as we did in the '90s that we are doing things 'behind the scenes'. It is now necessary for us to be in your face.'[407] By September

---

407 Bagraim, M. 2001/2. Quoted in 'SAJBD Cape conference faces the future'. *Cape Jewish Chronicle* 4, December/January.

2004, he had changed his approach: 'In order to fulfil our mandate of protecting South African Jewry, we need to influence those who are in a position to assist us. It is unreasonable for us to publicly attack someone one week and then ask him for favours the next.'[408]

The Board's new strategy did not preclude speaking out against the government. However, because the strategy was never formalised, the Board never adopted clear guidelines for when it should speak out and when it should use more discreet tactics. It seemed to discover its method by improvising in the course of events.

One example occurred in the weeks before the 2004 elections. On 21 March 2004, a rally of 1 000 mostly Muslim protesters was held at the Watsonia sports ground in Athlone, Cape Town to protest against Israel's 'targeted killing' of Yassin. One of the featured speakers was Ebrahim Rasool, at that time the finance minister for the Western Cape and the provincial leader of the ANC in the province. Rasool's speech was militant. He described Yassin as 'one of the greatest inspirations' to Muslims and quoted with approval Yassin's teaching that 'whoever dies, without having fought in the way of Allah or even having desire to fight in the way of Allah, dies on a twig of hypocrisy'. He also prayed that Palestinians 'stand up to these enemies and never succumb, that they fight and they fight under a flag of Islam', and he called on his audience to 'face the enemies—they are all over the world'.[409]

Nothing in Rasool's radical speech was explicitly antisemitic. Several of the speakers that followed Rasool, however, made remarks that clearly and explicitly were so. One Muslim cleric, for example, claimed that Jews had 'murdered and killed most of the prophets of God'. Citing the *Protocols of the Elders of Zion*, he claimed that Jews had established 'cinemas, bioscopes around the world to corrupt the gentiles'. Another speaker referred to Israel as 'the filthy Jewish nation' and instructed his audience: 'Do not go into any agreements with Jews; they are a filthy people.'[410]

The Board did not respond immediately. Instead it raised the matter in a private meeting with Rasool. It had done the same during the controversy surrounding the

---

408 Bagraim, M. 2004. 'Above Board: Reiterating Board's view'. *South African Jewish Report*, 5, 10 September.
409 Rasool, E. 2004. Speech at Watsonia sports ground, Athlone, Cape Town, 21 March. Voice of the Cape Radio broadcast. Unpublished transcript.
410 Abrahams, E. 2004. Speech at Watsonia sports ground, Athlone, Cape Town, 21 March. Voice of the Cape Radio broadcast. Unpublished transcript.

'A vote for the DA is a vote for Israel' posters, as well as after the inflammatory April 2002 rally at Athlone stadium, where Rasool had shared the stage with Kasrils. In this instance, as in previous cases, the Board accepted Rasool's assurances and took no public action. Most media outlets had failed to report the event in any case, save for the Islamic community radio station that had broadcast the proceedings.

In the wake of the incident, the Board continued to cultivate a close relationship with Rasool. He was invited to give an address at the Cape Council's centenary celebrations in August 2004 in his new capacity as Premier of the Western Cape. No opposition politicians were present or invited. On that occasion, Rasool gave a speech advocating religious tolerance. 'All of us', he argued, 'have to resolve to defeat and isolate fundamentalism as the worst expression of the uncertain among us as they strive to oppose us with violent methods and actions.'[411] No mention was made of the intolerant rally that Rasool had participated in exactly five months earlier. Rasool was later brought by Board members to a conference of the American Jewish Committee in 2006 as an exemplar of religious tolerance.

In September 2004, an article by myself appeared in the *South African Jewish Report* taking the Board to task for its decision not to criticise Rasool in public: 'It is entirely appropriate that the Board should seek to cultivate a close relationship with Rasool, not just because he governs the Western Cape but also because of his prominence within the Muslim community. Yet the price of that relationship should not be that the community forfeits its right to speak out openly against antisemitism or in favour of Zionism, which most South African Jews hold dear.'

The article also referred to the behaviour of the Board during the apartheid era, and opined that:

> *One cannot help but wonder whether the Board is playing the same game of former years, awed by the ANC's apparently unassailable political strength and fearful of being listed among its domestic opponents. If so, then the Board is squandering the very freedom that the advent of a democratic South Africa has provided it, and to all South Africans.*[412]

---

411 Rasool, E. 2004. Quoted in Bagraim, M. 'Above Board: United in fighting fundamentalism'. *South African Jewish Report*, 2. 27 August.
412 Pollak, J. 2004. 'Confronting contradictions'. *South African Jewish Report*, 10, 3 September.

The Board responded in an article of its own, signed by Bagraim, which ran on the same page.[413] Bagraim did not attempt to defend Rasool, but argued that 'the SAJBD is not a political party or body' and that 'confrontation' was not always the best response to the government's behaviour. 'Had the Board chosen ... to publicly confront Rasool regarding his participation at an anti-Semitic rally,' wrote Bagraim, 'we might have scored a few short-term publicity points, but it would have been at the long-term expense of the good working relationship we need to be building with him.'

There were few responses to this exchange, and none from Rasool himself. Keith Gottschalk of the University of the Western Cape wrote to defend Rasool's record as a 'moderate' who worked with Jews and stood up against extremism in the Muslim community.[414] Members of the Board interviewed for this book tended to share this view, and to support the quiet approach. 'Why condemn Rasool?' one asked. Some emphasised, and identified with, his difficulties in dealing with his Muslim supporters: 'If he loses that constituency,' one interviewee said, 'what good is he?'

In late 2004, further criticism of the Board's political behaviour came from Tony Leon, Leader of the Opposition. Invited to address a meeting of the Cape Council, Leon took the opportunity to criticise the Board's attitude towards the ANC government. Leon expressed concern about 'the growing reluctance of the community's leaders to speak out openly and publicly on matters of concern to its members'. He described 'a movement away from open debate and towards the politics of "influence"', pointing out that this was a movement occurring in many sectors of South African society owing to the 'vehement intolerance towards political and intellectual dissent' shown by President Mbeki.

Leon allowed that the Board was not a political party, that it could not be expected to speak out in public at every opportunity, and that 'the attempt by leaders of the Jewish community and other groups to explore a quieter and less confrontational approach' was 'quite understandable'. However, he pointed to the failures of ANC-aligned interest groups such as the TAC and Cosatu in lobbying for changes in the party's policy, as evidence that 'the prospects of the politics of

---

413 Bagraim, M. 2004. 'SAJBD's difficult tightrope'. *South African Jewish Report*, 10, 3 September.
414 Gottschalk, K. 2004. 'Rasool's voice of Muslim moderation'. *South African Jewish Report*, 10, 24 September.

'influence' would seem extremely dim indeed'. He concluded by warning that the Board 'appears to be slipping back toward a pattern of deferential behaviour' that had characterised its approach toward the government during the apartheid era. Furthermore, he added: 'Neither the Jewish community nor any other need ask the government for favours. We are not here on sufferance. It is the government's role and duty to live up the obligations and ideals of the Constitution. That, I believe, is what the Board should demand—that, and nothing less.'[415]

The Board responded in January 2005 in a four-page letter signed by Bagraim. It reiterated that it was not, like the Democratic Alliance, a political party. Bagraim argued that there were occasions 'where it has been appropriate for the Board to publicly speak out against the government', yet '[i]n the present climate, however, we believe that such an approach would be counter-productive'. Bagraim reiterated the Board's policy of neutrality and non-involvement: 'Any attempt to politicise the Board of Deputies, whether it comes from the DA or any other source, is something we will strongly resist, as indeed we must. The Board will not, and indeed cannot, take a stand on specific political issues.'

Much of the letter was devoted to a defence of the 'politics of influence'. Bagraim argued that groups such as Cosatu had failed to affect government policy on Zimbabwe because it 'chose to adopt a strongly confrontational approach in public on this issue when it could, and probably would, have achieved far more by bringing its concerns to the table in private'. Bagraim concluded: 'Given what we are seeking to achieve—not votes but on the ground results—we believe that the politics of influence are both more subtle and more effective.'

Bagraim did not contest Leon's suggestion that the Board had reverted to the behaviour of a previous era in terms of its relationship to its government. Instead, he defended that relationship by arguing that the post-apartheid government was different from the apartheid regime. 'Prior to 1994, as you well know, the Board was compelled by the circumstances of the day to deal with a minority government that had no legitimacy, either amongst the great majority of the population or internationally. This is diametrically opposed to the situation as it exists today.' Bagraim elaborated on this argument: 'Even though the ANC, with its 70 per cent of

---

415 Leon, A J. 2004. 'The creeping politics of influence'. Speech to Cape Council of South African Jewish Board of Deputies. Cape Town, South Africa, 7 December.

the national vote, would be quite entitled to amend the Constitution if it wished, it has shown no interest in doing so, whereas the brazen underhandedness through which the National Party changed the constitution in order to remove coloureds from the common voters' roll in the 1950s is deservedly notorious.' In closing, Bagraim cited examples in which the Board had been able to capitalise on its improved relationships with the government, such as the UN Palestinian rights conference of June 2004, and the Asian tsunami disaster of December 2004, when the Board led South Africa's relief, rescue and recovery efforts. He assured Leon that the Board would continue to try to engage all political parties on a regular basis.[416]

Leon responded a few days later in a 10-page letter in which he noted that Bagraim's response had seemed to confirm his fears that the Board was moving closer to the orbit of the government and the ruling party. Leon reiterated his argument that the 'politics of influence' were ineffective. He argued that Cosatu had turned to confronting the government over Zimbabwe only because quieter approaches had not worked. 'The point,' Leon wrote, 'is that lobby groups such as Cosatu and the Board have a variety of approaches—and that in some cases, public criticism can be used to stimulate greater private engagement.'

Leon observed that while it was 'important for the Board to maintain relations with all levels of government', certain successes that Bagraim had claimed as victories for the 'politics of influence' were in fact 'the minimum that citizens have a right to expect from their government'. The cooperation with the government in the UN Palestinian rights conference and the tsunami disaster were commendable, Leon noted, but added: 'We should not expect so little of our government that we see such efforts as extraordinary achievements.'

Leon acknowledged that the present government was far better and more legitimate than the apartheid government, but took issue with many of Bagraim's defences of the ANC. 'The most alarming statement in this section of your letter,' Leon wrote, 'is your assertion that 'the ANC, with its 70 per cent of the national vote, would be entitled to amend the Constitution if it wished…'. Here there seems to be a fundamental confusion between power and right. The fact that the ANC has the power to amend the Constitution does not mean that it is entitled to, or that it has a right to.'

---

416 Bagraim, M. 2005. Letter to Tony Leon. 20 January.

Leon concluded by commenting that the Board did not seem to have a mandate from the Jewish community for its new approach to the government. He wrote:

> *I cannot recall the Board inviting the Jewish community into its confidence to explain the reasons for its adoption of the 'politics of influence'. Nor does there seem to have been an open and democratic debate as to whether the 'politics of influence' should become the official programme of the Jewish polity in South Africa. A cursory reading of the letters submitted by Jewish correspondents to the newspapers, both Jewish and general, suggests that there is certainly a constituency of Jews who hold other positions and believe a judicious mix of strategies and tactics might be apposite.*[417]

Several months later, Leon's criticism was joined by criticism from Jewish intellectuals who had gathered at a monthly meeting organised by Milton Shain. Leon and Bagraim were guests at the meeting, and had been asked to comment on their correspondence, parts of which had been published in the *Cape Jewish Chronicle*. Several members of the audience expressed alarm at a letter Bagraim had written to the *Cape Times* supporting Rasool against public criticism. Referring to an earlier letter, and writing in his capacity as national chairman of the Board, Bagraim had written: 'Archbishop Njongonkulu Ndungane in his letter of April 25 writes that Ebrahim Rasool is 'genuine in his commitment to the Cape as a Home for All'.[418] From a Jewish point of view, I am happy to confirm that this has indeed been the case. Rasool has gone the extra mile in his efforts to foster warm relations with the Jewish community of Cape Town and this is greatly appreciated.'[419]

In Leon's presence, Bagraim was questioned and criticised by the audience about his eagerness to defend Rasool. Stung by this criticism from Leon and the community, the Board began reconsider its posture. In December 2004, the members of the Cape Council attended a *bosberaad* (retreat), at which the Board's interaction with the government was a key focus of discussion.[420]

---

417 Leon, A.J. 2005. Letter to Michael Bagraim. 25 January.
418 See Ndungane, N. 2005. 'Put ambition aside for the common good of the people'. *Cape Times*, 10, 25 April 2005) The letter was an explicit endorsement of Premier Ebrahim Rasool to remain as chairperson of the Western Cape ANC.
419 Bagraim, M. 2005. 'Home for all indeed'. *Cape Times*, 28 April.
420 Bagraim, M. 2004/5. 'A Board perspective and a personal glimpse of recent months'. *Cape Jewish Chronicle*, 5, December/January.

It was the first time that the Board's strategy had been explicitly discussed. Prior to the conference, in his monthly column in the *Cape Jewish Chronicle*, Bagraim explained that 'relationships between the Board and government have never been better', but that 'there are those who believe that the Board should not shy away from being critical of government'.[421]

Several months later, the Board began to show a more active and independent political stance. In May 2005, for example, the Board reacted to inflammatory statements in Parliament by ANC Chief Whip Mbulelo Goniwe. Goniwe had told the DA: 'One thing that you forget is that you are here because of the magnanimity of the ANC. If we had chosen the path of the Nuremberg Trials, all of you would be languishing in jail for the crime of apartheid that you committed.'[422] The Board responded by reminding the ANC that '[t]he Nuremburg Trials were instituted to punish those guilty of overseeing some of the most horrific atrocities ever committed' and declared that '[t]he intimation by Mr Goniwe that all South African whites are collectively guilty of similar crimes against humanity is offensive and uncalled for'.[423]

In July 2005, a scandal erupted in Cape Town when the ANC mayor's media adviser, Roderick Blackman Ngoro, was discovered to have made disparaging remarks about coloured and white South Africans on his personal website. In response, the Board issued a statement denouncing Ngoro's rhetoric. In a public statement, Bagraim called Ngoro's claims about coloured people 'outright racial stereotyping of a particularly offensive nature'.[424]

The Board seemed to be following Leon's advice that it should demand that the government live up to the ideals of the Constitution—'that, and nothing less'. The theme of the Board's 43rd National Conference in Johannesburg in August 2005 was 'Jews in a Democratic South Africa: Roles, Rights and Responsibilities'. At the Cape Council's conference in September 2005, where Leon was the keynote speaker, Board members acknowledged that they had taken his advice to heart—a claim some Board members also made in interviews for this book. At the Cape

---

421 Ibid.
422 Goniwe, M. 2005. Speech in the National Assembly, Parliament of South Africa, Cape Town, 25 May. Final Hansard.
423 Bagraim, M. 2005. Quoted in South African Press Association. 'Jewish Board slams ANC'. 28 May [online article].
URL: http://iafrica.com/news/sa/760173.htm; South African Jewish Board of Deputies. Press Release 27 May 2005.
424 Bagraim, M. 2005. Quoted in South African Press Association. 'Mayor orders probe into Ngoro's website'. 22 July [online article]. URL: http://www.iol.co.za/index.php?set_id=1&click_id=79&art_id=qw1122047280306B243

Council's conference, past national chairman Mervyn Smith commended Leon's stance: 'The days of 'Hofjude' [Court Jews] are long past—we're not lesser citizens of South Africa because we support [Leon].'[425]

At the same time that it began to adopt a more vocal posture, however, the Board continued to cultivate close relations with the ANC. Paradoxically, the debate with Leon had given greater definition and clarity to the Board's approach to government. The Board appropriated the term 'politics of influence' and now bore it proudly, as a concise expression of its strategy. In his message to the Board's 43rd conference, Bagraim wrote:

> *The Board is primarily a lobbying organisation, one that seeks to promote the interests of the Jewish community through the politics of influence. Through meeting with government at all levels, making known who we are, what we can offer and what concerns us, we have succeeded in forging strong contacts with those who are in a position to help us when needed. It has enabled us, as a Jewish community, to box far above our weight on the national stage. I am encouraged at how we have been able to increase our influence and make our mark in society, which in turn has enhanced our ability to function properly as the protectors of the Jewish community.*[426]

In practice this strategy meant that, while the Board was more active in its criticism of the government, it continued to organise special events for the ANC, such as its Freedom Charter dinner in June 2005 that brought ANC leaders together with members of the Board. In addition, despite earlier criticism from Leon and from Jewish intellectuals, Bagraim continued to publish letters in support of the government when controversy over its stance towards the Jewish community and Israel arose.

The Board's approach to the government can be understood in the context of the changing nature of minority group politics in South Africa. Increasingly, as the ANC enlarged its parliamentary majority and began to project ever-greater power in more and more sectors of South African life, minority groups began to feel greater pressure

---

425 Smith, M. 2005. Quoted in Schneider, M. 'Government must live up to Constitution'. *South African Jewish Report*, 5, 23 September.
426 Bagraim, M. 2005. 'National chairman's message'. South African Jewish Board of Deputies' 43rd National Conference programme, 7, August.

to align themselves with the government. The penalty for failing to do so would be social and political ostracisation—the same isolation the Jewish community felt during the Kasrils affair, and that other minority groups were subjected to on occasion.

One telling example was that of the Portuguese community. In November 2000, members of the Portuguese community organised a march in Pretoria under the banner of the 'Crime Awareness Committee' to protest against crime. The march ended at the Union Buildings in Pretoria, where a memorandum addressed to President Mbeki was handed over to officials:

> *It is our opinion that our Government simply does not have the political will to implement the same measures, which have been successfully deployed in other countries to combat crime and corruption at all the various levels of its existence ... There is no doubt that the African dream, or renaissance, has become a lifetime nightmare for many of our people, as the criminals continue to impose their brand of injustice on all levels of society ... We call upon the government to switch allegiance from the self-destructive anarchies of Zimbabwe and the Democratic Republic of Congo to focus all efforts on saving the lives of South Africans!*[427]

The vitriolic response that came several weeks later was signed by the then Minister of Safety and Security Steve Tshwete.[428] The letter stated:

> *It is perfectly clear to us that your initiative to march to the Union Buildings and deliver a memorandum addressed to our President was a conscious political act driven by your opposition to the government. I would even make bold to say that, in addition to your defining yourselves as our political opponents, you hold the government, our President and our continent in contempt ... Our country has had a considerable Portuguese community for some time, including the apartheid years. We know of no occasion when this community marched to the Union Buildings to present*

---

427 Gabriel, C M F. 2000. 'We, the citizens of a democratic nation ...' Memorandum to the President of the Republic of South Africa, delivered in Pretoria, 15 November [online text]. URL: http://www.anc.org.za/ancdocs/anctoday/docs/memorandum.htm
428 There has been some speculation that the letter was actually written by President Mbeki himself.

> a memorandum to the apartheid presidents demanding an end to the apartheid crime against humanity ...
>
> Some among the Portuguese community you claim to represent came to this country because they did not accept that the Mozambican and Angolan people should gain their freedom and independence from Portuguese colonialism. Accordingly, South Africa became a second home for these people, because our own people were not free.
>
> These came here because they knew that the colour of their skin would entitle them to join 'the master race', to participate in the oppression and exploitation of the black majority and to enjoy the benefits of white minority domination. It is perhaps because you have not outgrown these white supremacist ideas and practicses that you wrote your memorandum, which you delivered to the Union Buildings.[429]

The minister's letter created a media controversy and sent shock waves through South Africa's other minority communities. Effectively, the letter was interpreted as a warning not only to Portuguese South Africans but to organised minority groups in general.

White Afrikaners, who until 1994 had been in a position of political ascendancy, encountered some of the most acute difficulties of all. Many white Afrikaners felt that they were being made to bear the blame and punishment for apartheid, sometimes unfairly. Afrikaners in farming communities, where over 1 500 white farmers were killed in the decade after 1994, were convinced that they were being deliberately victimised,[430] notwithstanding the conclusion of an investigation in 2003 that found: 'By far the greater majority of cases are motivated by a desire to rob or steal. Very few cases have political overtones'.[431] The Afrikaans language, which had shared prominence with English for much of the 20th century, was pushed out in favour of English in most public spaces.

---

429 Tshwete, S. 2001. 'Where was the Portuguese community when the majority of South Africans suffered the crimes of apartheid?' [online text]. URL: http://www.anc.org.za/ancdocs/anctoday/docs/portuguese.htm
430 Graef, R. 2005. 'Murders foreshadow South African land war'. *Daily Telegraph*, 3 July [online article]. URL: http://www.telegraph.co.uk/news/main.jhtml;jsessionid=VWPBD0WZERADXQFIQMGSM5WAVCBQWJVC?xml=/news/2005/07/03/wsafr03.xml&sSheet=/portal/2005/07/03/ixportal.html
431 South African Police Service 2003. 'Report summary'. *Report of the Committee of Inquiry into Farm Attacks*, 31 July [online document]. URL: http://www.iss.co.za/CJM/farmrep/farmsummary.pdf

In addition, Afrikaans-speaking institutions, like all formerly white institutions in South Africa, came under pressure to 'transform'. The term 'transformation' was introduced by the ANC in the early 1990s but came to have several different meanings, including not only racial integration but ideological change as well. In the *Reconstruction and Development Programme White Paper* of September 1994, in which the government of the President Mandela set forth its economic vision, the purpose of 'transformation' was defined as 'to create a people-centred society which measures progress by the extent to which it has succeeded in securing for each citizen liberty, prosperity and happiness'.[432] This somewhat liberal definition gave way in the late 1990s, as the influence of Mbeki grew, to a definition that referred explicitly and emphatically to race. An ANC discussion document published at the time of the party's 50th National Conference in Mafikeng in 1997 described the goal and process of 'transformation' as 'a continuing battle to assert African [i.e., black] hegemony in the context of a multicultural and non-racial society'.[433]

In racial terms, the stated goal of 'transformation' was to achieve a state of demographic 'representivity', in which each institution in government, the economy and society, at every level, would reflect the racial and gender composition of South Africa as a whole. Ironically, this reflected the same logic of the proposal of Hendrik Verwoerd in 1937 to restrict Jewish economic participation to the Jewish share in the white population.[434] In political terms, the goal of 'transformation' was something larger. A senior ANC strategist, Joel Netshitenzhe, writing in the party's official journal, *Umrabulo*, in 1998, described the purpose of 'transformation' as follows: 'Transformation of the state entails, first and foremost, extending the power of the National Liberation Movement over all levers of power: the army, the police, the bureaucracy, intelligence structures, the judiciary, parastatals, and agencies such as regulatory bodies, the public broadcaster, the central bank and so on.'[435] The word 'transformation' does not appear once in the Constitution of South Africa, yet 'transformation' is

---

432 African National Congress 1994. *Reconstruction and Development Programme (RDP) White Paper*. Discussion document, September URL: http://www.anc.org.za/ancdocs/policy/white.html
433 African National Congress 1997. 'Nation-forming and nation-building: The national question in South Africa'. ANC discussion document, July [online text]. URL: http://www.anc.org.za/ancdocs/discussion/nation.html
434 Myburgh, J. 2001.'Solving the Jewish question: Racial nationalism in South Africa from Verwoerd to Mbeki'. Unpublished article.
435 Netshitenzhe, J. 1998. 'The state, property relations and social transformation'. *Umrabulo* [online journal]. URL: http://www.anc.org.za/ancdocs/pubs/umrabulo/articles/sprst.html

frequently described by government officials as a 'constitutional imperative' and is often enforced as such.[436]

The ANC's new 'transformation' ethos had profound implications for minorities. For Afrikaans educational institutions, it translated into pressure to abandon the exclusive use of the Afrikaans language, which few black students spoke or aspired to learn. This pressure came from the very top. In 2005, Bheki Khumalo, then working as the spokesperson for President Mbeki, wrote an op-ed in the *Sunday Times* in which he referred to single-medium Afrikaans schools as a form of 'apartheid-style influx control'.[437] Middle-class black parents often refused to send their children to Afrikaans schools, even when they were the closest and best-performing alternative, and pressured school governing bodies to adopt dual- or parallel-medium instruction in English and Afrikaans—though not, curiously, in another indigenous language. In the long run, dual- and parallel-medium arrangements frequently led to the wholesale substitution of English for Afrikaans. By 2005 only 3 per cent of schools in South Africa remained single-medium Afrikaans schools,[438] despite the fact that Afrikaans was the first language of over 13 per cent of the population.[439]

Often, pressure on minorities was explained as a necessary means of redress for the apartheid past. One example was a dispute that erupted over the decision by Stellenbosch University to award a posthumous honorary doctorate to Braam Fischer. The idea had been rejected by the university in 2001 and 2002, but was accepted in 2004.[440] A debate then ensued in the Afrikaans press, and in November 2004 a group of alumni formally requested that the university reconsider the award, on several grounds: first, that the university did not ordinarily award posthumous degrees; second, that the university had no connection with Fischer; and third, that notwithstanding his contributions to the struggle against apartheid, he had been a committed Stalinist until the end of his life.

The ensuing debate bore a strong resemblance to the debate among South African Jews over the Kasrils declaration. Just as Kasrils had accused his critics

---

436 Pahad, E. 2006. Speech in on the occasion of the Presidency Budget Vote, National Assembly, Parliament, Cape Town, 7 June 2006 [available online]. URL: http://www.polity.org.za/article.php?a_id=87862
437 Khumalo, B. 2005. 'Historical hangovers make a mockery of equal education.' *Sunday Times*, 23 January [online article]. URL: http://www.suntimes.co.za/Articles/TarkArticle.aspx?ID=1361845
438 Zille, H. Quoted in Philip, R & Van der Merwe, J. 2005. 'Six-year-olds trapped in political chess game'. *Sunday Times*, 3 July [online article]. URL: http://www.sundaytimes.co.za/Articles/TarkArticle.aspx?ID=1527414
439 Statistics South Africa. *Census 2001*. URL: http://www.statssa.gov.za
440 Giliomee, H. 2004. '*Vieser en Vieser* oor Fischer: A participant's notes on a controversy over an honorary degree'. Unpublished.

of being conservative, proponents of the Fischer doctorate accused those who disagreed with them of being 'neo-conservatives'[441], *verkrampte* 'reactionaries'[442] who were showing their reluctance to accept the new social and political order. South African Communist Party deputy secretary general Jeremy Cronin said: 'The reality is [that] an Afrikaner communist is just too indigestible for the conservatives. [The debate] has smoked out those individuals who remain stuck in a Cold War position—out of step with where young Afrikaners are going and out of step with a growing respect for the language.'[443]

However, this was a somewhat inaccurate portrayal of the opposition to Fischer's award. It was true that the movement to reconsider the doctorate had been led by Dr Tertius Delport, a DA MP who had also once served as a member of the Cabinet in the government of F W de Klerk. His membership of the old National Party was a matter of historical record, but other members of the opposition, such as sociologist Lawrence Schlemmer, had been firmly in the liberal political camp.

Historian Hermann Giliomee was the most outspoken critic of the university's decision. He accused the university's leadership of using Fischer 'to improve the image of US as a Politically Correct university'.[444] He elaborated:

> *At the heart of a PC University is a Manichean distinction between ... benign and evil forces as opposed to a tragic worldview in which both sides jointly accept their responsibility for a tragedy and agree to accept the past and work for a common future. In the Manichean moralistic view the one side condemns the other side totally and imputes all the blame and guilt to it for what had gone wrong. A clean break must be made with the pre-1994 past. There is nothing of any value that can be carried over from the old order to the new one.*[445]

Giliomee cited Anthony Holiday, who had previously suggested that Zionism should be outlawed in South Africa, and who had also commented on the Fischer debate. In an extensive defence of Fischer in the *Cape Times*, Holiday insisted that

---

441 Rabe, L. 2004. 'Not in the name of Stellenbosch'. *Mail & Guardian*, 8, 12 November.
442 Holiday, A. 2004. 'Fischer's spirit has triumphed'. *Cape Times*, 15 November.
443 Cronin 2004. Quoted in Merten, M. 'Will the real Afrikaners please rise?'. *Mail & Guardian*, 8, 12 November 2004.
444 Giliomee 2004.
445 Ibid, 5.

Stellenbosch had to 'cleanse itself' of the past by honouring Fischer.[446] The irony, to Giliomee and other critics, was that after having awarded honorary doctorates to many anti-apartheid luminaries—both within and beyond the Afrikaans community—in the years since 1994 (including Nelson Mandela, Desmond Tutu, Thabo Mbeki, Antjie Krog, Beyers Naude, Jakes Gerwel and others), Fischer's honorary doctorate was being described by some of its supporters as the litmus test of the university's commitment to the new political order and the imperative of 'transformation'.

Giliomee saw the debate as the inevitable outcome of increased ANC power, and what he described as the ANC's increased disregard for the terms of the constitutional settlement of the early 1990s: '[A] new, semi-official constitution has come into place. The rule is that there is less chance of the government acting to the detriment of an institution (or a corporation) if that institution pays obeisance to government and the ANC as a liberation movement.'[447] He added: 'The main tactic of the Fischer degree supporters was to attempt to occupy the high moral ground and to accuse their opponents of being obstructionist, selfish, reactionary, and intolerant.'[448]

In closing, Giliomee observed that the political pressures applied by the hegemonic ruling party to ethnic minority groups revealed its hostility towards any form of ethnic political mobilisation other than 'the black communal demand for economic empowerment and affirmative action'. He observed that many minority communities in addition to the Afrikaans community had also seen the emergence of 'follower-less ethnic leaders' who sought to appease the government in the hope of securing a minimalist compromise. These 'follower-less ethnic leaders in touch with government,' he wrote, 'runs [sic] the risk of being seen as representing government in their respective communities rather than the community in addressing themselves to government. Instead of mobilizing their community they want the community to demobilize for fear that it will antagonize.'[449]

A year later, Giliomee elaborated on this description of minority politics, citing the case of the Board of Deputies, as well as numerous examples from the Afrikaans community. In 2004, for example, a group of 112 Afrikaans-speaking

---

446 Holiday, A. 2004. 'Fischer's spirit has triumphed'. *Cape Times*, 15 November.
447 Giliomee 2004, 8.
448 Ibid, 9.
449 Ibid, 12.

business and academic leaders congratulated President Mbeki after the ANC's success in the general elections: 'You have made it possible for all South Africans, including us as Afrikaans-speakers, to be at home in our country and welcome in Africa and the world.'[450] Giliomee observed:

> *With the exception of Naspers, which publishes all Afrikaans newspapers and most magazines, no Afrikaans company presently supports Afrikaans cultural organizations and cultural festivals in a meaningful way. With the exception of Ton Vosloo, no Afrikaans business leader pleads for maintaining Afrikaans as a public language. None of them seems to support any Afrikaans cultural organization. Instead, the prevailing impression is that most Afrikaner business leaders have their respective corporate interests uppermost in mind when they meet the President as part of an 'Afrikaner delegation' to ensure him of their goodwill. Minority concerns seem to be raised only in a perfunctory way.*[451]

Giliomee ascribed the relationship between Afrikaans business and government to the fact that Afrikaners were in a 'post-nationalist phase', and to the 'trade-off' between business and government:

> *The government has given big business what it most wants, namely a conservative fiscal and monetary policy, which in recent years has helped to produce a growth rate last seen 20 years ago. In return, big business has raised no word of protest against the government's affirmative action policy and its demand for negotiated charters to facilitate black economic empowerment. There is a tacit understanding that business will help to resist any opposition to the government's policy of transformation. This understanding is policed by the government, which threatens to punish business by criticising it in a damaging way, imposing new regulations, withdrawing government contracts or nationalising sectors of the economy.*[452]

---

450 Giliomee, H. 2005. 'White-led opposition parties and white minorities under South Africa's 'liberal' dominant party system'. Paper prepared for Workshop on 'Dominant parties and democracy', European Consortium of Political Science, Granada, Spain, 14–19 April [online article]. URL: http://www.ever-fasternews.com/index.php?php_action=read_article&article_id=25
451 Ibid.
452 Ibid.

In other words, the vulnerable position of minorities was not simply a result of government pressure, but of self-seeking behaviour by minority leaders.

In accounting for the actions of Afrikaners and other minority-group leaders who opt for an obsequious approach to government, Giliomee arrived at an ironic conclusion:

> What looks like a puzzle at a first glance is that many of these opinion formers before 1990 were particularly close to the NP government and some were members of the Afrikaner Broederbond. By contrast several of the proponents of minority rights were public opponents of the NP government and of apartheid. The puzzle is solved if it is remembered that the appeasers simply perpetuate a particular style described by Leon as 'the creeping politics of influence'.[453]

Present closeness to the government, he suggested, was not associated with past sympathy for the struggle against apartheid. The opposite, he argued, was more likely to be true: minority-group leaders who had learned to appease the government in the past would continue to do so. He added that these leaders had no long-term political strategy—that they had staked their interests entirely on the incumbent government and its policies, and had no fallback plan in case power shifted to more radical hands.

Giliomee's analysis of minority politics in post-apartheid South Africa attributed many of the changes to the decline of political opposition parties representing minority communities. Indeed, the collapse of racial and ethnic parties was one of the most profound political changes in the first decade of South African democracy. The National Party, once the chief vehicle of Afrikaner national aspirations, saw its share of the national vote collapse from over 20 per cent in 1994 to under 2 per cent in 2004. In 2005 the New National Party dissolved entirely, as its leaders, already serving in government with the ANC, formally joined the majority party. The Inkatha Freedom Party, once a major Zulu political force under Chief Mangosuthu Buthelezi, also saw its support decline as the ANC applied relentless political pressure to the IFP voter base in KwaZulu-Natal. In the 2004 elections, it lost control of the

---

453 Ibid.

provincial government and left the national Cabinet; in 2005 the party began to fracture as several leaders opposed to Buthelezi broke away to form the National Democratic Convention (Nadeco). In the Muslim community, attempts to form separate Muslim parties were unsuccessful, save in Cape Town.[454]

Other smaller ethnic or social parties persisted but remained marginal. The Freedom Front (later renamed the Freedom Front Plus, after absorbing the remnants of the Conservative Party), with its programme of Afrikaner autonomy in a rural *volkstaat* in the western Northern Cape province, remained outspoken but tiny. The Pan Africanist Congress and its Afrocentric philosophies retained a small core of support but were considered little more than a fractious political sideshow. The Africa Muslim Party (AMP) won seats in the municipal elections of 2006 and joined Cape Town's municipal government, only to be ejected after one of its councillors attempted to oust Mayor Helen Zille.

Even after the decline of these parties, however, South African politics remained, broadly speaking, racially divided. In the 2004 general elections, the DA won approximately 75 per cent of the vote in predominantly white voting districts, while the ANC won 82 per cent of the vote in predominantly black areas.[455]

At the same time, while both parties campaigned vigorously in these constituencies, both also made conscious efforts to project at least the image of non-racialism. President Mbeki campaigned door-to-door in white Afrikaans neighbourhoods; the DA launched its election manifesto in Soweto.

The changes in minority politics seem to have been caused not only by the decline of minority political parties but by the ascendancy of the ANC in general. Though the number of votes received by the ANC continued to fall since 1994, its proportion of the votes cast continued to rise.[456] Its programme of 'transformation' had also succeeded in 'deploying' local ANC cadres to positions of power and influence throughout the state, the economy and society in general. In addition, it is clear from a brief survey of interest-group politics in the post-apartheid era that the constraints faced by minority communities, and the political strategies they chose, were not theirs alone. Other types of interest groups found themselves in similar circumstances and facing similar strategic choices.

---

454 Vahed & Jeppie, 277.
455 Leon, AJ. 2004. Speech in response to the State of the Nation Address. Parliament, South Africa, 25 May.
456 Independent Electoral Commission. URL: http://www.elections.org.za

One example was the Treatment Action Campaign (TAC), which had formed in the late 1990s to protest against the high prices charged by international pharmaceutical companies for anti-AIDS drugs. In 2000, however, after President Mbeki questioned the link between the human immunodeficiency virus (HIV) and acquired immune deficiency syndrome (AIDS), the TAC began protesting against the president's views and against the government's reluctance to provide antiretroviral drugs to AIDS patients.

Street demonstrations and protests were accompanied by court battles, including a landmark 2002 Constitutional Court victory for the TAC, in which the court required the government to provide the antiretroviral drug nevirapine to HIV-positive pregnant women in state hospitals.[457] The government, however, dragged its feet in implementing the court's decisions. The TAC then launched a campaign of civil disobedience in 2003, which was called off when the group was assured that the ANC would take its concerns seriously. Indeed, later that year, with the 2004 general elections undoubtedly in mind, the ruling party committed to a rollout of antiretroviral drugs.

However, the government continued to miss its own self-imposed treatment deadlines and to endorse denialist philosophies, such as the idea that changes in nutrition were an appropriate substitute for antiretroviral drugs. The government also sought to undermine the TAC by backing interest groups that opposed antiretroviral treatment, providing support to alternative organisations that backed the government's stance, such as the National Association of People Living with AIDS (NAPWA) and the Dr Rath Health Foundation.

Throughout these battles, the TAC continued to affirm close political ties with the ANC. Its leading members insisted that they remained ANC members. TAC chairperson Zackie Achmat proclaimed in 2000 that he was 'an ANC member in good standing—I attend all my branch meetings!'[458] Speculation within the organisation that the TAC might form its own political party or contest elections independently never came to fruition. Before the 2004 elections, TAC treasurer Mark Heywood said: 'I wouldn't advocate anybody to vote for a different political party, because at the end of the day, the ANC's going to come back

---

[457] Constitutional Court of South Africa. *Minister of Health v. Treatment Action Campaign*, CCT 8/02 (2002).
[458] Achmat, Z. 2000. Quoted in Treatment Action Group. 'Taking it to the street'. *The Body*, September [online article]. URL: http://66.102.9.104/search?q=cache:2f73SPP4jPsJ:www.thebody.com/tag/sept00/tac.html+tac+anc+members&hl=en

into power, and we've got to make sure that the ANC does what is necessary in terms of confronting this epidemic.'[459] After the 2004 elections, the TAC issued a message of congratulations to the ANC. It noted that 'a majority of TAC members voted for the ANC', and endorsed the government's platform: 'Support for the ANC across the country represents an unequivocal mandate from South Africa's citizens for the ANC government to deliver meaningful social improvements in our lives.'[460]

Given that the TAC's HIV/Aids positions were largely reflected in the policies of opposition parties, notably the DA, and that it had been in constant conflict with the ruling party over HIV/Aids, the organisation might have been expected to endorse the opposition rather than the government. But it did not, preferring to remain within the ruling party's fold. The organisation explained its political strategy: 'TAC did not make the 2004 election about HIV/Aids because we accepted the good faith of the change in government policy, the increased allocation of resources and the beginning of antiretroviral roll-out in key provinces. We refused to give succour to parties who wanted to make HIV/Aids a party-political issue.'[461]

It is this refusal to make key matters of policy—even life-and-death matters such as the HIV/Aids pandemic—into 'party-political' issues that has marked both minority groups and interest groups in general in Mbeki's South Africa. Groups of all kinds focus on lobbying the ruling party and its central executive, rather than on pursuing other political allies or forming issue-based political parties. There are a few exceptions: several anti-crime groups endorsed the DA in the 2004 general election.[462] By 2007, the TAC had begun to back away from the ruling party: 'The big lesson that the Treatment Action Campaign (TAC) learnt was that trying to solve the HIV/Aids problem within the ANC was as helpful as keeping incest in the family,' observed *Business Day* columnist Rhoda Kadalie. 'Recently, the TAC has joined hands again with civil society, willing political actors and faith communities to counter the cynicism that comes from the government.'[463]

---

459 Heywood, M. 2003. Quoted in Wilson, B. 'South Africa moves to distribute AIDS drugs'. National Public Radio, 27 August. [online broadcast]. URL: http://www.npr.org/templates/story/story.php?storyId=1413916
460 Treatment Action Campaign 2004. 'Statement on South African elections', 21 April [online newsletter]. URL: http://www.tac.org.za/newsletter/2004/ns21_04_2004.htm#Elections
461 Treatment Action Campaign, ibid.
462 Leon, AJ. 2004. 'Endorsement by anti-crime activists'. Press statement, Johannesburg, South Africa. 7 April.
463 Kadalie, R. 2007. 'Politicians score points as tik lays waste to coloured youth.' *Business Day*, 4 October [online article]. URL: http://www.businessday.co.za/articles/article.aspx?ID=BD4A578683

However, few groups are prepared to risk isolation and attack from the ANC. Partly due to the dominance of the ANC, and partly due to the timidity of interest groups, political parties in South Africa today do not compete for the support of those interest groups as they do in other, more established democracies. The Board of Deputies, then, was not unique in pursuing its new 'lobbying' strategy.

Leon's charge that the Board appeared to be 'slipping back toward a pattern of deferential behaviour' provoked some changes. Certainly, in the months after his criticism, the Board found its voice and spoke out against particular government actions. What the Board did not do was to chart a self-consciously independent course. As a 'lobby' group focused on the ANC, and no longer 'advocacy' group adopting a more assertive public stance, the Board had, like other interest groups, hitched its fortunes to those of the ruling party. It was doing no more and no less than what other minority groups and interest groups were doing when faced with the overwhelming power of the ANC.

In its failure to break beyond the boundaries of minority-group politics, the Board might therefore indeed be said to be repeating some of the patterns of the apartheid era. Shimoni had described Jewish politics under apartheid as '… characteristic minority-group behaviour—a phenomenon of self-preservation, performed at the cost of moral righteousness …'.[464] In the post-apartheid era, after a brief experiment with 'advocacy', Jewish leadership had begun to revert to a mode in which it sought to achieve its own narrow goals through 'lobbying' at the expense of contributing to the broader development of a vibrant South African democracy.

---

464 Shimoni 2003, 276.

CHAPTER SEVEN

CONCLUSIONS AND COMPARISONS

More than a decade after South Africa's first democratic elections, the South African Jewish community was still in a state of political transition. The central political question facing Jewish institutions remained whether the community should be more politically outspoken than it had been in the past, or whether it should behave once again as an intercessor, using quiet tactics to achieve influence. In effect, the answer was both. Souwth African Jews created alternative institutions and found new voices to articulate the community's point of view, while the Board set about cultivating a far closer relationship with the ruling party. The community affirmed its commitment to Israel, and began to incorporate and tolerate different and diverse voices. But the Board found itself in danger of 'capture' by the ruling party. To borrow Giliomee's terms, it began to represent the government to the community, often at the expense of representing the community to the government.

The Kasrils affair highlights the ambivalent nature of Jewish politics in the post-apartheid era, and of minority politics in South Africa more generally. It is possible to identify this ambivalence more precisely. In his eponymous treatise on modern Jewish politics, Ezra Mendelsohn constructed a 'typology of the various Jewish organisations active in Jewish politics' by posing seven 'key questions' that help 'to divide the Jewish world into a manageable number of schools or camps.'[465] The 'key questions' posed by Mendelsohn were as follows:

---

465 Mendelsohn, E. 1993. *On Modern Jewish Politics*. New York: Oxford University Press, 4–5.

1. How are the Jews, taken collectively, to be defined?

2. What should be the predominant cultural (meaning above all linguistic) orientation of the Jews?

3. Assuming the existence of a Jewish Question, where does the solution lie— 'here' in the Diaspora, where the Jews already live, or 'there' in Palestine/Eretz Yisrael or in some other Jewish territory to which they will go ...?

4. From a large number of potentially usable Jewish pasts ... which did the various Jewish organizations choose?

5. Which political forces in the non-Jewish world did these organizations identify with and seek out as allies?

6. What sort of political tactics did these various organizations favour ... the politics of loud and open protest or ... quiet, even secret diplomacy behind closed doors ...?

7. To what degree were the various organizations under consideration optimistic or pessimistic with regard to the collective future of the Jews in the Diaspora?

Many of these questions emerged in some form during the Kasrils affair. By referring to themselves as 'South Africans of Jewish descent', for example, Kasrils and Ozinsky challenged the community's prevailing opinion on the first question—how Jews were to be collectively defined—by reducing Judaism to a hereditary trait, rather than a complex interweaving of ethnicity, religion and culture. On the second question, regarding what defines Jews culturally, differences were again stark. In inter-war Poland—which provided the basis for Mendelsohn's typology—and even in South Africa until the 1950s, the question of Zionism was closely intertwined with the question of language. In South Africa, Hebrew fought Yiddish for supremacy (and triumphed, though both lost to English). Fifty years later, in the Kasrils affair, differences over language had long since subsided but differences over Zionism remained. Kasrils and many of his supporters viewed Zionism as a repugnant form of ethnic nationalism, and therefore antithetical to life in a diverse, multicultural society. Most Jews felt otherwise—that Zionism was a legitimate and even appropriate political creed in a multicultural South Africa.

Most of Mendelsohn's questions, however, were formulated to describe an era before the State of Israel existed. While it touched on many other issues, the debate around the Kasrils declaration was first and foremost about the Israeli–Palestinian conflict, and what attitude Jews should adopt towards it. That suggests the possible need for an 'eighth question', which could be termed as follows: Should Jews support Israel in her conflicts with her neighbours, particularly with the Palestinians, and to what extent? Different answers to this question (as well as different ways of posing it) abound, both in the Diaspora and in Israel, and were explored among South African Jews throughout the Kasrils affair.

While the 'eighth question' was at the core of the debate, however, it did not fully reflect the changing nature of politics within the Jewish community. Few opinions on Israel were shifted; Kasrils and his supporters remained in the minority. Mendelsohn's sixth question—the question of tactics—cut to the essence of the change that the Kasrils affair had provoked. The Board's shifting strategy—best symbolised by Bagraim's vow to pursue 'in-your-face' politics in 2001, and his call for the 'politics of influence' in 2005—reflected a movement away from what Mendelsohn referred to as the politics of 'loud and open protest' and towards the politics of 'quiet, even secret diplomacy behind closed doors'. This was not a complete switch from the former to the latter—the Board was by no means totally quiescent—but a marked change in emphasis. On social and constitutional issues, the Board felt confident enough to take on the government in public; on Israel, it began to delegate leadership to the revived SAZF and to other independent voices in the community. However, on broader political issues, it seemed determined to curry favour with the ruling party at virtually every opportunity until challenged by Leon and some of the community's intellectuals. Even on the issue of Israel, the Board shifted from criticising the government's approach to defending it in public. In doing so, the Board not only affirmed South Africa's apparent rapprochement with the Israeli government but also downplayed the government's past antagonism towards it (which had never completely subsided, and flared up again in the waning years of the Mbeki presidency).

The Board continued its pattern of reassuring the Jewish community about the government's stance on Israel in mid 2007, when the front page in the *South African Jewish Report* printed an article under the headline: 'Govt reassures Jews on ME'.[466] A delegation from the Board and the SAZF had met with the minister and deputy minister of foreign affairs to express their concerns about South Africa's stance at the UN, in particular its apparent support for Iran's nuclear programme and its absence from a vote condemning Holocaust denial. The ANC had also endorsed an anti-Israel campaign at home entitled 'End the Occupation' that called for, among other things, a boycott of Israeli goods (though the ANC distanced itself from the boycott).[467] The Board appeared to accept the government's pledges of even-handedness at face value. The *South African Jewish Report* even published a full-page letter from ANC presidential spokesperson Smuts Ngonyama to Israel United Appeal chairperson Motty Sacks in which Ngonyama pledged the ANC's support for Israel's right to exist.[468] Yet ANC hostility towards Israel persisted. In May 2008, on the occasion of Israel's 60th anniversary, the ANC endorsed, and several cabinet ministers (including Kasrils) signed, a letter entitled 'We fought apartheid; we see no reason to celebrate it in Israel now!' The letter was run as a paid advertisement in *The Citizen* and the *Mail and Guardian,* and provoked new frustration in the Jewish community.

Just how far the Board was willing to take the 'politics of influence' was revealed in a highly embarrassing episode involving the South African Broadcasting Corporation (SABC) and a Jewish journalist named Paula Slier. The controversy began when Dr Snuki Zikalala, SABC managing director of news and current affairs, was alleged to have 'blacklisted' certain commentators from appearing on the SABC because their political views were at odds with those of the ruling party and President Mbeki. The SABC conducted an internal investigation that was leaked to the media.[469] Among

---

466 Saks, D. 2007. 'Govt reassures Jews on ME'. *South African Jewish Report*,1, 30 June.
467 African National Congress 2007. 'Palestinian solidarity: Call to mobilize against Israeli occupation'. *ANC Today*, 25 May [online article]. URL: http://www.anc.org.za/ancdocs/anctoday/2007/at20.htm#art1
468 Ngonyama, S. 2007. 'Letter to Motty Sacks'. *South African Jewish Report*, 5, 30 June.
469 South African Broadcasting Corporation 2006. 'Commission of enquiry into blacklisting and related matters', 14 October. Copy by *Mail & Guardian* [online document]. URL: http://www.mg.co.za/ContentImages/286848/SABCBLACKLISTREPORT.pdf

the findings was the revelation that Zikalala had barred the SABC from using Slier as a news source regarding the ill health of Palestinian Authority Chairman Yasser Arafat, despite the fact that she was based in the Middle East at the time. The investigating commission quoted Zikalala's explanation verbatim:

> *Paula Slier, I'll give you an example. Paula Slier, why I said we should not use Paula Slier. What happened is that during the time of when Arafat passed away, when Arafat passed away Paula Slier used to work for us as a journalist and Paula Slier was much more biased towards what's happening in Israel. It was a Jewish war and especially the Middle East. We knew exactly her bias because she once wrote an article justifying the separation of the Palestinians, which was very, very negative towards us. From the movement where I come from we support PLO. But she supported what's happening in Israel. And then I said to them Paula Slier we cannot use her on the Middle East issue because we know where she stands. We need somebody who's impartial. We do have a correspondent there, I said let's use the correspondent ... that person is impartial, does not take sides. Paula Slier on the Middle East issue we can bring in all the tapes that she's written, she takes sides. I've got that editorial responsibility to do that. That's why I'm employed, to do checks and balance. I said no, you can't you can't undermine the Palestinian struggle, you can't. For me it's a principle issue.*[470]

The SABC's internal investigation recommended that the practice of blacklisting be ended, and expressed 'concerns about the particular management style of Dr Zikalala'.[471] However, it did not recommend any more tangible action against him, and none was taken.

In response, the Freedom of Expression Institute (FXI) filed a lengthy formal complaint with the Independent Communications Authority of South Africa, the statutory watchdog that is meant to regulate telecommunications and broadcasting in the public interest.[472] The Board also filed a complaint against the SABC on the basis of the evidence about the blacklisting of Slier. In July 2007,

---

470 Ibid. Ironically, Slier was regarded by some South African Jews as pro-Palestinian. It would be most accurate to say that she strove to understand both sides of the conflict.
471 Ibid.
472 Freedom of Expression Institute 2007. 'Action alert: Complain to ICASA for SABC violations of licence conditions and Broadcasting Act'. Press statement, 20 February [online document]. URL: http://www.fxi.org.za/content/view/35/

however, the Board suddenly withdrew its complaint after meeting with the SABC and striking a deal: it would agree to withdraw the complaint if the SABC would commit to more balanced coverage of the Middle East. An independent weblog entitled *It's Almost Supernatural* and run by community members Michael Kransdorff and Steve Magid sharply criticised the agreement:

> *The SAJBD is portraying this as a victory for their strategy of quiet diplomacy. In a Chamberlain-like statement in this week's South African Jewish Report (SAJR), they were reported to be 'upbeat over prospects of genuine even-handedness by the SABC'. While fair reporting at the SABC is welcomed, it is not something that we should have to bargain for. It is enshrined in the SABC's code of conduct.*
>
> *In securing a potential short-term lull in SABC anti-Israel coverage, the SAJBD has harmed democracy in South Africa long term ... It is becoming increasingly clear that the SAJBD, rather than lobbying the government on our behalf, is lobbying us on the government's behalf.*[473]

Kransdorff and Magid contacted the Board for their response, and Wendy Kahn, the Board's national director, outlined the details of the agreement with the SABC:

> *We asked for, and received, a number of concrete undertakings by the SABC to work with us in addressing the problem of anti-Israel bias within the organisation. These undertakings, which we now have in writing, are:*
>
> *1 An independent monitoring organisation will monitor the coverage of the SABC news on the topic of the Middle East for at least a year. The SABC is currently using Media Tenor, and this will most likely be the organisation used for this purpose. The SABC and the SA Jewish Board of Deputies will meet on a quarterly period to discuss the content of the coverage by Media Tenor. The latter will commence operation as from the 1 August 2007, and the first meeting will take place in the first week of November.*

---

473 Kransdorff, M & Magid, S. 2007. 'SAJBD cuts a deal with the SABC'. *It's Almost Supernatural*, 30 July [weblog entry]. URL: http://supernatural.blogs.com/weblog/2007/07/sajbd-cuts-a-de.html

2 The leadership of the Jewish Board of Deputies would meet with the editorial staff of the SABC, to provide an understanding of the SA Jewish community and its views on the Middle East.

3 The Jewish Board strongly recommended that where debates on the Middle East take place, moderates from both sides be used. They noted that there was no insight to be gained by allowing those who refuse to recognize the right of the other side to exist, to debate the Middle East. The suggestion was made that genuinely even-handed academics be used to discuss the situation. If the appropriate people were unavailable in South Africa the journalists should look elsewhere.

We have since already had the opportunity to address and engage with senior members of the SABC editorial staff in Johannesburg and nationally via teleconference facilities. This was an excellent forum for us to develop relationships with these key people in the SABC, answer their questions, bring to their attention our concerns over the way the Middle East conflict has been depicted and in general provide a face for the SAJBD and the SA Jewish community.

The process of engagement we have initiated with the SABC will be an ongoing one. The quarterly reports of Media Tenor will be of special significance since they will provide a considered analysis by a respected, wholly impartial media monitoring body, whose views cannot be casually dismissed as partisan.

So far as the broader question of the independence of the national broadcaster goes, this is indeed an issue of national importance, and it concerns Jews no less than it does other South African citizens. Addressing it, however, falls outside the mandate of the SAJBD, whose mission, as already noted, is to act as a lobbying body specifically on matters of Jewish concern. Addressing the wider implications of the blacklisting scandal rightfully falls within the purvey of such democratic watchdog groupings as the Freedom of Expression Institute. The latter is already dealing with the matter in a most dedicated and professional way.[474]

---

[474] Kahn, W. 2007. Quoted in *It's Almost Supernatural*, ibid.

These terms suggested that the Board actually received nothing in exchange for withdrawing its complaint except the promise of a few meetings. The SABC never apologised for its antisemitism, nor did it commit to any real change in its approach to the Middle East conflict.

Kahn's letter, posted on *It's Almost Supernatural*, triggered a minor national scandal. The FXI was outraged. It accused Zikalala of having 'agreed to another form of blacklisting' and said he was 'skating extremely close to allowing pre-broadcast censorship by a lobby group'.[475] It called on the SABC to confirm or deny the terms of the deal as reported by the Board. The SABC, in response, denied that any such deal had been struck:

> *At the meeting no agreement was reached regarding the use of commentators on the Middle East. The SAJBD proposed the use of 'moderates from both sides' whenever the Middle East issue was discussed and the SABC reiterated its commitment to the Editorial Code of the Corporation with specific reference to the need for balanced reporting.*
>
> *SABC did not agree to any form of pre-publication censorship, but agreed that the Jewish Board of Deputies could access quarterly content analysis provided to the SABC by an independent media monitoring company, to be used as a basis of discussion should concerns about bias remain.*
>
> *Editorial briefings are a regular feature in SABC news rooms and are used in order to provide editorial staff with a range of viewpoints on developments within the country and internationally. A wide variety of stakeholders and newsmakers have participated in these briefings, and the Jewish Board [is] no exception.*
>
> *Likewise, there was no undertaking on the part of News management to 'speak to the relevant people regarding getting coverage', for [Benjamin] Pogrund and [Bassem] Eid[476], merely that editorial staff would be informed of their presence in the country and of their availability to be interviewed. With the understanding that they are representing a particular view-point, they*

---

475 Freedom of Expression Institute 2007. 'From SABC's Zikalala—from one blacklist to another?' Press statement, 1 August [online document]. URL: http://www.fxi.org.za/content/view/128/1/

476 Pogrund, director of the Yakar Centre for Social Concern, and Eid, director of the Palestinian Human Rights Monitoring Group, visited South Africa together to speak about the peace process. Both opposed the Israel-apartheid analogy, and were well-received by the Jewish community.

too have been invited to an editorial briefing. They are as entitled to this as any other interest group within society.[477]

This left the Board in a highly embarrassing position, particularly after the story made national headlines. Faced with severe criticism from the Jewish community, the Board attempted to defend its position. Wendy Kahn wrote:

Let me state from the outset that the SA Jewish Board of Deputies shares our community's anger and frustration over some of the statements that emanate from time to time from government and the media …

However, over the years what the Board has learned is that confrontation and litigation are seldom the most effective ways of dealing with adversity.

While it does make us feel better in the short run to write nasty letters, threaten legal action and lambaste government personalities in the media, these tend to result at best in pyrrhic victories whose outcomes are short lived.

By contrast, far greater success has been achieved through the mechanisms of dialogue and conciliation. By engaging with government and the media, we have been able to achieve more sustainable and more meaningful outcomes that have enabled our community to benefit from solutions that are more forward thinking.

It is a far superior methodology to develop relationships with key personalities that we can work with going forward. …

The Board has worked tirelessly over the past few years investing in these relationships and developing effective channels of communication. Of course we still don't like everything that is said about us or about our beloved Israel, but at least we are able to challenge these statements and are given opportunities to put our case forward at the highest levels.

In summary, for the Jewish community to take its rightful place in South African society, we need to let go of our confrontational mindset and commit ourselves to a process of engagement with those around us. This does not

---

477 South African Broadcasting Corporation 2007. 'SABC responds to FXI statement on meeting with the SA Jewish Board'. Press statement, 2 August [online document]. URL: http://www.sabc.co.za:80/portal/binary/com.epicentric.contentmanagement.connectors.cda.CDADisplayServlet?connectorID=cda&moid=8b8430c324524110VgnVCM10000030d4ea9bRCRD

mean never being confrontational—there are times when we indeed need to speak out strongly and forthrightly, even if this means having to publicly attack those we are seeking to influence.

However, confrontation as opposed to constructive dialogue needs always to be seen as a last resort.[478]

This did not pacify those who opposed the Board's decision. The final blow was an op-ed by Slier herself in the *South African Jewish Report* entitled 'Please SAJBD, don't talk on my behalf!'[479] Slier wrote:

I never approached the SAJBD, nor did I ask them to represent me ... It's laughable that in exchange for protecting my rights and the potential damage to my reputation, the racist blacklisting and my loss of income, the Board views as a victory the fact that it strongly recommended that where debates on the Middle East take place, moderates from both sides be used.

Please, the national broadcaster needs to be informed of this? And to inform it is viewed as a victory? Objective, fair, precise, accurate journalism is not something to be bargained for ...

Not only have you thrown me to the dogs, you have insulted journalism as a whole by assuming that as journalists we should be beholden to groups with a very specific mandate and purpose. The fact that Zikalala agreed to this merely reinforces his poor judgment and conception of quality journalism ...

I was sold out. Simple. I was used by the Board for its purposes and now when it's convenient for it to toss me aside, it has no qualms doing so. This kind of 'representation' sends out a strong message to the South African Jewish community. Is it a sign of how one can expect to be looked after if one's rights are infringed?

What about the other journalists and commentators who were blacklisted? The SAJBD's mishandling of the issue misses a very real opportunity to challenge the shortcomings in our democracy.

---

478 Kahn, W. 2007. 'Confrontation often not the best way'. *South African Jewish Report*, 14, 17 August.
479 Slier, P. 2007. 'Please, SAJBD, don't talk on my behalf!'. *South African Jewish Report*, 10, 17 August.

> *The actions of the Board speak volumes about how they view the status of minorities in South Africa. Are we too frightened to speak out?*
>
> *This issue was never just about me or the other journalists who were blacklisted; it was about the very real threat to our country's democracy and our rights to freedom of speech which are being marred by a national broadcaster that has become the mouthpiece of the government.*[480]

Slier's riposte inspired a flurry of letters attacking the Board's stance. The letters were published on the eve of its national conference, much to the chagrin of the Board itself, which tried to minimise debate on Slier and the SABC during the proceedings. The new Board elected at the conference, headed by former national vice-chairman Zev Krengel, was expected to continue the 'politics of influence', as Krengel apparently prided himself on his connections with the ANC.[481]

The significance of the Board's shift towards the 'politics of influence' can be best understood by examining the responses of Jewish institutions in other Diaspora communities to public debates over the Israeli–Palestinian conflict. South African Jews were not alone in their exposure to new debates and new pressures in the months and years following the outbreak of the new *intifada* in September 2000. Jewish communities throughout the world were affected, directly and indirectly, by events in the Middle East and were caught up in internal and external debates about them. They were also the targets of a new wave of violence and abuse, dubbed by some observers as the 'new antisemitism.'

The new antisemitism was not a uniform phenomenon: antisemitism in North America differed in degree and in kind from antisemitism in Europe, and antisemitism in Britain differed from antisemitism in France and on the continent.[482] Some commentators also alleged that certain forms of anti-Israel rhetoric being expressed around the globe were antisemitic. Harvard University President Larry Summers spoke out on the subject in an address at Harvard's Memorial Church in September 2002:

---
480 Ibid.
481 Krengel was involved in another embarrassing episode in 2006 in which national director Yehuda Kay sent an e-mail report to a senior ANC member reporting on Tony Leon's visit to a Jewish school. The e-mail, which referred to Leon's speech as 'toilet reading material,' was forwarded to other ANC members with the subject line: 'look what the jewz think of leon'. Kay resigned as a result of the controversy, and Krengel's position on the Board was rumoured to have been challenged. See Bailey, C. 2006. 'Board dissociates itself from Leon e-mail'. *Cape Argus*, 7, 15 May.
482 Iganski, P & Kosmin, B (eds) 2003. 'Editors' introduction'. *A New Antisemitism?: Debating Judeophobia in 21st-Century Britain*. London: Profile/Institute for Jewish Policy Research, 1–2.

> ... [C]ertainly there is much to be debated about the Middle East and much in Israel's foreign and defense policy that can be and should be vigorously challenged. But where antisemitism and views that are profoundly anti-Israeli have traditionally been the primary preserve of poorly educated right-wing populists, profoundly anti-Israel views are increasingly finding support in progressive intellectual communities. Serious and thoughtful people are advocating and taking actions that are antisemitic in their effect if not their intent.[483]

Britain's Chief Rabbi Jonathan Sacks commented:

> What we are witnessing today is the second great mutation of antisemitism in modern times ... The mutation is this: that the worst crimes of antisemites in the past—racism, ethnic cleansing, attempted genocide, crimes against humanity—are now attributed to Jews and the state of Israel, so that if you are against Nazism, you must ipso facto be utterly opposed to Jews.[484]

In France, too, Israel was a key target of the new antisemitism. Pro-Palestinian groups became involved in a 'rhetorical bidding war', in which groups competed for attention by making more and more aggressive and inflammatory claims about Israeli actions.[485]

There were, however, debates about whether the new antisemitism was in fact 'new', or whether indeed it deserved to be called 'antisemitism' at all. Some observers argued that the wave of attacks against Jews and the vociferous criticism of Israel were not necessarily much greater, and in some ways was smaller, than in earlier decades.[486] Others wondered whether the surge of antisemitism was really motivated by hatred of Jews, or whether it represented a Diaspora extension of the Israeli–Palestinian conflict in countries with significant Arab immigrant communities. In some countries, the threat of antisemitic violence seemed to pale in comparison to the violence that erupted over ethnic rivalries that had little to

---

483 Summers, L. 2002. 'Address at morning prayers'. Memorial Church, Harvard University, Cambridge, MA. 17 September.
484 Sacks, J. 2003. 'A new antisemitism?' in Iganski & Kosmin, *A New Antisemitism?* 46.
485 Waintrater, M. 2003. 'France'. *American Jewish Year Book (2003)*. 385.
486 Julius, A. 2003. 'Is there anything 'new' in the new antisemitism?' in Iganski & Kosmin, *A New Antisemitism?*, 73–74.

do with Jews. In the same period that the new antisemitism peaked in Britain, for example, the country was experiencing severe tensions between white locals and Pakistani immigrants. These tensions erupted into violent race riots in 2001, and persisted after the London bombings of July 2005.

In October and November 2005, France experienced dramatic violent nationwide protests in which groups of North African immigrant youth clashed with police and destroyed cars and property. President Jacques Chirac declared a state of emergency, which was only lifted in January 2006.[487]

Other critics—particularly those hostile to the Israeli government—regarded the charges of antisemitism as exaggerated, and alleged that they were merely used to protect Israel from scrutiny. The controversial *Independent* commentator Robert Fisk, for example, wrote that 'a new theme has emerged. Reporters who criticise Israel are to blame for inciting antisemites to burn synagogues. Almost anyone who criticises US or Israeli policies in the Middle East is now in this free-fire zone'.[488]

Statistics, however, tended to support the view that the new antisemitism was real. France, for example, experienced the most serious wave of violent antisemitism within its borders since the Second World War—and, indeed, the worst contemporary antisemitism experienced by any Jewish community in the Diaspora. The violence—including attacks on Jewish property, institutions and individuals—reached a historic peak between the autumn of 2000 and the spring of 2002, when over 400 antisemitic attacks were reported.[489] The attacks differed from those in previous decades in that the suspected perpetrators were, in the main, not right-wing groups but Arab Muslims of North African origin. Britain also experienced a sharp rise in antisemitic attacks. The worst year was 2000, when the new *intifada* broke out, in which 405 antisemitic incidents were recorded, including vandalism, synagogue desecration, physical assault and attempted murder.[490]

---

487 BBC News 2006. 'France lifts state of emergency'. 4 January [web article] URL: http://news.bbc.co.uk/2/hi/europe/4576430.stm
488 Fisk, R. 2003. 'Why does John Malkovich want to kill me?' *The Politics of Antisemitism*, eds A Cockburn & J St. Clair. Petrolia: CounterPunch, 62.
489 The Stephen Roth Institute. 'France'. *Antisemitism Worldwide*. Annual Report 2001/2. URL: http://www.tau.ac.il/Antisemitism/asw2001-2/france.htm
490 Kochan, M & L. 2003. 'Great Britain'. *American Jewish Year Book*, eds D Singer & L Grossman, 366. New York: American Jewish Committee; and The Stephen Roth Institute. 'United Kingdom'. *Antisemitism Worldwide*. Annual report 2000/1. URL: http://www.tau.ac.il/Antisemitism/asw2000-1/united_kingdom.htm

South Africa was fortunate in that it recorded a relatively low number of antisemitic attacks, few of which were violent (at least until the record-breaking year of 2006). The major problem was antisemitic propaganda.[491] In the US, the surge in antisemitic attacks was less severe and did not occur primarily in Jewish communities but on university campuses across the country. There, Jewish students and faculty were confronted with hate and/or violence and vandalism that grew out of strident campus activism against Israel and American foreign policy in the Middle East in general.

In each of the above cases, there were certain distinct similarities. In each, the sudden estrangement of Israel from at least some parts of the international community was seen as a powerful metaphor for Jewish fears about, and experiences of, isolation from broader society in the Diaspora. For many Diaspora Jews, the 'normalisation' of relations between Israel and her neighbours that had occurred during the Oslo peace process had symbolised the normalisation, or resolution of the tension (felt by some more than others) between the identity of the Jewish individual as a Jew and as a citizen.

The *intifada* threatened this 'normalisation'. But, in each case, Jews regrouped to assert both their rights as citizens in the Diaspora and the case for Israel against her enemies. Jews around the world developed similar responses to antisemitic and anti-Israel rhetoric—and, thanks to the Internet, were often able to cooperate. Rallies, petitions and media campaigns, as well as more discreet methods of persuasion and intercession, were employed. In France, a large portion of Parisian Jews joined the pro-Israel demonstration organised by community leaders in April 2002. In Britain, campaigns conducted by such groups as HonestReporting.com organised pro-Israel responses in public debates, often in coordination with central Jewish authorities. Attempts to organise anti-Israel boycotts were largely failures. When the department store Harrods took Israeli goods off its shelves in 2002, its actions were greeted by such vehement protests that it ended the boycott (but identified Israeli goods with stickers).[492] Various academic boycotts of Israeli scholars or institutions were attempted, but were largely defeated or repealed. The most notorious of these was the vote by the British Association

---

491 The Stephen Roth Institute for the Study of Contemporary Antisemitism and Racism. 'South Africa'. *Antisemitism Worldwide*. Annual report 2003/4. URL: http://www.tau.ac.il/Antisemitism/asw2004/sth-africa.htm
492 Kochan, 378.

of University Teachers (AUT) in April 2005 to boycott two Israeli universities. The British government strongly criticised the boycott, and in a subsequent vote in June it was cancelled.[493] Further boycotts, however, were attempted in the months and years that followed.

In each case, as in South Africa, there was a minority of Jews who dissented with the communal mainstream and supported vociferous criticism of Israel. In Britain, the Jewish Labour MP Gerald Kaufman called for sanctions against Israel in 2004.[494] Groups such as Jews for Justice for the Palestinians and other left-wing Jewish groups dissented from the Jewish political mainstream, provoking debate both within and outside the community.[495] In 2007, a group calling itself Independent Jewish Voices emerged with a declaration—perhaps modelled after, but somewhat more moderate than, the Kasrils declaration—calling on British Jews to 'speak out'. Such dissent posed a challenge for centralised Jewish institutions. In August 2002, the Board of Deputies of British Jews (the progenitor of the South African Board) publicly distanced itself from remarks attributed to Chief Rabbi Sacks in an interview with the *Guardian* in which he expressed shame over certain actions committed against Palestinians by Israeli soldiers in the occupied territories.[496]

In the US, Jewish criticism of Israel was partly led by Tikkun, a San Francisco-based group founded and led by Rabbi Michael Lerner. Lerner caused great controversy within the Jewish community in 2002 by placing a full-page advertisement in the *New York Times* that attacked Israel's occupation but did not criticise the Palestinians.[497] Despite this stance, in February 2003, with the Iraq War looming, Lerner was barred from speaking at a demonstration in San Francisco against the war by one of the groups organising the event. The group, ANSWER[498]—an offshoot of the socialist Workers World Party—had attacked Israel in harsh terms and questioned its right to exist. Lerner had in the past criticised ANSWER 'for using antiwar demonstrations to put forward what he

---

493 Pollak, J. 2005. 'An own goal against the Palestinian cause'. *Mail & Guardian*, 13 June.
494 Kaufman, G. 2004. 'The case for sanctions against Israel.' *Guardian*, 12 July [online article]. URL: http://www.guardian.co.uk/comment/story/0,3604,1259087,00.html
495 Kochan, 572–3.
496 Kochan, 373.
497 Ibid, 111–2.
498 ANSWER - Act Now to Stop War and End Racism

consider[ed] anti-Israel propaganda'.[499] Lerner still encouraged his supporters to attend the rally, but the affair raised a warning flag about the collapsing boundary between criticism of Israel and antisemitism.

The South African case also had some additional unique features. One was the fact that Kasrils was leading criticism of Israel as a senior government minister and as a Jew. The closest analogue in any other case was Britain's Kaufman—but he was not a minister, and had maintained a lifelong connection to left-wing Zionism in any case, which Kasrils had not.[500] Kasrils's political prominence strengthened the force of his critique, and his Jewish origin was used both to give his views extra weight and to blunt charges of antisemitism. Indeed, in the South African case, perhaps more than any other, there was a conspicuous attempt by the government to distinguish between anti-Zionism and criticism of Israel on the one hand from antisemitism on the other. Kasrils was seen as the personification of that distinction, and was in a unique position to exert political pressure on the Jewish community and its institutions.

In addition to these similarities, there were also some important differences between different cases. Different countries, for example, experienced different degrees and kinds of antisemitism. Antisemitism in France was accompanied by a resurgence in anti-American sentiment, exacerbated by public dislike of US President George W Bush, hostility towards globalisation and harsh criticism of the American-led wars in Afghanistan and Iraq. The right-wing Front National of Jean-Marie Le Pen took full advantage of this situation—hostility toward Jews and America on the one hand, popular fear of violent Islamic extremism on the other—to score small but significant electoral gains in the 2002 presidential race that dislodged Socialist Prime Minister Lionel Jospin in the first round of ballots.[501]

Many French Jews were frustrated by what they perceived as the slow response of French leaders to the violence. 'Faced with an increasing number of press reports of violence', wrote Meir Waintrater, editor-in-chief of the French Jewish monthly *L'Arche*, 'some left-wing politicians, including members of the government, responded with simple denials.'[502] There were various reasons

---

499 Corn, D. 2003. 'The banning of Rabbi Lerner'. *The Nation*, 10 February [weblog]. URL: http://www.thenation.com/capitalgames/index.mhtml?bid=3&pid=385
500 Watt, N. 2002. 'MP accuses Sharon of "barbarism"'. *Guardian* 17 April [web article]. URL: http://www.guardian.co.uk/politics/2002/apr/17/houseofcommons.israel
501 Ibid, 379.
502 Waintrater, 382.

suggested for this slow response. One was the widespread sympathy on the left for Muslim African immigrants as a vulnerable community. Another was post-colonial guilt, which made it harder for some to criticise immigrants from former French colonies. Still another reason was electoral considerations, since there were more votes to be won (or lost) among roughly five million French Muslims than among about 600 000 French Jews.[503]

The new centre-right government of Prime Minister Jacques Chirac and Prime Minister Jean-Marie Raffarin, which took office in 2002, felt considerable pressure to clamp down on public violence, lest it be used by the far right to rally support.[504] By the time the government succeeded in rolling back the attacks, however, the damage had been done, and the relative comfort of post-war French Jewry had been punctured. In spite of communal solidarity, French Jews still felt increasingly isolated from the French political mainstream. There were some issues on which Jews could, and did, find common ground with Arabs and Muslims. These included common concerns about right-wing racism and xenophobia, as well as common concerns about new French legislation, effected in 2004, to ban religious garb—including headscarves and yarmulkes as well as crucifixes—from public schools. Yet hostility towards Israel among Arabs, Muslims and left-wing groups limited the scope of these alliances.[505]

In the mid 1990s, Pierre Birnbaum had described right-wing antisemitism in France as a force that encouraged Jews to stand apart from the rest of French society—a communitarianism, he said, that was reinforced from below by the increasing religiosity and insularity of French Jews.[506] To Birnbaum, the major consequence of 'the temptation toward communal isolation' was that the Republican ideal—'the universalistic practices as well as the emancipatory strategies adopted by generation after generation of Jews'—was being challenged by both internal and external pressures.[507]

A decade later, in the wake of the new antisemitism, Samuel Trigano described the problem in opposite fashion, contending that the new antisemitism, with its anti-Zionist character, was denying Jewish communal identity, forcing Jews to

---

503 Ibid, 382–3.
504 Ibid, 383.
505 Ibid, 389–90.
506 Birnbaum, P. 1995. *Jewish Destinies: Citizenship, State and Community in Modern France.* Trans. A Goldhammer. New York: Hill & Wang / Farrar, Straus & Giroux, 7–8.
507 Birnbaum 7–8.

abandon the post-war paradigm and return to the old, failed Republican model of assimilation.[508] French Jews, he said, faced a choice: 'Either they revert to the prewar mould of Jewish identity, in which their peoplehood is sacrificed to an indiscriminate definition of Judaism … or they can affirm their Jewish peoplehood by choosing to live more complete Jewish lives somewhere other than France.'[509]

There was some disagreement, then, about the nature of the challenge posed by antisemitism in France. Some saw it as a challenge to the emancipation of the revolution; others felt Jews were being forced back into its conformist strictures. Yet there was near-universal agreement that the new antisemitism presented a potential existential threat to the community. French Jews responded to the threat in a variety of ways. Some joined marches or letter-writing campaigns. Some emigrated to Israel. But many did not know what to do. 'Called on to endorse grossly exaggerated accusations against Israel or to disavow crimes that might well be imaginary,' Waintrater wrote, 'they chose the path of silence.'[510]

In Britain, while there were some physical attacks, much of the antisemitism experienced by British Jews tended to be political, expressed through the media, in partisan political debates and clashes among activists on university campuses. Some of the antisemitic rhetoric was of the 'traditional', right-wing variety; the failed libel case of Holocaust denier David Irving against American historian Deborah Lipstadt in 2000 (and failed appeal in 2001) was one example.[511] Much of the hatred, however, was spawned by militant Islam.

Concerns about the rise of anti-Israel rhetoric on the left were given weight by the occasional antisemitic outbursts of left-wing, anti-Israel British politicians. Labour MP Tam Dalyell, for example, claimed in May 2003 that Prime Minister Tony Blair was surrounded by 'a cabal of Jewish advisers'. Less than two weeks after the London bombings of July 2005, Labour mayor Ken Livingstone described Palestinian suicide bombings as the only means of defence against Israel.[512] He later called a Jewish journalist a 'concentration camp guard[513].'

---

508 Trigano, 59.
509 Ibid, 60.
510 Waintrater, 388.
511 Pallister, D. 2001. 'Irving's tag as "Holocaust denier" upheld'. *Guardian* 21 July [web article] URL: http://www.guardian.co.uk/uk/2001/jul/21/books.irving
512 'London mayor defends the use of Palestinian suicide bombers' 2005. *Ha'aretz*, 20 July [online article].
513 Muir, H. 2005. 'Livingstone faces inquiry over Nazi guard jibe at Jewish reporter.' *Guardian*, 12 February [online article]. URL: http://www.guardian.co.uk/media/2005/feb/12/pressandpublishing.londonpolitics

British media coverage of the Israeli–Palestinian conflict and the Iraq War played a significant role in shaping public debate, and in some cases fanned hostility toward Israel. The low point was the coverage of the Jenin battles of Israel's Operation Defensive Shield in April 2002. Palestinian allegations of a 'massacre' were faithfully reported by many British news outlets, some of which failed to apologise for the error.[514] Negative portrayals of Israel in the media were widely celebrated. A cartoon in the *Independent* depicting Ariel Sharon devouring a baby won a national award for 'Political Cartoon of the Year' from the Political Cartoon Society.[515] The *New Statesman* published a cover in January 2002 with a Jewish Star of David atop a prone Union Jack underneath the headline 'A kosher conspiracy?'[516]

The American experience of the new antisemitism was more moderate, with attacks occurring most visibly and frequently on university campuses. Antisemitic incidents at American university campuses rose for three straight years from 2000 to 2002—a development that was watched with great concern by Jewish communities.[517]

On many campuses, student groups opposed to Israeli policy started divestment campaigns—based on those used in the 1980s to convince some universities to divest from South Africa—in an attempt to isolate and stigmatise Israel. Nowhere were these campaigns successful, but they did create a tense and polarised atmosphere at many universities. The broader political effect of such campaigns may have been dampened somewhat after 9/11, when the US found itself squaring up to military and ideological enemies that were the enemies of Israel as well. Hostility toward the Jewish state was also checked by the emergence of evangelical Christian fundamentalists as staunch supporters of Israel—albeit supporters that some Jews were determined to keep at arm's length. These activists countered criticism of Israel in the media and gave Zionism a broader political base, which may have helped restrain antisemitism, at least indirectly.

The fractured and decentralised nature of American Jewry made formulating a coherent response to anti-Israel agitation more difficult. At the same time, however, it made dissent within the Jewish community less extraordinary. The

---

514 'Rules of war' 2002. *Economist*, 8 August.
515 '*Independent* cartoonist wins award' 2003. *Independent*, 27 November [online article]. URL: http://news.independent.co.uk/uk/media/story.jsp?story=467627
516 Pickett, W. 2003. 'Nasty or Nazi? The use of antisemitic topoi by the left-liberal media' in Iganski & Kosmin, *A New Antisemitism?*, 152–3.
517 The Stephen Roth Institute. 'US'. *Antisemitism Worldwide*. Annual report 2003/4. URL: http://www.tau.ac.il/Antisemitism/asw2003-4/usa.htm

views of Lerner's *Tikkun* may have been contentious, but few perceived them as threatening. In relation to the broader American public, the controversy over the Israeli–Palestinian conflict was barely a factor in shifting perceptions of Israel or Jews. A 2005 survey by the Anti-Defamation League of B'nai Brith confirmed that Americans favoured Israel over the Palestinians by wide margins and supported a continued strong US-Israel relationship.[518] Jewish fears about the potential violent consequences of public debates about Jews and Israel were largely unrealised. One such case was the controversy surrounding the Mel Gibson film *The Passion of the Christ*. Several Jewish groups criticised the film for its portrayal of Jews, and suggested it might lead to worsening interfaith relations, yet this reaction failed to materialise when the film opened to great box-office success despite Gibson's own antisemitic views.[519]

Perhaps the most important difference between the various cases is the way in which different Jewish communities and their leaders experienced antisemitism. In France, the rise in anti-Israel rhetoric and antisemitic attacks was so dramatic that Jews perceived them as an existential threat—not only to Israel but also to their Diaspora community. Jews often felt the need to defend themselves against prejudices that associated Jews with Israeli misdeeds, real and imagined. As Waintrater observed:

> *Simply invoking the name of Ariel Sharon conjured up the spectre of evil, and representatives of the Jewish community were suspected of collusion with the government identified by that name before they even opened their mouths to speak ... And the experience of the public representatives of the community was increasingly extended to every Jew—even down to schoolchildren who were called on by classmates and sometimes by teachers to account for 'the Sharon government's policies'.*[520]

In South Africa, similar pressure existed and was given an official imprimatur when it was promoted by Kasrils as a senior member of the ruling party and

---

518 Anti-Defamation League of B'nai Brith 2005. 'ADL poll shows strong American support for Israel continues'. Press release, 10 April. URL: http://www.adl.org/PresRele/IslME_62/4687_62.htm
519 The Stephen Roth Institute 2003/4. 'US'.
520 Ibid, 388.

the government. Despite the low number of violent incidents, the community's major organ expressed the belief that there was 'genuine cause for concern' for the safety and future of Jews in South Africa.[521] Ironically, survey data reported that South Africans in general supported Israel ahead of the Palestinians, as did most predominantly Christian countries in Africa.[522] However, the later resurgence of violent antisemitism may have proven that Jewish fears were well founded.

In Britain and the US, the situation was rather different. Pressure on Jews was exerted in portions of the British media and by politicians on the left, but was hardly overwhelming. And, in the US, the eagerness with which many legislators in Congress, the vast majority of them not Jewish, rushed to affirm support for Israel reassured American Jews in their own support for Israel. Indeed, vocal portions of American Jewry felt quite confident speaking out against Israeli policies—not just against the occupation but also, in 2004 and 2005, against Sharon's policy of disengagement, which was deeply unpopular among many Orthodox Jews. Jews were united in support of Israel but divided, sometimes deeply, over particular Israeli policies. Whereas Jews in South Africa and France felt perhaps (more strongly in the latter) that they had to trade Zionism for full acceptance into society, Jews in the US and Britain seemed to face such trade-offs only in certain spheres, such as in the academy or on the political left. The commercial success of anti-Israel books such as Jimmy Carter's *Palestine Peace Not Apartheid* and John J Mearsheimer and Stephen M Walt's *The Israel Lobby and US Foreign Policy* caused heated debates on university campuses but seemed to have no effect on general American attitudes towards Israel, which remained very positive.[523]

The differences in the experiences of Jewish communities during the rise of anti-Israel rhetoric and the 'new antisemitism' during the new *intifada* may have reflected underlying differences in the way different countries define citizenship and national identity. Both the US and Britain are liberal democracies with relatively amorphous and multicultural notions of national identity. American society is more decentralised and more successful than Britain at integrating immigrant communities. Both, however, shy away from the state imposition of identity and tend towards minimalist notions of citizenship, seeing it as a basic set of rights and obligations.

---

521 South African Jewish Report, Ibid.
522 Pew Research Center 2007. 'Global unease with major world powers: 47-nation pew global attitudes survey', 27 June [Online document]. URL: http://pewglobal.org/reports/pdf/256.pdf. 96.
523 Jewish Telegraph Agency 2007. 'Poll finds US support for Israel soaring'. *Jerusalem Post*, 7 May [online article]. URL: http://www.jpost.com/servlet/Satellite?cid=1178431587241&pagename=JPost%2FJPArticle%2FShowFull

South Africa and France, by contrast, are both 'statist' republics with strong central governments that see it as their duty to determine the identity of the citizen beyond simple rights and duties. In France, the ideal is of a universalistic, republican identity with racial, ethnic and religious differences relegated to the private sphere—though multiculturalism has begun to take root in recent decades. In South Africa, the idea of an overarching national identity is still a fresh one, but the state has claimed a great role in determining it. The ideal of a 'rainbow nation' of equal yet diverse groups, expressed often during the Mandela era, has retreated in the face of the 'Africanism' or 'African hegemony' of the Mbeki era, which views minorities as secondary to the racial majority. In both France and South Africa, Jews were forced to face a 'Jewish Question' about where they, as a minority, fit into the national whole. By contrast, Jews in Britain and the US were not facing a 'Jewish Question' about their relationship to the nation or the state. Rather, they faced a prejudice that was largely social and circumstantial in nature, confined to particular political and intellectual spheres.

The fact that South African Jews had to confront a 'Jewish Question' during the Kasrils affair relates directly to the new constraints of minority politics in South Africa. The apartheid government used threats and coercion to ensure the compliance of minority communities; Verwoerd's invocation of antisemitism was but one example. As was observed at the time, the NP was attempting to draw Jews, along with other minorities, into an ethnic *laager*. The post-apartheid government did not use threats or coercion, but the prospect of isolation. Manifestos such as the Kasrils declaration and the 'Home For All' campaign sought to pressure leaders of minority communities to demonstrate their allegiance to the ruling party's ideological worldview and policy programme, if not directly to the party itself. In the economic sphere, the ANC's programme of 'transformation' involved a series of 'charters' and 'codes of good practice' through which firms would demonstrate their commitment to policies of black economic empowerment (BEE). These charters and codes were voluntary, but non-compliance meant that companies would be at a disadvantage in competing for contracts in both the public and private sectors. Similarly, in civil society, interest groups like the TAC feared that they would receive less attention from the government if they failed to pay homage to the ANC. In place of the *laager*, then, the post-apartheid government sought to impose a kind of 'social contract' on minorities and on interest groups within civil society as well. The penalty for failure to join was political, social and economic isolation.

As for the Kasrils initiative itself, it was both a success and a failure. It failed, in that the declaration never gathered more than 300 signatures, as against the 13 000 signatures on the pro-Israel counter-petition. It never convinced a significant number of South African Jews to break with the Zionist beliefs of the mainstream. In terms of Kasrils's own personal ambitions, if his own political advancement had been his main goal—as some had claimed—then he can be said to have succeeded to some extent. After the 2004 general elections, Kasrils retained his Cabinet seat and moved to the Department of Intelligence, where he and the Board found themselves forging a new relationship. However, he failed to win re-election to the Central Committee of the South African Communist Party in 2007—owing largely to rivalries in the ANC succession race (see Epilogue)—and had to be co-opted back into the leadership structure.

The Kasrils initiative and the groups that formed in its wake failed to maintain their ideological coherence and were eventually overtaken by events. When the Israeli government announced its 'disengagement' policy of withdrawing soldiers and settlers from Gaza in 2003, and carried out the policy in 2005, neither Kasrils nor 'Not In My Name' formally responded, even though the policy conformed to some of what the Kasrils declaration had demanded. The only comment came from Ozinsky, who claimed that Israel's disengagement from Gaza was merely an excuse to expand settlements in the West Bank and surround Gaza with an impenetrable boundary (not knowing, apparently, that Gaza was already surrounded by such a boundary).[524]

Nevertheless, Kasrils's opinion on Middle East affairs continued to be sought, both at home and abroad, albeit somewhat less frequently than before. In April 2005, he was invited to address a conference of academics, diplomats and policymakers at a forum on the Israel-Palestinian conflict at Goedgedacht, near Cape Town.[525] His language moderated considerably, if temporarily. Kasrils returned to a more radical and activist line after the Second Lebanon War. This led him into a thicket of controversies: accusations of 'hate speech' in his

---

524 Ozinsky, M. 2005. Remarks at seminar, 'The apartheid wall: Palestine and beyond', Salt River, Cape Town, 28 July.
525 Kasrils, R. 2005. 'What hope for Middle East peace?' Speech at the Goedgedacht Forum, Western Cape, 6 April [online text]. URL: http://www.intelligence.gov.za/Speeches/WhatHope.htm

published articles; allegations that he supported Iran's nuclear programme; endorsements of and invitations to Hamas's leadership in Gaza; and questions about his speech at Birzeit University in the West Bank, among other contentious episodes. These public relations debacles may have convinced him to withdraw once more.

In any event, the effect of the Kasrils declaration on South African foreign policy turned out to be somewhat ambivalent. The government's policies towards the Israel-Palestinian conflict returned to a more even-handed posture in the latter half of 2004. The pendulum swung back again, however, amidst concerns about the government's apparent eagerness to establish itself as one of the key defenders of Iran's nuclear programme.[526] In 2007, when South Africa took up a temporary seat on the UN Security Council, it drew criticism by shielding autocratic governments—Zimbabwe, North Korea, Sudan, Myanmar, and Iran, to name a few—from international intervention, though it eventually supported sanctions against Iran.[527] Yet South Africa and the ANC remained committed, at least in principle, to the two-state solution to the Israeli–Palestinian conflict. President Thabo Mbeki even made a surprise visit to an Israeli Yom Ha'atzmaut (Independence Day) celebration in Durban in April 2007.[528]

Kasrils's effect on Jewish opinion was limited. Yet while Kasrils did not convince many Jews to desert Israel, he did convince Jewish leaders that the price of isolation from the ruling party and the government was too high to pay. The Board began to work diligently to cultivate its relations with senior members of the ANC. And while the Board certainly did not abandon Israel, it adopted a more discreet approach to defending Israel from criticism. One Board member said in an interview: 'The Board is focused on the best outcome for the Jewish people and Israel.' Another, however, commented that, in his own role on the Board, he had 'moved away from the case for Israel' and that he was 'not making the case for Israel or for Israeli actions'.

Some Board members defended the new approach as a sign of the maturation of Jewish politics in South Africa. One even described public debate and

---

[526] See Smillie, S. 2005. 'SA dismisses report of nuclear deal with Iran'. *Cape Times*, 8 November [online article]. URL: http://www.capetimes.co.za/index.php?fSectionId=271&fArticleId=2984862
[527] Kirchik, J. 2007. 'Going south'. *Azure*, 29 [online version]. URL: http://www.azure.org.il/magazine/magazine.asp?id=389
[528] *It's Almost Supernatural* 2007. 'Mbeki continues to surprise', 30 April [weblog entry]. URL: http://supernatural.blogs.com/weblog/2007/04/mbeki_continues.html

criticism as an old and outdated approach: 'We have achieved a better outcome today than the "old style" of antagonism and insult.' Others agreed, arguing that the Board's relationship with the democratic government was far better than its relationship had been with the apartheid regime. 'Before, the Board would pose for photographs, make friends, say "yes sir, no sir",' one interviewee argued. 'We never met to get something done. It was all just superficial. Today, we meet to get something done. It's a big difference.'

Some interviewees compared the Board's new approach to the lobbying methods used by pro-Israel organisations such as the American Israel Public Affairs Committee (AIPAC) in the US, widely regarded as one of the strongest and most effective lobbying organisations in Washington, DC. One explained: 'The DA attack on the Board was to some extent unfair. We're using the AIPAC strategy. You have to get whomever is in power on your side.' Others, however, were more critical. One interviewee described the new approach as 'a move to be more connected to the ANC, to become "Hofjude" [Jews at the medieval Court]'. Another speculated that some Board members may have confused their personal interests with those of the broader community they were meant to represent.

The Board, like other minority groups and interest groups, had chosen to become a 'lobbying' organisation because of the ANC's overwhelming strength. But that strength began to show cracks in 2005, as political rivalries within the ANC began to boil over the issue of succession. President Mbeki was due to step down as national president following the expiration of his second—and constitutionally final—term in 2009. According to party tradition, ANC and national Deputy President Jacob Zuma would move into Mbeki's position. But Zuma had rivals within the party—including Mbeki himself, who was contemplating retaining the presidency of the ANC at the ruling party's congress in 2007 even as he relinquished the presidency of the country two years later.

In June 2005, President Mbeki dismissed Zuma as South Africa's Deputy President over allegations of corruption in the government's controversial multibillion-rand arms deal. This only strengthened Zuma's popularity as his trial began in the Durban High Court, and pro-Mbeki and pro-Zuma factions formed at every level of the party and even within government departments, including the security services and the National Intelligence Agency under

Kasrils's administration. Kasrils himself was known to be in the Mbeki camp, as were many former ANC exiles. But many of the party's former 'in-ziles' and disaffected leftist interest groups, including Cosatu and the SACP, backed Zuma. Their support began to wane later in the year when Zuma was charged with rape and suspended from his party office as deputy president of the ANC. Zuma was acquitted in 2006, however, and the corruption case was temporarily withdrawn, sending his popularity to new heights. Mbeki loyalists such as Kasrils found themselves suddenly vulnerable.

The rivalries took their toll at the provincial and local levels. In June 2005, Rasool was ousted as the Western Cape provincial leader of the ANC by a so-called 'Africanist' faction. Led by James Ngculu and Mcebisi Skwatsha, the faction argued that, because the majority of ANC voters in the Western Cape were black, the leader of the party in the province should also be black and not coloured. Rasool was also damaged by his support for Mbeki; the 'Africanist' faction pledged its loyalty to Zuma. Ironically, one of the key ringleaders of this faction was Max Ozinsky, who overlooked a shared passion for the Palestinian cause in orchestrating Rasool's downfall.

A major risk of the Board's strategy became apparent: it could back one ANC leader, only to find itself isolated from a new leader who might emerge from the ANC's internal struggles. One Board member interviewed for this book described the marginalisation of Rasool, now a lame-duck premier, as 'frightening'. Indeed, the relationship that the Board had so carefully cultivated with Rasool was now virtually worthless, barring a dramatic reversal of the premier's political fortunes. One interviewee said the Board could simply cultivate relations with the Skwatsha faction if it took office. In practice, however, such rapid realignments may be difficult to achieve (Rasool was dismissed as premier in 2008.)

Another risk appeared in the form of old-style Jewish conspiracy theories, spun by the internal party antagonists in the Mbeki-Zuma fight. In late 2005, an anti-Mbeki e-mail hoax suggested the existence of a conspiracy against Jacob Zuma that involved Kasrils, Tony Leon, the Scorpions anti-crime unit and Israel's Mossad.[529] The e-mails, which were circulated among senior ANC members, quoted Kasrils as saying: 'What is wrong with me organising metings

---

529 Mde, V & Brown, K. 2005. 'Sinister anti-Zuma e-mails stoke tensions'. *Business Day*, 1, 25 November.

[sic] with Mossad since it is known I am a jew [sic]?'⁵³⁰ This hoax suggested that the Mbeki-Zuma split could lead to the political scapegoating of Jews, as has happened in other cases throughout history.

Yet another risk is that which was pointed out by Giliomee—the emergence of 'follower-less ethnic leaders'. If Jewish institutions are 'captured' by the ruling party, they may actually lose their ability to lobby effectively for the community's concerns. They may also risk losing their mandate and support from the community they are meant to represent. One interviewee claimed that Jewish leaders had convinced the government that the community is 'the X-factor in South African development', essential to South Africa's economic future. Whether this is true or not, and what it implies for the broader content of relations with the government into the future, remains to be seen.

It is clear is that the Board, like other minority and interest groups, continues to cultivate closer relations with the ANC in spite of the party's internal turmoil. What is unclear is whether the Board's current approach represents a viable strategy, and whether its leaders have considered the long-term possibility of political change in South Africa and its potential consequences.

It is impossible to know exactly how that change would happen—whether an opposition party would become strong enough to challenge for power at the national level, or whether the ANC itself would split into different parties based on rival factions, or some combination of both. In March 2006, the DA's Helen Zille won election to the position of Mayor of Cape Town, the first time since 1994 that an ANC government had been toppled through the ballot box. In May 2007, having survived several ANC challenges to her fragile coalition in the city council, Zille was elected the DA's new leader following the departure of Tony Leon. Picking up where her predecessor left off, she aimed to increase the DA's nationwide presence in black communities while retaining its traditional minority constituencies. These developments could herald the emergence of a new and more contested era in South African politics.

Alternatively, they could be the prelude to a more centralised and repressive age. There are warning signs emerging that this may be possible—that South

---

530 Sole, S & Dawes, N. 2005. 'Spy-war e-mails: What they really say.' *Mail & Guardian*, 15 December [online article]. URL: http://www.mg.co.za/articlePage.aspx?articleid=259263&area=/insight/insight__national/

Africa could follow the authoritarian path that has enticed so many emerging democracies in Africa and beyond. In late 2004, the ANC began introducing new proposals for constitutional amendments that would severely restrict the independence of the judiciary by giving the executive greater control over its affairs. It persisted with these proposals through 2005 and into 2006, despite protests from senior judges. And, regardless of the self-professed tolerance of the new government, it still shows severe hostility towards political opposition, whether in Parliament or in civil society. In 2007 President Mbeki fired his outspoken Deputy Health Minister, Nozizwe Madlala-Routledge, who had pushed for a stronger response to the HIV/Aids pandemic. He also suspended National Director of Public Prosecutions Vusi Pikoli after he issued a warrant for the arrest of national police commissioner Jackie Selebi, an Mbeki ally allegedly linked to the criminal underworld. Meanwhile, senior ANC and government officials continued to express frequent hostility towards the independent press.[531] South Africa is not yet a fully open democracy and there is the risk that it may even be moving back towards a more closed, centralised and race-conscious system.

It would seem that the Board has reckoned neither with the fact that national political change could happen nor with the possibility that such political change will have to happen if South Africa is to entrench and strengthen its democracy. The Kasrils affair may have helped to encourage this myopia.

At the same time, Kasrils may have performed a great service to the community by increasing the boldness of dissenting voices. The Kasrils initiative, for all its failings, succeeded in reviving the anti-Zionist critique that had lain dormant within South African Jewry since 1948. In the wake of the Kasrils declaration, critics of the Israeli occupation arguably enjoyed somewhat greater tolerance in the community than they had before.

Kasrils had—perhaps unwittingly—created space for new, moderate voices to emerge. The new moderates included several former anti-apartheid activists who had refused to sign the declaration, frustrating Kasrils's attempt to draw parallels between Israel and apartheid. Other moderates were those who disagreed with

---

531 Da Silva, I S. 2007. 'South Africa: ANC media policy under scrutiny'. *Bizcommunity.com*, 25 October [online article]. URL: http://www.bizcommunity.com/Article/196/15/19170.html

the declaration but argued vehemently in defence of Kasrils's right to state his views. Some of those who had signed the declaration later dissented, complaining of Kasrils's 'grandstanding'. Several attended house meetings in Cape Town in a short-lived attempt to organise a peace movement outside of the 'Not In My Name' initiative. Jewish Voices SA was reported to have distanced itself from the tactics of the Kasrils campaign.[532] As erratic and ephemeral as these moderate voices sometimes were, they demonstrated the potential for increased political diversity on Israel-related issues within the Jewish community as Jews began to search for their place, not with one side or another but within a broadening spectrum of views on Israel and other issues.

That diversity may hold the key to the political future for South African Jewry. During the Kasrils affair, Jewish leaders struggled to deal with internal dissent and external challenges at the same time. But the community's greatest successes occurred when institutions besides the Board—such as the SAZF and the American Jewish Committee—played a role, and when independent voices from the community stepped forward to defend its views. Sometimes the Board supported these alternative efforts; sometimes it attempted to discourage or co-opt them. But they were essential to the achievement of the Board's aims. By encouraging greater internal debate—not just on Israel, but on broader political and religious matters—and by involving multiple institutions in tackling common problems, the Board may perform its leadership function in the community far more effectively in future.

The corollary lesson for other minority groups and interest groups is that allowing for greater internal diversity may provide greater leverage in policy debates in South Africa's single-party-dominant democracy. Centralised leadership is necessary, and close relationships with the ruling party can be useful, but the combination can also lend itself to co-option. Minority groups are strengthened when they develop a diverse range of institutions. Interest groups are strengthened when they lobby a diverse spectrum of political parties. And diverse relationships between diverse institutions reinforce a robust social structure that looks more like a web and less like a pyramid, one that is more democratic and less hierarchical.

---

532 Isaacs, D. 2004. 'Finding a liberal voice in Jewish community'. *South African Jewish Report*, 12 March.

For now, the future of the South African Jewish community, like that of South Africa itself, remains cautiously optimistic. The Kasrils affair rocked the foundations of South African Jewry, but it may eventually prove to have strengthened the institutions and the viability of this long-established, prosperous and patriotic community. The long-term question remains whether South African Jewry will seek accommodation as a somewhat protected and detached minority within an increasingly centralised polity and unequal, divided society, or whether South African Jews will help contribute to the fulfilment of the Constitution's vision of a free, liberal and equal society fundamentally different from that which came before.

EPILOGUE

THE ZUMA ERA

Two months after the manuscript of this book was completed in November 2007, South African politics went through a major change. At the ANC's 52nd National Conference, held in Polokwane from 16-20 December 2007, the delegates elected Jacob Zuma over incumbent Thabo Mbeki as president of the organisation. They also voted many of Mbeki's allies off the ANC's National Executive Committee (NEC).

One of those who lost was Kasrils. He was deeply resented by Zuma loyalists who accused him of manoeuvring to undermine their candidate.[533] Kasrils had apparently expected that Mbeki would be re-elected and that he himself would be returned to the NEC. At the conference, he also submitted a motion that the ANC boycott the 'Zionist state of Israel'.[534] But his days in the ANC's senior leadership were over.

On 21 September 2008, Mbeki was forced by the new ANC leadership to resign as president of the country – a development that had hardly been imaginable less than a year before. The man at the core of the ANC's 'democratic centralism' was suddenly gone from the political arena. Zuma would come to power in the 2009 elections unless an opposition coalition could be assembled to thwart his ambitions.

The ascent of Jacob Zuma worried many Jews, as well as other South Africans. Zuma, a practising polygamist with a rudimentary education, was well liked but drew his support from the ANC's radical left and its traditionalist right. His reputation

---

[533] Monare, M. 2006. 'Kasrils denies bid to bring down Zuma'. *The Star*, 3, 12 May.
[534] South African Press Association 2007. 'Kasrils casts his vote', 18 December [online article]. URL: http://www.int.iol.co.za/index.php?set_id=1&click_id=6&art_id=nw20071218104329570C319651

had been clouded by accusations of corruption and a criminal trial for rape (he was acquitted of the latter charge and charges of corruption were dismissed on procedural grounds in September 2008). He was, essentially, a populist with uncertain views.

On the one hand, Zuma's rise represented an opening of democratic possibilities. As a Zulu, he punctured the Xhosa dominance of the ANC hierarchy. He also relieved the ANC of Mbeki's stifling authoritarian leadership. At the same time, his supporters challenged the independence of the judiciary and opposed South Africa's stable, market-friendly macroeconomic policies, causing worry among investors.

In June 2008, ANC Youth League President Julius Malema announced that his party would 'Kill for Zuma', provoking alarm at home and abroad.

Zuma's views on Israel were thought to be influenced by the ANC's left wing, which included the Palestine Solidarity Committee. In June 2007, in a message to the End Israeli Occupation Campaign, Zuma equated Israel with both apartheid South Africa and Nazi Germany:

> *We who have experienced the racism of Apartheid colonialism will fail in our international duty if we do not strongly condemn the Israeli government and its many international backers for the brutal oppression of the Palestinian people ... Israel has ignored all international laws and conventions, which were put in place after the atrocities of the Second World War to prevent the very type of situations that exist in Israel today.*[535]

South African Jewish Board of Deputies Chairman Zev Krengel—architect of the community's new relationship with the ANC—and Chief Rabbi Warren Goldstein both attended the Polokwane conference. Feeling the need to reassure the community about the outcome of the ANC election, and to defend their strategy of close engagement with the ruling party, Krengel released the following message to members of the Jewish community:

> *I have just returned from Polokwane, where I attended the ANC conference as an observer. Both Chief Rabbi Goldstein and myself were warmly*

---

[535] Quoted in Kransdorff, M & Magid, S. 2008. 'Is Zuma good for the Jews?' *It's Almost Supernatural*, 6 January [weblog]. URL: http://supernatural.blogs.com/weblog/2008/01/is-zuma-good-fo.html

welcomed, and the fact that representatives of the Jewish community were present at this important event was clearly much appreciated. The conference itself resulted in major leadership changes within the ruling party. The long-term implications of this for the country as a whole will obviously only start to become apparent in the course of time. What is nevertheless extremely encouraging is that the change was accomplished in a fair, transparent and scrupulously democratic manner. No matter which side one might have supported, it could not be denied that what one saw at all times was a vibrant democracy in action. (Tokyo Sexwale even remarked to me that the robust give-and-take of opposing views reminded him of Israel's Knesset).

In short, a majority of delegates were dissatisfied with the current party leadership and, following open and extensive debate, voted to replace it. This is a sign of a normal, healthy democratic society, and let us never forget how few countries in the world are similarly in a position to bring about so fair and peaceful a transition.

Naturally, as is always the case with the passing of the old guard and the ushering in of the new, there will be a degree of uncertainty over what the future holds. I would like to urge all members of our community to keep things in perspective and give the incoming ANC leadership—who in all likelihood will in due course become the leadership of the country as a whole—a chance to find its feet and prove itself.

As always, the SA Jewish Board of Deputies will seek to engage with the government of the day, as well as the leadership of the ANC, in order to represent the interests of the Jewish community. We congratulate the newly elected office bearers of the ANC and look forward to working with them in the future.[536]

Despite Krengel's reassurances, the effects of a Zuma presidency on the South African Jewish community have yet to be seen. Whether or not Krengel is correct that 'few countries in the world are similarly in a position to bring about so fair and peaceful a transition', the fact is that democratic changes of power are the norm in most countries in which Jews live, and to which South African Jews emigrate.

---

536 Krengel, Z. 2007. 'Open letter to the Jewish community.', 19 December [e-mail].

As Kasrils prepared to leave the political scene, the Board's policy 'to engage with the government of the day, as well as the leadership of the ANC' remained firmly entrenched. Whether South African politics becomes more open, more closed, or more chaotic, Jewish leadership has been 'tamed' by the Kasrils affair. It may be that those Jews who seek to play a more active political role will do so—as ever—on their own.

They will do so in the face of great challenges, to the Jewish community and to South Africa in general.[537] The rise of antisemitism is again a pressing concern. A study released in September 2008 indicated that 31 per cent of South Africans have a 'very unfavourable' opinion of Jews and 15 per cent have a 'somewhat unfavourable' view. At the same time, the community is struggling once again to deal with difficult debates about Israel. In July 2008, left-wing Jews organised a brief tour of the West Bank for a group of South African human rights activists. The delegation issued strong condemnations of Israeli policy, which were in turn met by vociferous criticism in the Jewish community. The 'eighth question' of Jewish politics remains a potent symbol of a community still struggling, alongside other minorities, to secure its place in the fragile South African body politic.

---

[537] Pew Research Center 2008. 'Unfavorable Views of Jews and Muslims on the Increase in Europe'. 17 September [web document]. URL: http://pewglobal.org/reports/pdf/262.pdf

APPENDIX

THE KASRILS DECLARATIONS

October Version:
ADDRESS TO THE NATIONAL ASSEMBLY, CAPE TOWN
BY MR RONNIE KASRILS, MP
MINISTER OF WATER AFFAIRS AND FORESTRY
23 OCTOBER 2001[538]

1. The Fundamental Causes of the Conflict:
Successive Israeli governments and the world Zionist movement have consistently denounced their critics as anti-semites and blamed the Palestinians for the failure to reach a negotiated settlement. We emphatically reject these assertions. We do not dispute that sectors of the Palestinian population have resorted to terror and we condemn indiscriminate killings of civilians from whatever quarter. Yet this is not the root cause of the on-going violence. The fundamental cause of the conflict is Israel's occupation of Palestine, and the suppression of the Palestinian struggle for national self-determination.

---

538 [Online text]. URL: http://www.dwaf.gov.za/Communications/MinisterSpeeches/Kasrils/2001/Address%20to%20 National%20Assembly%20about%20Israeli%20Government%20on%2023%20Oct%2001.doc

In November 2000 the Israeli cabinet considered a document prepared by the Prime Minister's office on alleged transgressions by the Palestinians. The Acting Foreign Minister, Shlomo Ben-Ami, opposed the distribution of the document on the grounds that no one would be surprised that a people under occupation had failed to honour its agreements with its occupier: 'Accusations made by a well-established society about how a people it is oppressing is breaking rules to attain its rights do not have much credence'.

Henry Siegman, former Executive Director of the American Jewish Congress, observes correctly that this statement 'goes to the very heart of the conflict and extracts the poison buried there'. The establishment of the State of Israel in 1948 inflicted a great injustice on the Palestinian people, compounded by the subsequent Israeli rule of the Occupied Territories and denial of the legitimate claims of the Palestinian refugees.

A recognition of the fundamental causes of the on-going violence does not constitute antisemitism. Nor does it amount to a denial of Israel's right to exist. Rather, it constitutes an urgent call on the Israeli government to redress injustice and satisfy legitimate claims, without which peace negotiations will fail.

2. The Holocaust Compels us to Speak Out:

All Jews live in the shadow of the Holocaust. For some of them, the overriding lesson is that survival is the highest morality. They seek to justify Israel's intransigence in peace negotiations and application of excessive force against the Palestinians on these grounds. Other Jews believe that the Holocaust compels them to support justice and freedom from persecution for all people, regardless of their nationality, ethnicity or religion. We stand firmly in this camp.

3. Repression Intensifies Resistance:

After the suffering experienced by Jews in Europe during Nazism we are utterly appalled at the ruthless security methods employed by the Israeli government against Palestinians. These include the deployment of bull-dozers, machine guns, tanks and helicopter gunships and the use of lethal force, as a matter of policy, even against civilians armed with stones and slings; targeted assassination of opponents, the doctrine of 'collective punishment' of Palestinian communities, demolition of homes and olive groves, the stringent curfews, and roadblocks making normal life impossible; the ritual of control and humiliation. These intolerable strategies together with the growing number of provocative Jewish settlements in the West Bank, undermine the legitimacy of the Israeli government and its negotiating position and give rise to intensified resistance that will continue to grow.

We take note of the fact-finding report by members of South Africa's Parliament who visited the Middle East in July 2001. Their report observes: 'It becomes difficult, particularly from a South African perspective, not to draw parallels with the oppression experienced by Palestinians under the hand of Israel and the oppression experienced in South Africa under Apartheid rule'.

We are committed to justice and freedom for pragmatic as well as ethical reasons. Oppression almost always gives rise to rebellion and thereby threatens the security of the oppressor. Repression and reprisals in response to rebellion provide no relief. They only deepen, broaden and prolong the cycle of violence and counter-violence. The notion that security can be achieved through reliance on force is demonstrably false as the struggle against Apartheid testified.

4. The Security of Israelis and Palestinians is Inseparable:

We understand the fears of Jews in Israel and their longing for security. The security of Israelis and Palestinians, however, is inescapably intertwined. Neither group will be secure for as long as the other is insecure. There is consequently no viable alternative to a negotiated settlement that is just, that recognises both Palestine and Israel as fully independent sovereign states, and that provides for peaceful coexistence and co-operation between these states. It is only on this basis that peace and security can be achieved. Shimon Peres recently stated: 'We want to see an independent Palestinian State successful, flourishing. We think that the better the Palestinians will have it, the better neighbour we shall have'. We fully agree, but it is incumbent on Israel, the dominant force and power over the Palestinians to demonstrate its serious intent in this respect.

What is more if Israel is to become a respected society it must grant full, equal rights to all who dwell within its borders—Christians, Muslims and non-believers alike who are victims of discriminatory treatment and laws.

5. A Call for Peace and Security:

Israel carries a great responsibility to improve the dangerous state of affairs, in the Middle East and internationally, by recognising the legitimate rights of the Palestinian people and creating the basis for peace and stability.

We fully support the joint call to the international community by Presidents Bouteflika of Algeria and Mbeki of South Africa in October 2001 to ensure that peace be restored to the region through dialogue and negotiations. We support their call for the withdrawal of the Israeli forces from the Palestinian Territories.

We call on South Africans of Jewish descent, and Jews everywhere, to raise their voices and join with all governments and people in support of justice for Palestine and peace and security for all in the Holy Land. This is a vital step towards reducing the grave threat of international disorder and anarchy.

6. As an Immediate Step toward Peace We Call on the Government of Israel:

- To resume and sustain negotiations with the Palestinian authority in good faith.
- To conduct negotiations within the framework of the relevant resolutions of the United Nations Security Council, and of Resolution 242 of 1967 in particular.
- To conduct its security operations with restraint and in accordance with international humanitarian law.
- To work in partnership with the Palestinian leaderships to build a lasting peace on the basis of reconciliation.

November/December Version:
DECLARATION OF CONSCIENCE ON THE ISRAELI–PALESTINIAN CONFLICT BY SOUTH AFRICANS OF JEWISH DESCENT[539]

We the undersigned are compelled to express ourselves on the Israeli–Palestinian Conflict as a matter of conscience and concern for the safety and well being of the Israeli and Palestinian Peoples and for world peace.

---

539 [Online text]. URL: http://www.ajds.org.au/intifada/sa.htm

1. The Fundamental Causes of the Conflict

We assert that the fundamental causes of the current conflict are Israel's suppression of the Palestinian struggle for national self-determination and its continued occupation of Palestinian lands.

We do not dispute that certain sectors of the Palestinian population have resorted to terror and we condemn indiscriminate killings of civilians from whatever quarter. Yet this is not the root cause of the problem.

The state of Israel was founded as a homeland for the persecuted Jews of Europe. It came into being as a result of a war of independence. The action of the British in assuming that Palestine was theirs by colonial mandate to dispose of, inflicted a great injustice on the Palestinian people. This was compounded by the subsequent Israeli rule of the Occupied Territories and the denial of the legitimate claims of the Palestinian refugees.

Recognition of the fundamental causes of the ongoing violence does not constitute antisemitism. Rather, it constitutes an urgent call on the Israeli government to redress injustice, uphold human rights, and satisfy legitimate claims, without which peace negotiations will fail. Nor does it amount to a denial of Israel's right to exist. It recognises that such negotiations require that the Western Powers, the Arab States and the Non-aligned States through the aegis of the United Nations guarantee the mutual security of the state of Israel and the state of Palestine.

2. Our History Compels Us to Speak Out

All Jews live in the shadow of the Holocaust. For some of us, the lesson of that tragedy has been that survival is the highest morality. For others of us, the lesson is that Jews must support justice and freedom from persecution for all people. Many feel torn between these two. But we believe that Jewish survival and the fulfillment of Palestinian national aspirations are not mutually exclusive goals. We believe that the path forward is through championing the legitimate desires of the Palestinian people, and we reject an approach that is guided by existential fear and which sacrifices principles of justice in the name of collective survival.

3. Repression Intensifies Resistance

In light of the suffering that we Jews have experienced ourselves, especially in the past century, we object to the ruthless security methods employed by the Israeli government against Palestinians. These include the deployment of bulldozers, tanks, helicopter gunships, and fighter planes; the use of lethal force, as a matter of policy, even against civilians armed with stones and slings; the targeted assassination and extra-judicial killing of political leaders and activists; the 'collective punishment' of Palestinian communities; the demolition of homes, destruction of farms, and uprooting of olive groves; and the stringent curfews and roadblocks that make normal life impossible and create a daily ritual of control and humiliation. These intolerable practices, together with the expansion of illegal Israeli settlements, invite condemnation of the Israeli government and give rise to further resistance against it.

In November 2000 the Israeli cabinet considered a document prepared by the Prime Minister's office on alleged transgressions by the Palestinians. The Acting Foreign Minister, Shlomo Ben-Ami, opposed the distribution of the document on the grounds that no one would be surprised that a people under occupation had failed to honor its agreements with its occupier: 'Accusations made by a well-established society about how a people it is oppressing is breaking rules to attain its rights do not have much credence.'

We take note of the fact-finding report by members of South Africa's Parliament who visited the Middle East in July 2001. The report observes: 'It becomes difficult, particularly from a South African perspective, not to draw parallels with the oppression experienced by Palestinians under the hand of Israel and the oppression experienced in South Africa under apartheid rule.'

We are committed to justice and freedom for pragmatic as well as ethical reasons. Oppression almost always gives rise to rebellion and thereby threatens the security of the oppressor. Repression and reprisals in response to rebellion provide no relief. They only deepen, broaden and prolong the cycle of violence and counter-violence. The notion that security can be achieved through reliance on force is demonstrably false, as the struggle against apartheid testified.

The struggle against apartheid also demonstrated that successful resistance to oppression depends on a coherent non-violent strategy alongside the armed struggle. Palestinian intellectual and activist Edward Said recently wrote: 'The answer to our needs is in principled resistance, well-organised civil disobedience against military occupation and illegal settlement, and an education system that promotes co-existence.' We also note that the key to successful resistance in South Africa was a commitment in good faith by the resistance movement to the suspension of the armed struggle once negotiations had begun. This commitment has also recently been made by the Irish Republican Army in Northern Ireland.

We note that Palestinian Authority Chairman Yasser Arafat has repeatedly condemned terrorism and we call on him to pursue every effort to end terrorist acts committed by some sectors of the Palestinian population. President Mbeki has provided moral guidance by stating that 'no circumstances whatsoever can ever justify resort to terrorism'. We note that Chairman Arafat is only able to rule with great difficulty in the Palestinian areas and hope that the situation in the Occupied Territories improves to the point where the Palestinian leadership can offer security guarantees to the Israeli people. But this will be impossible to achieve in the context of current Israeli policies—especially the expansion of settlements, the aggressive and pointless reprisals, and the collective punishment of the Palestinian people for individual acts of terror.

4. The Security of Israelis and Palestinians is Inseparable

We understand the fears of Jews in Israel and their longing for security. The security of Israelis and Palestinians, however, is inseparably intertwined. Neither group will be secure as long as the other is insecure. There is consequently no alternative to a negotiated settlement that is just, that recognises both Palestine and Israel as fully independent sovereign states, and that provides for peaceful coexistence and co-operation between these states. It is only on this basis that peace and security can be achieved. Shimon Peres recently stated: 'We want to see an independent Palestinian state successful, flourishing. We think that the better the Palestinians have it, the better neighbour we shall have.' We fully agree, and stress that it is incumbent on Israel, the dominant force and power over the Palestinians, to demonstrate its serious intent in this respect.

We also call attention to the insecure status of Palestinians and non-Jews living within Israel's 1948 boundaries. We insist that Israel take steps to guarantee the full and equal rights of all who dwell within its borders—Jews and non-Jews alike.

5. A Call For Peace and Security

Israel carries a great responsibility to improve the dangerous state of affairs, in the Middle East and internationally, by recognising the legitimate rights of the Palestinian people and creating the basis for peace and stability.

We fully support the joint call to the international community by President Bouteflika of Algeria and President Mbeki of South Africa in October 2001 to ensure that peace be restored to the region through dialogue and negotiations. We support their call for the withdrawal of the Israeli forces from the Palestinian Territories.

We call on South Africans of Jewish descent, and Jews everywhere, to raise their voices and join with all governments and people in support of justice for Palestine and peace and security for all in the Holy Land. This is a vital step towards reducing the grave threat of international disorder and anarchy which the September 11 terrorism in the USA has so horrifically demonstrated.

6. As an Immediate Step Toward Peace, We Call on the Government of Israel:

- To resume and sustain negotiations with the Palestinian Authority in good faith.
- To conduct negotiations within the framework of the relevant resolutions of the United Nations—Resolutions 242 and 338 in particular—and expanding on the proposals tabled at negotiations in early 2001.
- To conduct its security operations with restraint and in accordance with humanitarian law.
- To work in partnership with the Palestinian leadership and the international community to build a lasting peace on the basis of reconciliation and realising the solution of two independent states living side by side in friendship and cooperation.

BIBLIOGRAPHY

Abrahams, E. 2004. Speech at Watsonia sports ground, Athlone, Cape Town, 21 March. *Voice of the Cape*. Radio broadcast. Unpublished transcript.
Adam, H & Moodley, K. 2005. *Seeking Mandela: Peacemaking between Israelis and Palestinians*. Johannesburg: Witwatersrand University Press.
Adler, T. 1978. 'Lithuania's diaspora: The Johannesburg Jewish Workers' Club, 1942–1948'. *Journal of Southern African Studies*, 6, 1, 70–92.
African National Congress 1994. *Reconstruction and Development Programme (RDP) White Paper*. Discussion document. September. URL: http://www.anc.org.za/ancdocs/policy/white.html
African National Congress 1997. 'Nation-forming and nation-building: The national question in South Africa'. ANC discussion document, July [online text]. URL: http://www.anc.org.za/ancdocs/discussion/nation.html
African National Congress 2004. 'Tony Leon challenged to resign'. Press statement, 23 February [online archive]. URL: http://www.anc.org.za/ancdocs/pr/2004/pr0223b.html
African National Congress 2007. 'Palestinian solidarity: Call to mobilize against Israeli occupation'. *ANC Today*, 25 May [online article]. URL: http://www.anc.org.za/ancdocs/anctoday/2007/at20.htm#art1
Agence France-Presse 1998. 'With Sharon's encouragement, settlers seize another West Bank hill.' 16 November.
Aggrieved Orthodox Jew (pseudonym) 1995. 'Chief Rabbi charged with political expediency.' *South African Jewish Times* letter, 21, 24 February.
Akhalwaya, A. 1993. 'A love–hate relationship: Jews and Muslims in South Africa'. *The Jewish Quarterly*, 17–9, Spring.
Anti-Defamation League of B'nai Brith 2005. 'ADL poll shows strong American support for Israel continues'. Press release, 10 April. URL: http://www.adl.org/PresRele/IslME_62/4687_62.htm
Apfel, S. 2001. 'Can there be Jewish anti-Semites?' *South African Jewish Report*, 7, 9 November.

Associated Press 2002. 'U.N. report: No massacre in Jenin'. *USA Today* 1 August [web article] URL: http://www.usatoday.com/news/world/2002-08-01-unreport-jenin_x.htm

Auerbach, F. 1997. 'Should we apologise? South African Jewish community responses to apartheid'. *Jewish Affairs*, Autumn.

Auerbach, F. 2001. 'Demonising the other side'. *South African Jewish Report*, 6, 16 November.

Bagraim, M. 2004. 'Above Board: Board ready to meet CEIRP issues'. *South African Jewish Report*, 2, 2 July.

Bagraim, M. 2004. 'Above Board: Moderation prevails at CT UN conference'. *South African Jewish Report*, 2, 9 July.

Bagraim, M. 2004. 'Above Board: Reiterating board's view'. *South African Jewish Report*, 5, 10 September.

Bagraim, M. 2004. 'Above Board: United in fighting fundamentalism'. *South African Jewish Report*, 2, 27 August.

Bagraim, M. 2004. 'All about lekhotla and ubuntu'. *South African Jewish Report*, 2, 24 September.

Bagraim, M. 2004. 'Friends wherever they can be found'. *South African Jewish Report* 14, 22 October.

Bagraim, M. 2004. 'Govt misses point'. *South African Jewish Report*, 2, 5 March.

Bagraim, M. 2004. 'Guard against being sidelined'. *South African Jewish Report*, 2, 30 April.

Bagraim, M. 2004. 'SAJBD's difficult tightrope'. *South African Jewish Report*, 10, 3 September.

Bagraim, M. 2004. 'Politics of engagement' lauded.' *South African Jewish Report*, 2, 29 October.

Bagraim, M. 2004/5 'A board perspective and a personal glimpse of recent months'. *Cape Jewish Chronicle*, 5, December/January.

Bagraim, M. 2005. 'Don't incite a lone wolf'. *South African Jewish Report*, 2, 3 June.

Bagraim, M. 2005. 'Home for all indeed'. *Cape Times*, 28 April.

Bagraim, M 2005. 'MJC vitriol an eye-opener'. *South African Jewish Report*, 2, 10 June.

Bagraim, M. 2005. 'National chairman's message'. South African Jewish Board of Deputies' 43rd National Conference programme, 7, August.

Bagraim, M. 2005. 'This memorandum wrongly addressed'. *South African Jewish Report*, 2, 27 May.

Bagraim, M. 2005. Letter to Tony Leon. 20 January.

Bagraim, M. 2006. 'Mbeki and Israel'. *Cape Times*, 13 January.

Bagraim, M. 2006. 'The Palestinians have no Freedom Charter'. *Sunday Times*, 16, 15 January.

Bailey, C. 2006. 'Board dissociates itself from Leon e-mail'. *Cape Argus*, 7, 15 May.

Baldauf, S. 2007. 'Murder of a reggae star spurs reflection in South Africa'. *Christian Science Monitor*, 26 October [online article]. URL: http://www.csmonitor.com/2007/1026/p04s01-woaf.html

Barrell, H. 2000. 'Rasool's brothers linked to anti-Semitic poster'. *Mail & Guardian*, 24 November [online article]. URL: http://www.mg.co.za/articledirect.aspx?articleid=162924&area=%2farchives__print_edition%2f

Barron, C. 2002. 'Not In My Name'. *Fairlady*, 38, 22 May.

Baruch, I. 2007. 'Economic and diplomatic boycotts of Israel are destructive and misguided'. *Cape Times*, 9, 25 June.

Baruch, I. 2007. 'SA needs to know too'. *Cape Times*, 10, 3 July.

Bastos, M. 2002. 'Muslim anti-Zionism and antisemitism in South Africa since the Second World War, with special reference to Muslim news/views'. Unpublished MA dissertation. University of Cape Town.

Battersby, J & Gordin J. 2001. 'Ronnie Kasrils launches declaration of conscience'. *Sunday Independent* 1–2, 9 December.

BBC News 2006. 'France lifts state of emergency'. 4 January [web article] URL: http://news.bbc.co.uk/2/hi/europe/4576430.stm

Belling, M. 2002. 'S. African rabbi blasts pro-Palestinian Jewish politico'. *Jewish Bulletin News of Northern California*, 3 May [web article]. URL: http://www.jewishsf.com/bk020503/ip17a.shtml

Belling, S. 2005. 'MJC picks fight on spurious grounds'. *South African Jewish Report*, 8, 27 May.

Berger, M. 2001. 'Of rhetoric and resistance'. *Mail & Guardian*, 21, 14 December.

Bernstein, E. 1968. 'A bird's-eye view of South African Jewry today'. *South African Jewry (1967–68 edition)*, ed L Feldberg. Johannesburg: Fieldhill. Reprinted by South African Jewish Board of Deputies c. 1975

Birnbaum, P. 1995. *Jewish Destinies: Citizenship, State and Community in Modern France*. Trans. A Goldhammer. New York: Hill & Wang / Farrar, Straus & Giroux.

Bordiss, B et al. 2001. 'Kasrils: We stand by him'. *The Citizen*, 21 November.

Bordiss, B et al. 2001. 'Support for Kasrils' stand'. *South African Jewish Report*, 8, 23 November.

Bordiss, B et al. 2004. 'Tribute to Yasser Arafat'. *South African Jewish Report*, 14, 19 November.

Bosch, M. 2007. 'S. African reggae star's murder puts focus on crime'. Reuters, 19 October [online article]. URL: http://www.canada.com/ottawacitizen/news/arts/story.html?id=b152651f-7702-4270-af37-7dedc98a04e3&k=80440

Bradlow, E. 1978. *Immigration to the Union, 1910–1948: Policies and Attitudes.* Unpublished PhD dissertation. University of Cape Town.

Brodovcky, N. 2001. 'Not In My Name: Ronnie Kasrils launch of declaration'. Transcript and notes of presentation, District Six Museum, Cape Town, 7 December.

Brother Mangash 2002. Speech at Vygieskraal stadium, Athlone, Cape Town, South Africa. 21 April.

'Capetonians flock to public meeting' 1990. *Cape Jewish Chronicle*, 1, April.

Chazan, N. 1987. 'Israeli perspectives on the Israel–South Africa relationship'. *Institute of Jewish Affairs, London: Research Report*, nos 9 & 10, December.

Clegg, J. 2003. Personal communication with the author. 31 October.

Constitutional Court of South Africa. *Minister of Health v. Treatment Action Campaign*, CCT 8/02 (2002).

Corn, D. 2003. 'The banning of Rabbi Lerner'. *The Nation*, 10 February [weblog]. URL: http://www.thenation.com/capitalgames/index.mhtml?bid=3&pid=385

'Declaration of conscience giant step to dialogue' 2001. Editorial. *Sunday Independent*, 9 December.

Da Silva, I S. 2007. 'South Africa: ANC media policy under scrutiny'. *Bizcommunity.com*, 25 October [online article]. URL: http://www.bizcommunity.com/Article/196/15/19170.html

Davis, D. 2005. 'Listen to the many Jewish voices'. *South African Jewish Report*, 8, 9 December.

Davis, D. 2005. 'SA Jewish Board of Deputies (Cape Council) Chairman's Report: 2004–2005'. Presented at the annual conference of the Cape Council of the South African Jewish Board of Deputies, Cape Town, 18 September.

'Declaration of conscience challenges roots of mistrust' 2001. *ANC Today*, 7 December [online newsletter]. URL: http://www.anc.org.za/ancdocs/anctoday/2001/at46.htm#art1

DellaPergola, S & Dubb, A A. 1988. 'South African Jewry: A sociodemographic profile' in *American Jewish Year Book 1988*, eds D Singer & R R Seldin, vol. 88. 66–7. New York: American Jewish Committee.

Derfner, L. 2005. 'New Jews in a new South Africa'. *Jerusalem Post*, 22 September.

Dershowitz, A. 2005. *The Case for Peace: How the Arab–Israeli Conflict can be Resolved*. Hoboken, NY: Wiley.

Dubb, A A & Shain, M. 1993. 'South Africa' in *American Jewish Year Book 1993*, eds D Singer & R R Seldin, vol. 93. New York: American Jewish Committee.

Ebrahim, E I. 2001. Speech in the National Assembly, Parliament of South Africa, Cape Town. 23 October. *Debates of the National Assembly* no. 19 (23 to 26 October 2001): 6836.

'Emigration drops dramatically'. 2005. *South African Jewish Report*, 1, 2 September.

Fabricius, P. 2006. 'Kasrils triggers seminar flutter'. *The Star* 12 October.

Feuerstein, S. 2001. 'Re: Not in My Name'. E-mail to Bradley Bordiss. 20 September. Provided by Ebrahim Fakir.

Fisk, R. 2003. 'Why does John Malkovich want to kill me?' in *The Politics of Antisemitism*, eds A Cockburn & J St Clair. Petrolia: CounterPunch, 62.

'Flood of ANC rebels quit to go independent'. 2006. *Dispatch Online*, 23 January [online article]. URL: http://www.dispatch.co.za/2006/01/23/southafrica/

Freedom of Expression Institute 2002. 'Minister receives death threats on his stand on Palestinian/Israeli conflict'. Press release 28 May [online text]. URL: http://fxi.org.za/archives/press/2002/28-5-2002.0.htm

Freedom of Expression Institute 2007. 'Action alert: Complain to ICASA for SABC violations of licence conditions and Broadcasting Act'. Press statement, 20 February [online document]. URL: http://www.fxi.org.za/content/view/35/

Freedom of Expression Institute 2007. 'From SABC's Zikalala—from one blacklist to another?' Press statement, 1 August [online document]. URL: http://www.fxi.org.za/content/view/128/1/

Freedom of Expression Institute. n.d. 'On Jewish Report's censoring of Ronnie Kasrils' [online statement]. URL: http://www.fxi.org.za/index.php?option=com_content&task=view&id=38&Itemid=1

Friedman, S. 1999. 'Jewish leadership during and after apartheid: Double standards?' *South African Jewish Report*, 6, 6 August.

Friedman, S. 2001. 'Kasrils' statement a cause for hope'. *South African Jewish Report*, 9, 23 November.

Gabriel, C M F. 2000. 'We, the citizens of a democratic nation …' Memorandum to the President of the Republic of South Africa, delivered in Pretoria, 15 November [online text]. URL: http://www.anc.org.za/ancdocs/anctoday/docs/memorandum.htm

Gaddin, R. 2002. 'Above Board'. *South African Jewish Report*, 2, 15 March.

Gaddin, R. 2003. 'Above Board'. *South African Jewish Report*, 2, 25 April.

Gastrow, S. 2001. 'Kasrils recognises both sides' right to safety'. *Sunday Independent*, 4 November.

Geldenhuys, B L. 2001. Speech in the National Assembly, Parliament of South Africa, Cape Town. 23 October. *Debates of the National Assembly* no 19 (23 to 26 October 2001): 6829.

Ghanem, Y. 2002. 'Insulted by Israel'. *Al-Ahram Online*, 28 March.

Giliomee, H. 2004. 'Vieser en vieser oor Fischer: A participant's notes on a controversy over an honorary degree'. Unpublished article.

Giliomee, H. 2005. 'White-led opposition parties and white minorities under South Africa's 'liberal' dominant party system'. Paper prepared for workshop on 'Dominant parties and democracy', European Consortium of Political Science, Granada, Spain, 14–19 April [online article]. URL: http://www.ever-fasternews.com/index.php?php_action=read_article&article_id=25

Goldstein, W & Mandela, D. 2005. *African Soul Talk: When Politics is Not Enough*. Johannesburg: Jacana Media.

Goniwe, M. 2005. Speech in the National Assembly, Parliament of South Africa, Cape Town, 25 May. Final Hansard.

Gordin, J. 2001. 'Kasrils defends call for 'Jews to raise their voices''. *Sunday Independent*, 3, 28 October.

Gordon, J. 1994. 'SA, Israel have much in common'. *SA Jewish Times*, 2 September.

Gottschalk, K. 2004. 'Rasool's voice of Muslim moderation'. *South African Jewish Report*, 10, 24 September.

Government Communication and Information System 2004. 'Statement on cabinet meeting'. 3 November [online press release]. URL: http://www.info.gov.za/speeches/2004/04110318001001.htm

Gqiba, F. 2007. Interview by the author. Tel Aviv, Israel, 13 August.

Graef, R. 2005. 'Murders foreshadow South African land war'. *Daily Telegraph*, 3 July [online article]. URL: http://www.telegraph.co.uk/news/main.jhtml;jsessionid=VWPBD0WZE RADXQFIQMGSM5WAVCBQWJVC?xml=/news/2005/07/03/wsafr03.xml&sSheet=/portal/2005/07/03/ixportal.html

Halle, C. 2005. 'SA chief rabbi refused to attend Rabin memorial'. *Haaretz*, 11 November [web article]. URL: http://www.haaretz.com/hasen/objects/pages/PrintArticleEn.jhtml?itemNo=647027

Harris, C et al. 2001. 'What about the truth?: Rabbis respond to Ronnie Kasrils'. Press release, 20 December.

Harris, C et al. 2004. 'Insidious assault on democratic ideals that underpin our society'. *Cape Times*, 2 April [online article]. URL: http://www.capetimes.co.za/index.php?fSectionId=273&fArticleId=390549

Hartley, W. 2005. 'Mbeki lauded by group of leading Afrikaners'. *Business Day*, 3, 9 November.

Hellig, J. 1984. 'Religious expression'. *South African Jewry: A Contemporary Survey*, ed M Arkin. Cape Town: Oxford University Press, 95–116.

Hellig, J. 2001. 'Why impugn Ronnie Kasrils' motives?' *South African Jewish Report*, 6, 9 November.

Herzl, T. 2001. 'To call the inequalities apartheid is sheer nonsense'. *Cape Argus*, 14, 5 December.

'Hijacking of a grand idea' 2001. *South African Jewish Report*, 6, 31 August.

Hirschberg, P. 2002. 'Sharon talks regional peace to American Jews'. *Ha'aretz*, 24 April [online article]. URL: http://news.haaretz.co.il/hasen/pages/ShArt.jhtml?itemNo=155134

Hoffman, T & Fischer, A. 1998. *The Jews of South Africa: What Future?* Johannesburg: Southern.

Holiday, A. 2004. 'Fischer's spirit has triumphed'. *Cape Times*, 15 November.

Holiday, A. 2004. 'Local federation promotes Zionism: Patriotism of SA Jews undermined'. *Cape Times*, 30 March.

Holiday, A. 2006. 'Has Mbeki changed line on Israel?' *Cape Times*, 10 January.

Hurwitz, H. 1995. 'Menachem Begin and Nelson Mandela…'. *SA Jewish Times*, Rosh Hashanah.

Iganski, P & Kosmin, B (eds) 2003. 'Editors' introduction'. *A New Antisemitism? Debating Judeophobia in 21st-Century Britain*. London: Profile/Institute for Jewish Policy Research, 1–2.

'*Independent* cartoonist wins award' 2003. *Independent*, 27 November [online article]. URL: http://news.independent.co.uk/uk/media/story.jsp?story=467627

Independent Electoral Commission of South Africa 2005. 'By-election detailed results report for 27 July 2005' [online report]. URL: http://www.elections.org.za/InternetReportsIEC/DetailedReport/ByElectionDetailReport.asp?lWardID=79400074&lElectionID=91

Independent Electoral Commission. n.d. URL: http://www.elections.org.za

International Court of Justice 2004. 'Legal consequences of the construction of a wall in the occupied Palestinian territory (request for advisory opinion)'. Press release, 25 June [online text]. URL: http://www.icj-cij.org/icjwww/ipresscom/ipress2004/ipresscom2004-23_mwp_20040625.htm

Isaacs, D. 2004. 'Finding a liberal voice in Jewish community'. *South African Jewish Report*, 5, 12 March.

Isaacson, B. 2001. 'Isaacson's challenge to Ronnie Kasrils'. *South African Jewish Report*, 6, 16 November.

Isaacson, B. 2001. 'Give me a worthy opponent'. *South African Jewish Report*, 8, 30 November.

'Israel has window of opportunity' 2006. *Sunday Times*, 8 January.

'Israel's ambassador Alon Liel: No stranger among us' 1993. *Cape Jewish Chronicle*, 10, 3, April, 8.

Jassat, I. 2001. 'Kasrils slams Israel. *Muslim Views*' 13, November.

Jassat, I. n.d. 'Jewish weekly slaps ban on Kasrils' [online statement]. URL: http://www.mediareviewnet.com/newnote_new.asp?ID=1856

Jeter, J. 2001. 'South African Jews polarized over Israel'. *Washington Post*, A35, 19 December.

Jewish Telegraph Agency 2007. 'Poll finds US support for Israel soaring'. *Jerusalem Post*, 7 May [online article]. URL: http://www.jpost.com/servlet/Satellite?cid=1178431587241&pagename=JPost%2FJPArticle%2FShowFull

Joffe, H. 2001. 'Biased, one-eyed criticism'. *South African Jewish Report*, 7, 23 November.

Jordan, P. 2001. Speech during President's debate, National Assembly, Parliament, Cape Town, 14 February [online text]. URL: http://www.anc.org.za/ancdocs/speeches/2001/sp0214.html

Josselowitz, B. 2003. 'React to biased letters, programmes'. *South African Jewish Report*, 14, 18 July.

Julius, A. 2003. 'Is there anything 'new' in the new antisemitism?' in Iganski & Kosmin, *A New Antisemitism?*

Kahn, W. 2007. 'Confrontation often not the best way'. *South African Jewish Report*, 14, 17 August.

Kane-Berman, J. 2006. 'Capitalism itself may be the loser'. *South African Institute of Race Relations: Fast Facts*, 1, January.

Kapelianis, A. n.d. 'Who was Walter Sisulu?' *SABC news* [online article]. URL: http://www.sabcnews.com/features/walter_sisulu/bio.html

Kasrils, R. 2001. 'Don't condemn the rape victim'. *The Citizen*, 19 December.

Kasrils, R. 2001. 'Few of struggle's Jewish heroes were Zionists'. *Sunday Independent* 12 August.

Kasrils, R. 2001. 'Low intellectual level of Jewish soothsayers.' *South African Jewish Report*, 6, 23 November.

Kasrils, R. 2001. 'Speaking out against Israel'. *Sowetan*, 1 November.

Kasrils, R. 2001. Speech in the National Assembly, Parliament of South Africa, Cape Town, 23 October. *Debates of the National Assembly* no 19 (23 to 26 October 2001).

Kasrils, R. 2002. 'Inequity of distribution of resources in Palestine: Apartheid in the Holy Land.' Speech at Justice in Palestine Conference, Sandton, Johannesburg, 20 July. URL: http://www.dwaf.gov.za/Communications/Articles/Israel/2002/Justice%20in%20Palestine%20Conference%20 20%20July%2002.doc

Kasrils, R. 2002. Speech at Vygieskraal stadium, Athlone, Cape Town, South Africa, 21 April.

Kasrils, R. 2004. *Armed and Dangerous: From Undercover Struggle to Freedom* (New Updated Edition). Johannesburg: Jonathan Ball, 342-43.

Kasrils, R. 2004. 'Israel's wall a prison by any name'.*Business Day*, 9 March.

Kasrils, R. 2004. 'My lunch with Arafat'. *This Day*, 8 March.

Kasrils, R. 2005. 'What hope for Middle East peace?' Speech at the Goedgedacht Forum, Western Cape, 6 April [online text]. URL: http://www.intelligence.gov.za/Speeches/WhatHope.htm

Kasrils, R. 2006. 'David and Goliath: Who is who in the Middle East'. *Umrabulo* 27, November [online article]. URL: http://www.anc.org.za/ancdocs/pubs/umrabulo/umrabulo27/art11.html

Kasrils, R 2006. 'Land and peace.' *Socialist Worker Online*, 21 January [online article]. URL: http://www.socialistworker.co.uk/article.php?article_id=8113

Kasrils, R 2006. 'Rage of the elephant'. *Mail & Guardian*, 2 September [online version]. URL: http://www.mg.co.za/articlePage.aspx?articleid=282802&area=/insight/insight__comment_and_analysis/

Kasrils, R 2006. 'Myths of Zionism'. *Mail & Guardian*, 21, 27 January.

Kasrils, R 2007. 'Contents of my lecture misquoted and spun out of context'. *Cape Times*, 8, 9 July.

Kasrils, R 2007. 'David and Goliath: Who is who in the Middle East / Part 2'. *Umrabulo* 28, March [online article]. URL: http://www.anc.org.za/ancdocs/pubs/umrabulo/umrabulo28/art12.html

Kasrils, R 2007. Speech at Birzeit University, Ramallah, Palestinian Authority. 5 May [available online]. http://www.intelligence.gov.za/MediaStatements/Birzeit2.wmv

Kasrils, R 2007. 'Solidarity with Palestinians is not a call to murder Israelis'. *Cape Times*, 8, 28 June.

Kasrils, R & Brittain, V 2002. 'No room for justice'. *Guardian*, 21 December [online article]. URL: http://www.guardian.co.uk/israel/comment/0,10551,864049,00.html

Kasrils, R & Brittain, V. 2005. 'Silence from academe'. *Mail & Guardian*, 29, 27 May.

Kasrils, R & Ozinsky, M. 2001. 'Declaration of conscience on the Israeli–Palestinian conflict by South Africans of Jewish descent'. Final draft of declaration, 19 November.

Kasrils, R & Ozinsky, M. 2001. 'In a propaganda war, truth is the victim'. *South African Jewish Report*, 7, 9 November.

Kasrils, R & Ozinsky, M. 2001. 'Statement on the Israeli–Palestinian conflict'. Address by Kasrils to the National Assembly, Cape Town, 23 October.

Kasrils, R & Ozinsky, M. 2002. '"Not In My Name": One year on'. Press release, 28 November.

Kasrils, R & Pahad, A. 2001. 'We're trying to help settle M-E conflict'. *The Citizen*, 31 October.

'Kasrils incenses with ME remarks' 2001. *South African Jewish Report*, 2, 26 October.

Katz, K. 2001. 'I will not be joining you, Mr Kasrils…'. *South African Jewish Report*, 7, 2 November.

Kaufman, G. 2004. 'The case for sanctions against Israel'. *Guardian*, 12 July [online article]. URL: http://www.guardian.co.uk/comment/story/0,3604,1259087,00.html

Kessler, S. 1995. 'The South African rabbinate in the apartheid era'. *Jewish Affairs*, 31, Autumn.

Kessler, S. 2004. 'Should we open our institutions?' *South African Jewish Report*, 7, 16 January.

Khumalo, B. 2005. 'Historical hangovers make a mockery of equal education'. *Sunday Times*, 23 January [online article]. URL: http://www.suntimes.co.za/Articles/TarkArticle.aspx?ID=1361845

Kirchik, J. 2007. 'Going South'. *Azure* 29 [online version]. URL: http://www.azure.org.il/magazine/magazine.asp?id=389

Kochan, M & Kochan.L. 2003. 'Great Britain'. *American Jewish Year Book*, eds D Singer & L Grossman, 366. New York: American Jewish Committee

Kosmin, B A et al. 1998. 'Jews of the "new South Africa": Highlights of the 1998 national survey of South African Jews'. Institute for Jewish Policy Research, 3, September.

Kransdorff, M & Magid, S. 2007. 'GAP under fire'. *It's Almost Supernatural*, 19 October [weblog]. URL: http://supernatural.blogs.com/weblog/2007/10/gap-under-fire.html.

Kransdorff, M & Magid, S. 2007. 'SAJBD cuts a deal with the SABC'. *It's Almost Supernatural*, 30 July [weblog entry] URL: http://supernatural.blogs.com/weblog/2007/07/sajbd-cuts-a-de.htm

Kransdorff, M & Magid, S. 2008. 'Is Zuma good for the Jews?' *It's Almost Supernatural* 6 January [weblog]. URL: http://supernatural.blogs.com/weblog/2008/01/is-zuma-good-fo.html

Krengel, A. 2002. 'No! Mr Minister'. *South African Jewish Report*, 16, 5 March.

Krengel, Z. 2005. 'A letter from a South African Jewish community leader'. *Ha'aretz* 27 April.

Krengel, Z. 2007. 'Open letter to the Jewish community.' 19 December [e-mail].

Legum, C. 2001. 'No peace until both sides forgo victory by force'. *Sunday Independent*, 4 November.

Leon, A J. 2004. 'The creeping politics of influence'. Speech to Cape Council of South African Jewish Board of Deputies. Cape Town, South Africa, 7 December.

Leon, A J. 2005. Letter to Michael Bagraim. 25 January.

Leon, A J. 2005. Speech to Democratic Alliance members in Citrusdal, Western Cape, 18 May.

Leon, A J. 2004. 'Endorsement by anti-crime activists'. Press statement, Johannesburg, South Africa, 7 April.

Leon, A J. 2004. Speech in response to the State of the Nation Address. Parliament, South Africa, 25 May.

Levy, F. 2001. 'Israel is not to blame …' *Sowetan*, 14 December.

'London mayor defends the use of Palestinian suicide bombers' 2005. *Ha'aretz*, 20 July [online article].

Macfarlane, D. 2002. 'Israeli forces take over Wits'. *Mail and Guardian*, 5 September [online article]. URL: http://www.mg.co.za/Content/l3.jsp?a=59&o=8607

Mandela, N. 1993. Address at the opening of the 37th national conference of the South African Jewish Board of Deputies, Johannesburg, 21 August [online text]. URL: http://www.anc.org.za/ancdocs/history/mandela/1993/sp930821.html

Mandela, N. 1995. *Long Walk to Freedom*. London, Abacus.

Maughan, K & Dolley, C. 2006. 'Double murder leaves arts community in tears'. *The Star*, 1, 17 April.

Mbeki, T. 2003. Address at the Centenary Conference of the South African Jewish Board of Deputies. Johannesburg, 7 September.

Mbeki, T. 2004. Speech at the memorial meeting for Minister Dullah Omar, 24 March.

Mbeki, T. 2004. Statement at the opening of the United Nations African meeting in support of the inalienable rights of the Palestinian people, Cape Town. 29 June [online text]. URL: http://www.dfa.gov.za/docs/speeches/2004/mbek0701.htm

Mbeki, T. 2005. Letter to Israeli Prime Minister Ariel Sharon. Provided by Israeli Ministry of Foreign Affairs, August [online text]. URL: http://www.mfa.gov.il/MFA/Government/Communiques/2005/P M+Sharon+receives+letters+from+Moroccan+King+and+South+African+President+17-Aug-2005.htm

'Mbeki disappoints' 2002. *South African Jewish Report*, 3, 5 April.

Mde, V & Brown, K. 2005. 'Sinister anti-Zuma e-mails stoke tensions'. *Business Day*, 1, 25 November 1.

Mendelsohn, E. 1993. *On Modern Jewish Politics*. New York: Oxford University Press, 4–5.

Merten, M. 2004. 'Will the real Afrikaners please rise?'. *Mail & Guardian*, 8, 12 November.

'Minutes of the meeting of the management committee of the South African Jewish Board of Deputies held on Thursday, 25 October 2001, at 15.00 pm'. Provided by South African Jewish Board of Deputies, Johannesburg. Unpublished document.

'Minutes of the meeting of the management committee of the South African Jewish Board of Deputies held on Thursday, 25 October 2001, at 15.00 pm'. Provided by South African Jewish Board of Deputies, Johannesburg. Unpublished document.

'Minutes of the meeting of the management committee of the South African Jewish Board of Deputies held on Thursday, 6 December 2001, at 15.00 pm'. Provided by South African Jewish Board of Deputies, Johannesburg. Unpublished document.

Mizroch, A. 2006. 'S. African Jewish paper causes storm'. *Jerusalem Post*, 22 November.

Modise, T R. 2001. Speech in the National Assembly, Parliament of South Africa, Cape Town, 23 October. *Debates of the National Assembly*, no 19 (23 to 26 October 2001).

Moeng, S. 2001. "Declaration shows 'not all Jews are bad people'". *Sunday Independent*, 16 December.

Monare, M. 2006. 'Kasrils denies bid to bring down Zuma'. *The Star*, 3, 12 May.

'Mpahlwa, business delegation on three-day visit to Israel' 2005. *Business Day*, 3, 12 November.

Mufson, S. 1988. 'South African Jews'. *Tikkun*, 3, 1.

Muir, H. 2005. 'Livingstone faces inquiry over Nazi guard jibe at Jewish reporter.' *Guardian*, 12 February. [online article]. URL: http://www.guardian.co.uk/media/2005/feb/12/pressandpublishing.londonpolitics

Myburgh, J. n.d. 'Solving the Jewish question: Racial nationalism in South Africa from Verwoerd to Mbeki'. Unpublished article.

Nathan, L. 2001. 'The declaration of commitment by white South Africans'. Presentation to Harold Wolpe Forum, Cape Town, 20 February [online notes]. URL: http://www.wolpetrust.org.za/show.asp?inc=forums/2001/debate20.htm&menu=forummnu.htm

Nathan, L. 2001. Presentation to portfolio committee on foreign affairs, Parliament of South Africa, 10 October URL: http://www.pmg.org.za/viewminute.php?id=1010

Ndungane, N. 2005. 'Put ambition aside for the common good of the people'. *Cape Times*, 10, 25 April.

Netshitenzhe, J. 1998. 'The state, property relations and social transformation'. *Umrabulo* [online journal]. URL: http://www.anc.org.za/ancdocs/pubs/umrabulo/articles/sprst.html

Newsmakers 2001, SABC, 27 October.

Ngonyama, S. 2007. 'Letter to Motty Sacks'. *South African Jewish Report*, 5, 30 June.

'Open debate in troubled times' 2001. *South African Jewish Report*, 6, 9 November.

Ozinsky, M. 2001 'Jewish debate on Mid-East crisis a healthy sign'. *Cape Times*, 12, 30 November.

Ozinsky, M. 2001. Speech at launch of Kasrils declaration, District Six Museum, Cape Town, 7 December.

Ozinsky, M. 2002. 'Left out'. *Cape Times*, 6 February.

Ozinsky, M. 2005. Remarks at seminar, 'The apartheid wall: Palestine and beyond,' Salt River, Cape Town, 28 July.

Pahad, A. 2004. Statement at International Court of Justice, The Hague, Netherlands. 23 February [online text]. URL: http://www.dfa.gov.za/docs/2004/icj0223.htm

Pahad, E. 2006. Speech in on the occasion of the Presidency Budget Vote, National Assembly, Parliament, Cape Town, 7 June [available online]. URL: http://www.polity.org.za/article.php?a_id=87862

'Pahad, Kasrils stirring it up' 2001. Editorial. *The Citizen*, 12, 25 October.

Pallister, D. 2001. 'Irving's tag as "Holocaust denier" upheld'. Guardian 21 July [web article]. URL: http://www.guardian.co.uk/uk/2001/jul/21/books.irving

Parliament of South Africa (Hansard) 2001. 'Consideration of report of fact-finding mission to Israel and Palestine from 9 to 19 July 2001'. *Debates of the National Assembly* no 19 (23 to 26 October): 6813–6864.

Parliament of South Africa 2001. 'Report of the fact-finding mission to Israel and Palestine from 9 to 19 July 2001' [online article]. URL: http://www.parliament.gov.za/committees/report/repjuly01.htm (link defunct)

Patten, J. 2001. 'Are Kasrils and co helping to solve the Middle East problem?' *Cape Times* 8, 13 December.

Pew Research Center. 2007. 'Global unease with major world powers: 47-nation pew global attitudes survey', 27 June [online document]. URL: http://pewglobal.org/reports/pdf/256.pdf. 96.

Philip, R & Van der Merwe, J. 2005. 'Six-year-olds trapped in political chess game'. *Sunday Times*, 3 July [online article]. URL: http://www.sundaytimes.co.za/Articles/TarkArticle.aspx?ID=1527414

Pickett, W. 2003. 'Nasty or Nazi? The use of antisemitic topoi by the left-liberal media' in Iganski & Kosmin, *A New Antisemitism?* 152–3.

Podbrey, P. 2004. 'Holiday's article is a dangerous diatribe, based on prejudice'. *Cape Times*, 8 April.

Pollak, J. 2004. 'Confronting contradictions'. *South African Jewish Report*, 10, 3 September.

Pollak, J. 2005. 'An own goal against the Palestinian cause'. *Mail & Guardian*, 13 June.

Press TV 2007. 'S. Africa says Iran visit positive', 18 April [online article]. URL: http://www.presstv.ir/detail.aspx?id=6515&sectionid=351020101

Rab, A P et al. 2001. 'An open letter to Minister Ronnie Kasrils by five former Soviet Jews'. *South African Jewish Report*, 7, 2 November.

Rabe, L. 2004. 'Not in the name of Stellenbosch'. *Mail & Guardian*, 8, 12 November.

Rabiner, A P et al. 2001. 'Minister fuels violence cycle'. *The Citizen*, 20 November.

Rabinowitz, R. 2004. 'A memorable and tasteful event'. *South African Jewish Report*, 23 April.

Rabinowitz, R. 2004. 'SAJDB "tagging onto ANC"'. *South African Jewish Report*, 14, 11 October.

Rabinowitz, R & Grinker, A. 2004. "Liliesleaf Freedom Seder 'inappropriate'". *South African Jewish Report*, 14, 2 April.

Rasool, E. 2004. Speech at the launch of the Home For All logo, Cape Town, 16 December [online text]. URL: http://www.polity.org.za/pol/speech/2004/?show=61019

Rasool, E. 2004. Speech at Watsonia sports ground, Athlone, Cape Town, 21 March. Voice of the Cape Radio broadcast. Unpublished transcript.

Roberts, R S. 2005. *No Cold Kitchen: A Biography of Nadine Gordimer*. Johannesburg: STE .

Robins, S. 2001. 'Voices of reason older than Israel'. Sunday Independent, 7, 25 November.

Rosenberg, A. et al. 2003. "Above Board and 'below the belt'". South African Jewish Report, 16, 2 May.

Roussouw, R. 2006. 'Using religion to muzzle society'. Business Day: Weekender Edition, 6, 14 October.

'Rules of war' 2002. *Economist*, 8 August.

'SA slams Israel' 2001. *The Citizen*, 1. 24 October.

Sacks, J. 2003. 'A New Antisemitism?' in Iganski & Kosmin, *A New Antisemitism?* 46.

Saenger, H & Sherman, J. 1997. 'Shouting from the grandstand: By way of an afterword'. *Jewish Affairs*, Autumn.

'SAJBD Cape Conference faces the future' 2001/2. *Cape Jewish Chronicle*, 4, December/January.

'SAJBD to celebrate adoption of Freedom Charter' 2005. *South African Jewish Report*, 3, 6 May.

Saks, D & Romain, M (eds) 2005. 'Helping hands across the ocean: South African Jewry and the tsunami disaster'. Johannesburg: South African Jewish Board of Deputies.

Saks, D. 1999. 'Jewish leftists: SA Jewry's lost tribes?' *South African Jewish Report*, 7, 30 July 1999.
Saks, D. 1999. 'No shame in Jewish lobbying'. *South African Jewish Report*, 6, 20 August.
Saks, D. 2002. 'Personal attack'. *Cape Times*, 11 February.
Saks, D. 2003. 'South African Jewry: A contemporary portrait'. Institute of the World Jewish Congress, Policy Study no 25.
Saks, D. 2003/4. 'South Africa'. *Antisemitism Worldwide: Annual Report 2003/4* [online report of the Stephen Roth Institute]. URL: http://www.tau.ac.il/Anti-Semitism/asw2003-4/south_africa.htm.
Saks, D. 2005. 'Activists commemorate Freedom Charter anniversary'. *South African Jewish Report*, 3, 17 June.
Saks, D. 2006. 'Letter to Jane Duncan, director: Freedom of Expression Institute', 29 November.
Saks, D. 2007. 'Govt reassures Jews on ME' *South African Jewish Report*, 1, 30 June 2007.
Saron, G. 2001. *The Jews of South Africa: An Illustrated History to 1953*, ed N Musiker. Johannesburg: Scarecrow Books.
Saron, G & Hotz L (eds) 1955. *The Jews in South Africa: A History*. Cape Town: Oxford University Press.
Saunders C. 1995 (ed). *Illustrated History of South Africa: The Real Story*. Cape Town: Reader's Digest.
Sawant, G. 2001. 'SA takes stand against Israeli oppression'. *Muslim Views*, 13, November.
Schkolne, T. 2001. 'A Jewish Uncle Tom'. *South African Jewish Report*, 8, 23 November.
Schneider, M. 2005. 'Goldstein sticks to his guns'. *South African Jewish Report*, 1, 16 December.
Schneider, M. 2005. 'Government must live up to Constitution'. *South African Jewish Report*, 5, 23 September.
Schwartz, P. 2002. 'There is no moral high ground'. *Mail & Guardian*, 19, 26 April.
Segal, R M & Jacobson, D. 1957. 'Apartheid and South African Jewry'. *Commentary*, November, 424–31.
Shain, M. 1983. Jewry and Cape Society: The Origins and Activities of the Jewish Board of Deputies for the Cape Colony. Cape Town: Historical Publication Society.
Shain, M. 1994. *The Roots of Antisemitism in South Africa*. Johannesburg: Witwatersrand University Press.
Shain, M. 1996. 'South Africa'. *American Jewish Year Book 1996* (vol 96), eds D Singer & R R Seldin. New York: American Jewish Committee.
Shain, M. 1997. 'South Africa'. *American Jewish Year Book 1997* (vol 97), eds D Singer & R R Seldin. New York: American Jewish Committee.
Shain, M. 1998. 'South Africa'. *American Jewish Year Book 1998* (vol 98), eds D Singer & R R Seldin. New York: American Jewish Committee.
Shain, M. 1999. 'South Africa'. *American Jewish Year Book*, eds D Singer & R R Seldin. New York: American Jewish Committee.
Shain, M. 2001. 'Please, Ronnie Kasrils, not in my name' *Sunday Independent*, 16 December.
Shain, M. 2001. 'South Africa'. *American Jewish Year Book 2001* (vol 101), eds D Singer & L Grossman. New York: American Jewish Committee, 466.
Shain, M. 2002. 'South Africa'. *American Jewish Year Book 2002* (vol 102), eds D Singer & L Grossman. New York: American Jewish Committee.
Shain, M. 2002. 'South African Jewry: Emigrating? At risk? Or restructuring the Jewish future?' *Continuity, Commitment, and Survival: Jewish Communities in the Diaspora*, eds S Encel & L Stein. Praeger Series on Jewish and Israeli Studies. Westport: Praeger.
Shain, M. 2004. 'South Africa'. *American Jewish Year Book 2004* (vol 104), eds D Singer & L Grossman. New York: American Jewish Committee.

Shain, M. 2005. 'Humpty Dumpty was pushed: Anti-Jewish conspiracies and the South African experience'. 17th Jacob Gitlin Memorial Lecture, Cape Town, 28 June.

Shain, M & Mendelsohn, R. (eds) 2000. *Memories, Realities and Dreams: Aspects of the South African Jewish Experience*. Johannesburg: Jonathan Ball.

Shain, M et al. 2001. *Looking Back: Jews in the Struggle for Democracy and Human Rights in South Africa*. Cape Town: Isaac and Jesse Kaplan Centre for Jewish Studies and Research, University of Cape Town.

Sharon, A. 2005. Personal communication with the author, Jerusalem, Israel. 12 January.

Shimoni, G. 1980. *Jews and Zionism: The South African Experience 1910–1967*. Cape Town: Oxford University Press.

Shimoni, G. 2003. *Community and Conscience: The Jews in Apartheid South Africa*. Hanover, NH: New England University Press.

Slier, P. 2007. 'Please, SAJBD, don't talk on my behalf!' *South African Jewish Report*, 10, 17 August.

Smetheram, J-A. 2002. '10 000 turn up at Palestinian solidarity rally'. *The Star*, 22 April.

Smillie, S. 2005. 'SA dismisses report of nuclear deal with Iran'. *Cape Times*, 8 November [online article]. URL: http://www.capetimes.co.za/index.php?fSectionId=271&fArticleId=2984862

Smuts, D. 2001. Speech in the National Assembly, Parliament of South Africa, Cape Town, 23 October. *Debates of the National Assembly* no 19 (23 to 26 October 2001): 6819.

Sole, S & Dawes, N. 2005. 'Spy-war e-mails: What they really say'. *Mail & Guardian* 15 December [online article]. URL: http://www.mg.co.za/articlePage.aspx?articleid=259263&area=/insight/insight__national/

South African Broadcasting Corporation 2006. 'Commission of enquiry into blacklisting and related matters'. Copy by *Mail & Guardian* [online document]. URL: http://www.mg.co.za/ContentImages/286848/SABCBLACKLISTREPORT.pdf

South African Broadcasting Corporation 2007. 'Hamas has "no problem with Jews"',16 May [available online]. URL: http://www.sabcnews.com/politics/government/0,2172,149239,00.html

South African Broadcasting Corporation 2007. 'SABC responds to FXI statement on meeting with the SA Jewish Board'. Press statement, 2 August [online document]. URL: http://www.sabc.co.za:80/portal/binary/com.epicentric.contentmanagement.connectors.cda.CDADisplayServlet?connectorID=cda&moid=8b8430c324524110VgnVCM10000030d4ea9bRCRD

South African Communist Party 2007. 'SACP Central Committee press statement', 19 August [online document]. URL: http://www.sacp.org.za/main.php?include=docs/pr/2007/pr0819a.html

South African Department of Health 2005. 'National HIV and syphilis antenatal sero-prevalence survey in South Africa 2004', 20 July [online report]. URL: http://www.doh.gov.za/docs/reports/2004/hiv-syphilis.pdf

South African Human Rights Commission 2007. 'In re: Referral by Mr. Ronnie Kasrils', 23 March [available online]. URL: http://www.sahrc.org.za/sahrc_cms/publish/article_247.shtml

South African Jewish Board of Deputies 1990. *Press Items of Jewish Interest*, 16 February. Quoted in Dubb, A A & Shain, M. 'South Africa'. *American Jewish Year Book 1992* (vol 92), eds D Singer & R R Seldin 1992. New York: American Jewish Committee.

South African Jewish Board of Deputies 2001. Press release, October.

South African Jewish Board of Deputies (Cape Council) Cape Committee Meeting: Tuesday, 27 November 2001'. Minutes of meeting.

South African Ministry of Intelligence 2007. 'Ruling from the Human Rights Commission on "Ronnie Kasrils and his critique of Israel"'. Press statement, 23 March [available online]. URL: http://www.intelligence.gov.za/MediaStatements/SAHR%20Media%2023%20Mar%2007.doc

South African Police Service 2003. 'Report summary'. *Report of the Committee of Inquiry into Farm Attacks*, 31 July. [online document]. URL: http://www.iss.co.za/CJM/farmrep/farmsummary.pdf

South African Press Association 2003. 'Israel wants better relations with SA: D-G', 27 June.

South African Press Association 2005. 'Jewish Board slams ANC', 28 May [online article]. http://iafrica.com/news/sa/760173.htm; South African Jewish Board of Deputies. Press Release 27 May 2005.

South African Press Association 2005. 'Mayor orders probe into Ngoro's website', 22 July [online article]. URL: http://www.iol.co.za/index.php?set_id=1&click_id=79&art_id=qw1122047280306B243

South African Press Association 2007. 'Kasrils refutes Iranian media claim',20 April [online article]. URL: http://iafrica.com/news/sa/792748.htm

South African Press Association and Associated Press 2007. 'Palestinian leader invited to visit SA', 3 May.

South African Press Association 2007. 'Kasrils casts his vote', 18 December [online article]. URL: http://www.int.iol.co.za/index.php?set_id=1&click_id=6&art_id=nw20071218104329570C319651

Sparks, A. 2005. 'The boys who cried "antisemite"'. *The Star*, 5 October.

Speeches at MJC March, Cape Town, 25 May 2005. Radio 7886 broadcast. Unpublished transcript.

Statistics South Africa 2001. *Census 2001*. URL: http://www.statssa.gov.za

Summers, L. 2002. 'Address at morning prayers'. Memorial Church, Harvard University, Cambridge, MA, 17 September.

Suttner, I. (ed) 1997. *Cutting Through the Mountain: Interviews with South African Jewish Activists*. Johannesburg: Penguin, 275.

Suzman, H. 2002. 'Israel as apartheid state is ludicrous'. *Sunday Independent*, 5 January.

Suzman, H. 2006. 'Antisemitism the issue'. *Business Day: Weekender Edition*, 5, 21 October.

'Talking to Jews in the ANC' 1994. *Jewish Affairs*, Autumn, 17–24.

Tanner, J. 2001. 'Stop, analyse and wonder'. *South African Jewish Report*, 8, 14 December.

'The PLO in S Africa' 1995. *South African Jewish Times*, 3, 10 March.

The Stephen Roth Institute 2000/1. 'United Kingdom'. *Antisemitism Worldwide*. Annual report. URL: http://www.tau.ac.il/Anti-Semitism/asw2000-1/united_kingdom.htm

The Stephen Roth Institute 2001/2. 'France'. *Antisemitism Worldwide*. Annual report. URL: http://www.tau.ac.il/Anti-Semitism/asw2001-2/france.htm

The Stephen Roth Institute 2003/4. 'United States'. *Antisemitism Worldwide*. Annual report. URL: http://www.tau.ac.il/Anti-Semitism/asw2003-4/usa.htm

The Stephen Roth Institute for the Study of Antisemitism and Racism at Tel Aviv University. n.d 'South Africa 2006' [online article]. URL: http://www.tau.ac.il/Antisemitism/asw2006/sth-africa.htm

The Stephen Roth Institute for the Study of Contemporary Antisemitism and Racism 2003/4. 'South Africa'. *Antisemitism Worldwide*. Annual report. URL: http://www.tau.ac.il/Anti-Semitism/asw2004/sth-africa.htm

Tim Modise Show 2001. SAfm, 23 November.

'Time to reject Sharon' 2004. Editorial, *Mail & Guardian*, 25 March.

Treatment Action Campaign 2004. 'Statement on South African elections', 21 April. [online newsletter]. URL: http://www.tac.org.za/newsletter/2004/ns21_04_2004.htm#Elections

Treatment Action Group 2000. 'Taking it to the street'. *The Body*, September [online article]. URL: http://66.102.9.104/search?q=cache:2f73SPP4jPsJ:www.thebody.com/tag/sept00/tac.html+tac+anc+members&hl=en

Trigamo, S. 2005. 'Is there a future for French Jewry?' *Azure*, 20, 59.

Tshwete, S. 2001. 'Where was the Portuguese community when the majority of South Africans suffered the crimes of apartheid?' [online text]. URL: http://www.anc.org.za/ancdocs/anctoday/docs/portuguese.htm

Tutu, D & Urbina, I. 2002. ‚Against Israeli apartheid', July [online article]. URL: http://www.merip.org/newspaper_opeds/Tutu_IU_Israeli_Apartheid.html.

UNAIDS/WHO 2004. 'UNAIDS 2004 report on the global AIDS epidemic'. [online report]. URL: http://www.unaids.org/bangkok2004/GAR2004_html/GAR2004_17_en.htm#TopOfPage

'United Kingdom'. n.d. *Antisemitism Worldwide: Annual Report 2000/1* [online report of the Stephen Roth Institute]. URL: http://www.tau.ac.il/Anti-Semitism/annual-report-00-01.html

United States Navy 2001. 'People against Gangsterism and Drugs (PAGAD)'. From *Patterns of Global Terrorism, 2001*. [online article]. URL: http://library.nps.navy.mil/home/tgp/pagad.htm

Vahed, G & Jeppie, S. 2004/5. 'Multiple communities: Muslims in post-apartheid South Africa'. *State of the Nation: South Africa 2004–2005*. Human Sciences Research Council [online document]. URL: http://www.hsrcpress.ac.za/download.asp?filename=2055_10_State_of_the_Nation_2004-2005-16112004105739AM.pdf. 278–9.

Van der Merwe, J H. 2001. Speech in the National Assembly, Parliament of South Africa, Cape Town, 23 October. *Debates of the National Assembly* no 19 (23 to 26 October 2001): 6824.

Van Hees, B. 2001. 'Ministers hold Middle East vigil'. *The Citizen,* 1–2, 29 December.

Waintrater, M. 2003. 'France'. *American Jewish Year Book* (2003), 385.

Watt, N. 2002. 'MP accuses Sharon of "barbarism"'. *Guardian* 17 April [web article]. URL:http://www.guardian.co.uk/politics/2002/apr/17/houseofcommons.israel

Weisbord, R G. 1967. 'The dilemma of South African Jewry'. *The Journal of Modern African Studies*, 5, 2.

Wilson, B. 2003. 'South Africa moves to distribute AIDS drugs'. National Public Radio, 27 August. [online broadcast]. URL: http://www.npr.org/templates/story/story.php?storyId=1413916

'World cannot ignore the plight of the Palestinian people' 2004. *ANC Today*, 1, 31 (24 August) [online newsletter]. URL: http://www.anc.org.za/ancdocs/anctoday/2001/at31.htm#art1

World ORT 2008. 'How ORT began'. [online article]. URL: http://www.ort.org/asp/article.asp?id=117

'Zionism in new SA: The experts debate' 1993. *Zionist Record—and SA Jewish Chronicle*, 6, 6 August.

INDEX

1967 War, 32, 33, 63
9/11 attacks, 1, 6, 59, 64, 81, 153
A vote for the DA is a vote for Israel, 57, 116
Africa Muslim Party (AMP), 131
African National Congress, 2, 6, 7, 8, 11, 15, 17, 42, 47, 56, 59, 60, 67, 94, 99, 131, 132, 156–161, 166
    and Kasrils declaration, 67
    and Middle East, 42, 43, 47
    relations with Israel, 34, 35, 44, 55–58, 94–99, 106, 138
    relationship with SA Jewish Board of Deputies, 100, 101, 107, 110–113, 117–122, 161
Afrikaans, 4, 7, 28, 124, 125, 126, 128, 129, 131
Afrikaners, 19, 24–26, 28–30, 52, 74, 124, 128–130
Afrikaner Weerstandbeweging (AWB), 42

Afro-Asian bloc, 31, 36
Alexander, Morris, 23
Al-Husseini, Haj Amin, 70
Aliens Act, 1937, 25
American Israel Public Affairs Committee (AIPAC), 112, 159
American Jewish Committee, 18, 97, 106, 116
American Nation of Islam, 47
ANC Youth League, 43, 166
Anglo-Boer War, *see* South African War
ANSWER, 150
antisemitism, 3, 5, 6, 8, 9, 16, 21, 22, 25–27, 42, 50, 57–59, 62, 73–76, 79, 105, 109, 110, 115, 145–148, 150–156
anti-Zionism, 19, 57, 150
apartheid, 2, 5, 8 10, 16, 18, 23, 27–31, 33–38, 40, 41, 43, 49, 51–55, 71, 78, 114, 116, 119, 130,

131, 134, 135
'reformed' apartheid, 16
Arafat, Yasser, 33, 42, 47, 66, 84, 89, 92, 98, 102, 139
Athlone, Cape Town, 86, 115, 116
Auerbach, Franz, 51, 78

Bagraim, Michael, 10, 11, 82, 85, 97, 99–102, 104, 105, 111, 114, 117–120, 122, 137
Barak, Ehud, 55
Baruch, Ilan, 91
Batavian Republic, 21
Battersby, John, 68
Begin, Menachem, 41
Behr, Saul, 82
Berger, Mike, 69
Betar, 19
Beth Din, 14, 69
Bethlehem, Marlene, 57
Biran, Yoav, 95
Birnbaum, Pierre, 151
black economic empowerment (BEE), 156, 157
Bloom, Richard, 109
Board of Deputies, *see* South African Jewish Board of Deputies (SAJBOD)
Braude, Claudia, 52
British Association of University Teachers (AUT), 149
Brittain, Victoria, 89
Buthelezi, Chief Mangosuthu, 100, 130, 131

Cape Town Holocaust Centre, 49
Chabad, *see* Lubavitch Chabad
Chevra Kadisha 15
Chirac, Jacques, 147, 151
Class Areas Bill, 1924, 23
Clegg, Johnny, 68
Community Security Organisation (CSO), 15, 49, 55
Congress of Democrats, 17
Congress of South African Trade Unions (Cosatu), 58, 59, 118, 119, 160
crime 39, 49–50, 55, 109, 123, 124, 133

Dalyell, Tam, 152
Davis, Justice Dennis, 11, 34, 75, 80, 106
Davis, Uri, 58, 64, 76
De Klerk, F W, 39, 40, 127
De la Rey, 7
Democratic Alliance (DA), 16, 17, 42, 43, 60, 68, 118, 131
Democratic Party (DP), 2, 16, 17
Durban Conference, *see* United Nations World Conference Against Racism, Xenophobia and Other Related Forms of Intolerance
Dutch East India Company, 21

Ebrahim, Ismail, 2
emigration, *see* Jewish community

fact-finding mission to Israel and Palestine, 1–3

Feinstein, Andrew, 55
Fischer, 76, 78, 126–128
Fisk, Robert, 147
Freedom Front/Freedom Front Plus, 131
Freedom of Expression Institute (FXI), 90, 139, 142
Friedman, Steven, 53–56, 78, 81

Gaddin, Russell, 68, 71, 80–84
Gandhi, Mahatma, 23
Gastrow, Sheilagh, 70, 73
Geldenhuys, Dr B L 'Boy', 2, 3
Gesher, 49, 51
Gesuiwerde National Party, 25, 26
Giliomee, Hermann, 127–130, 135, 161
Glenhazel Active Patrol (GAP), 49
Goethe Institute, 90–91
Goldin, Brett, 109
Goldstein, Chief Rabbi Dr Warren, 14, 106, 166
Goniwe, Mbulelo, 121
Gordimer, Nadine, 66
Gottschalk, Keith, 117
Gqiba, Major General Fumanekile, 112
Green and Sea Point Hebrew Congregation, 46, 55
Grinder, Anthony, 100
Gulf War, 42

Habonim, 19, 20
Hamas, 91, 158
Haniyeh, Ismail, 91
Harris, Chief Rabbi Cyril, 46, 47, 51–53, 55, 69, 87

Hashomer Hatza'ir, 19
Hellig, Prof Jocelyn, 78
Hertzog, Barry, 25
Herzl, Tova, 72, 96, 97
HIV/Aids, 39, 40, 59, 106, 110, 132, 133, 163,
Hoffman, Rabbi David, 55, 58
Hofmeyr, Jan H, 24
Holiday, Anthony, 103, 104, 110, 111, 127
Holocaust, 3, 31, 50, 55, 138, 150, 152
Home for All campaign, 6, 7, 64, 156

Immigration Act, 1913 22, 23
Immigration Quota Act, 1930 24
immigration, *see* Jewish community
Independent Democrats (ID), 17
Independent Jewish Voices, 149
Inkatha Freedom Party (IFP), 46, 100, 130
International Court of Justice, 101
intifada, see Palestinian intifada
Iran, 47, 91
Iraq War, 149
Irving, David, 152
Isaac and Jesse Kaplan Centre for Jewish Studies, 52, 56, 70, 81
Isaacson, Rabbi Ben, 70, 72
Islam, *see* Muslims
Israel, 3–7, 20, 32, 33, 35, 37, 39, 42, 44, 47, 56, 58, 61–66, 71, 79, 87–89, 94–96, 98, 101, 105, 106, 111, 112, 135, 137, 146–148, 150, 152, 153, 155, 158

Israel United Appeal-United
  Communal Fund, 15
Israel–apartheid analogy, 2, 8, 35, 43,
  64, 71, 72, 78, 79, 87, 166
It's Almost Supernatural, 140, 142

Jacobson, Dan, 18
Jeenah, Na'eem, 90
Jenin 'massacre', 87, 153
Jewish anti-apartheid activists, 5, 28,
  29, 35, 36
Jewish community
  emigration, 20, 45, 103, 108, 109
  immigration, 22–25
  post-apartheid, 38–60
  pre 1994 politics, 12–37
Jewish Media Network (JMN),
  83, 84, 106
Jewish Question, 20, 26, 31, 36, 156
Jewish Voices, SA, 92, *see* SA
  Jewish Voices
Jewish vote, 17, 40
Jews for Justice, 35, 149
Jews for Social Justice, 35
Jospin, Lionel, 150
Justice in Palestine Conference, 88

Kacev, Rabbi Craig, 108
Kadalie, Rhoda, 133
Kahn, Wendy, 140, 142, 143
Kasrils declaration, 62–85, 169–176
Kasrils, Ronnie, 4–6, 11, 16, 53,
  60, 62, 63, 64–67, 70–72, 74–78,
  81–94, 97, 99, 107, 109, 110, 126,
  136, 150, 157, 158, 160, 163

Katsav, Moshe, 84
Katz, Ken, 75
Katzew, Henry, 30, 74
Kaufman, Gerald, 149
Kay, Yehuda, 81, 98
Kessler, Solly, 81, 82
Kransdorff, Michael, 140
Krawitz, Philip, 11, 85
Krengel, Avrom, 102, 108
Krengel, Zev, 108, 112, 145,
  166, 167
Kruger, Paul, 22

Le Pen, Jean-Marie, 150
Lebanon
  crisis, 34, 62, 80, 92
  second Lebanon War, 89, 158
Legum, Colin, 69, 72
Leon, Tony, 16, 42, 55, 60,
  117, 118, 119, 120, 121,
  122, 160
Lerner, Rabbi Michael, 149
Lerner's Tikkun, 154
Levy, Felicia, 69
Liberal Party, 16
Lieberman, Hyman, 21
Liel, Alon, 39
Likud Party (Israel), 96, 101
Liliesleaf Farm, 100
Lipstadt, Deborah, 152
Lithuania, 12, 19, 24, 25
Litvaks, 13, 19, 24
Livingstone, Ken, 152
Louw, Eric, 8, 9, 26, 32
Lubavitch Chabad, 14, 45

MaAfrica Tikkun, 15, 48, 110
Madlala-Routledge, Nozizwe, 162
Magid, Steve, 140
Malan, David Francois, 25–27
Malema, Julius, 166
Mandatory Palestine, 28
Mandela, Nelson, 39, 42, 43, 44, 46, 47, 54, 55, 59, 62
Mann, David, 34
Mbeki, Thabo, 7, 39, 54, 57, 59, 63, 84, 87, 88, 93–95, 97, 99, 110–112, 117, 125, 133, 158, 159, 161, 162, 165
Mendelsohn, Ezra, 135–137
Modise, Thandi, R 2
Moeng, Solly, 75
Mugabe, Robert, 60
Muslim Judicial Council, 113
Muslims, 2, 4, 34, 42, 47, 50, 56, 57, 67, 82, 86, 110, 115–117, 147, 150, 151

Nathan, Laurie, 64
Nathan, Sir Matthew, 21
National Democratic Convention (Nadeco), 131
National Party (NP), 16, 17, 25–28, 31, 33, 36, 47, 52, 61, 119, 130
  antisemitic policies of, 16, 25, 26, 27, 31
Nazism, 24, 26, 27, 31, 71, 74, 87, 89
Ndugane, Archbishop Njongonkulu, 120
Netanyahu, Benjamin, 47

Netshitenzhe, Joel, 125
new antisemitism
  Britain, 145, 147, 152, 153, 155, 156
  France, 145–148, 150–152, 154, 156
  South Africa, 5, 148, 155, 156
  United States, 148, 153, 155, 156
New National Party, 17, 60, 130
Ngculu, James, 160
Ngonyama, Smuts, 138
Ngoro, Robert Blackman, 121
Nine-Point Programme, 26
Not In My Name campaign, 4, 67, 71, 73, 75, 92, 157, 163

Olmert, Ehud, 96, 97
Operation Defensive Shield, 87, 153
Organisation for Rehabilitation and Training (ORT), 46
orthodox Judaism, 13, 14
Oslo peace process, 44, 108, 148
Ozinsky, Max, 3, 5, 62, 64, 71, 73, 75–78, 92, 136, 160

Pahad, Aziz, 68, 70, 84, 94, 113
Palestine Liberation Organisation (PLO), 3, 33, 44, 62
Palestine National Authority, 47
Palestinian intifada, 1, 35, 42, 56, 59, 60, 88, 145, 147, 148, 155
Pan Africanist Congress (PAC), 42, 131
Patten, John, 68
People Against Gangsterism and Drugs (PAGAD), 50

Peres, Shimon, 98
Pikoli, Vusi, 163
Pilger, John, 64, 83
Pinshaw, Issy, 41
Podbrey, Pauline, 68, 72, 104, 106
Portuguese community, 123
Pretoria–Jerusalem axis, *see* South Africa Israel Alliance
Progressive Party (Progressive Federal Party or PFP), 8, 16, 31, 39, 79

Rabin, Yitzchak, 44, 47, 106
Rabinowitz, Chief Rabbi Louis I, 30
Rabinowitz, Ruth, 100
Raffarin, Jean-Marie, 151
Rasool, Ebrahim, 57, 101, 115–117, 120, 160
Red Scare, 24
Revisionist Zionism, 20
Rivonia Trial, 28
Robins, Steven, 73, 78
Robinson, C P, 24
Robinson, Mary, 58
Roussouw, Rehana, 90

SA Jewish Voices, 4, *see* Jewish Voices, SA
Sabra, 61, 80
Sacks, Chief Rabbi Jonathan, 146, 149
Saenger, Hanns, 52
Saks, David, 53, 54, 77, 98
Schkolne, Theo, 76, 77
Schlemmer, Lawrence, 127
Schwartz, Pat, 75

Schwarz, Harry, 43
Segal, Hagai, 89
Segal, Ronald M, 18
Selebi, Jackie, 163
Shain, Milton, 70, 120
Sharon, Ariel, 56, 94–97, 102, 111, 153, 155
Shatila, 61, 89
Sherman, Dr Joseph, 52
Shimoni, Gideon, 9, 10, 23–25, 28, 29, 48, 54, 61, 134
Sifrin, Geoff, 56, 90
Six Day War, *see* 1967 War
Skwatsha, Mcebisi, 160
Slier, Paula, 138, 139, 140, 144, 145
Slovo, Joe, 16, 29, 53
Smith, Mervyn, 83, 122
Smuts, Dene, 3, 27
Smuts, Jan, 25
Someach, Ohr, 45
South Africa Israel Alliance, 36, 41, 72, 92, 138
South African Broadcasting Corporation (SABC), 138–142, 145
South African Communist Party (SACP), 16, 17, 127, 157
South African Human Rights Commission, 90
South African Jewish Board of Deputies (SAJBOD)
    advocacy approach, 10, 54, 110, 114, 115, 54
    Cape Council, 34, 101
    denunciation of apartheid, 18, 35
    Kasrils declaration, 68, 81–84

lobbying, 10, 105, 86, 159
policy of non-involvement, 9, 17, 18, 23, 24, 27–30, 35, 36, 54
relationship with ANC, 100, 101, 107, 110–113, 117–122, 161
Verwoerd affair, 31, 32, 33
South African Party, 25
South African Union of Jewish Students (SAUJS), 43
South African Union of Progressive Judaism, 14
South African War, 22
South African Zionist Federation (SAZF), 4, 14, 15, 24, 33, 75, 83, 84, 88, 92, 102, 103, 137, 163
Soviet Union, 33
Sparks, Allister, 103
Spier conference, 87
Steinhorn, Rabbi Jack, 49
Stuttgart, 25
Summers, Larry, 146
Suzman, 72, 90

Tikkun, 48, 45, 55, 110, 149, *see* MaAfrika Tikkun
transformation, 125, 126, 131
Treason Trial, 28
Treatment Action Campaign (TAC), 106, 110, 132, 133, 157
Tripartite Alliance, 59
Truth and Reconciliation Commission (TRC), 51
Truth in the Middle East (TIME), 83
Tshwete, Steve, 123, 124
tsunami, 110, 119

Tutu, Archbishop Emeritus Desmond, 68

Umkhonto we Sizwe, 100
uitlanders, 21
Ungar, Andre, 30
Union of Orthodox Synagogues (UOS), 14, 55
Union of South Africa, 15, 22
Unionist Party, 22
United Democratic Front, 35
United Nations Africa Meeting in Support of the Inalienable Rights of the Palestinian People (CEIRP), 95, 105
United Nations Palestinian Rights Conference, 119
United Nations World Conference against Racism, Xenophobia and Other Related Forms of Intolerance, 6, 57, 58, 81, 105
United Party (UP), 16, 26–28
United South African National Party, 25

Vally, Salim, 90
Van Blerk, Bok, 7
Verwoerd affair, 8, 31, 32, 61, 79
Verwoerd, Hendrik, 8, 9, 26, 31, 32, 43, 61, 79, 80, 156
Vorster, B J, 34

Weinstein, Julius, 43
World Summit on Sustainable Development (WSSD), 98

World Zionist Organisation, 18

Yassin, Ahmed, 94
Yom Kippur War, 33
Yutar, Percy, 74

Zikalala, Snuki, 138, 139, 142
Zille, Helen, 131, 161
Zimbabwe, 60, 158
Zionism, 5, 8, 14, 18–21, 28–30, 32, 35, 41–44, 52, 87, 103, 106, 127, 137, 153
Zuma, Jacob, 159, 160, 161, 165–167